Readings on
Catholics
in
Political Life

Readings on

Catholics

in

Political Life

TASK FORCE ON CATHOLIC BISHOPS AND CATHOLIC POLITICIANS
UNITED STATES CONFERENCE OF CATHOLIC BISHOPS

United States Conference of Catholic Bishops
Washington, D.C.

The document *Readings on Catholics in Political Life* is a publication of the Task Force on Catholic Bishops and Catholic Politicians of the United States Conference of Catholic Bishops (USCCB). It was approved by the members of the Task Force, including the chairmen of the USCCB Committees on Doctrine, Pro-Life, International Policy, Domestic Policy, Communications, Migration, and Education. It was also reviewed and approved by the Vatican Congregation for the Doctrine of the Faith. It has been authorized for publication by the undersigned.

Msgr. William P. Fay

General Secretary, USCCB

First Printing, January 2006

ISBN 1-57455-703-3

Contents

Documents of the Bishops of the United States

Introduction

In June 2004, the United States Conference of Catholic Bishops (USCCB) issued *Catholics in Political Life*, a statement on the responsibilities of Catholics who serve in public life. In this statement, the bishops acknowledged their responsibility to teach clearly about the obligations that all Catholics have in the public arena and to affirm their unequivocal commitment as a community of faith to the protection of human life from the moment of conception until natural death. This compendium, *Readings on Catholics in Political Life*, has been developed as part of the bishops' efforts to fulfill their commitment to share this important teaching. This book is intended to help Catholics—including those who serve in public life—to understand more fully how the church's teachings should shape everyone's participation in the political process.

Readings draws from a wide range of papal documents, other statements of the universal Church, and statements from the United States Conference of Catholic Bishops. It brings together excerpts and full documents that express important aspects of the Church's teaching on the responsibilities of Catholics in political life.

Readings is not a comprehensive compilation of Catholic teaching on these matters. It does not address questions regarding worthiness to receive Holy Communion, as this topic falls under the jurisdiction of the USCCB Committee on Doctrine and the Committee on Pastoral Practices, which continue to develop teaching and guidance in this area. Instead, *Readings* highlights key ideas from Catholic teaching about the responsibilities of Catholics in public life, the role of the Church in relationship to the political order, and the values and principles that have shaped how the Church responds to public issues affecting human life and human dignity.

As the Second Vatican Council said in its *Decree Concerning the Pastoral Office of Bishops in the Church* (*Christus Dominus*):

> In exercising their duty of teaching—which is conspicuous among the principal duties of bishops[2]—they should announce the Gospel of Christ to men, calling them to a faith in the power of the Spirit or confirming them in a living faith. They should expound the whole mystery of Christ to them, namely, those truths the ignorance of which is ignorance of Christ. At the

same time they should point out the divinely revealed way to give glory to God and thereby to attain to eternal happiness.[3]

They should show, moreover, that earthly goods and human institutions according to the plan of God the Creator are also disposed for man's salvation and therefore can contribute much to the building up of the body of Christ.

Therefore, they should teach, according to the doctrine of the Church, the great value of these things: the human person with his freedom and bodily life, the family and its unity and stability, the procreation and education of children, civil society with its laws and professions, labor and leisure, the arts and technical inventions, poverty and affluence. Finally, they should set forth the ways by which are to be answered the most serious questions concerning the ownership, increase, and just distribution of material goods, peace and war, and brotherly relations among all countries.[4] (Second Vatican Council, Decree Concerning the Pastoral Office of Bishops in the Church [Christus Dominus] [Rome: October 28, 1965], no. 12), at *www.vatican.va*.

This book is intended to help bishops carry out their essential roles as leaders and teachers on these important matters, to help Catholic politicians understand their responsibilities to act on their faith, and to help all Catholics learn about their obligations in public life. A wide range of documents and statements on these topics, from the universal Church and from the bishops of the United States, could not be included here. We encourage Catholics to explore these documents more deeply. A list of websites where many of these documents can be found is provided in an appendix. We hope that *Readings on Catholics in Political Life* will only be the first step in a process of learning and reflecting on the Church's teaching about political life.

> Cardinal Theodore McCarrick
> Chairman, Task Force on
> Catholic Bishops and Catholic Politicians

2,3,4 Cf. Second Vatican Council, *Dogmatic Constitution on the Church* (*Lumen Gentium*), no. 22: AAS. 57 (1965) pp. 25-27.

Papal
Documents

✠ ✠ ✠

On the Occasion of the Eightieth Anniversary of *Rerum Novarum* (*Octogesima Adveniens*)

Pope Paul VI, 1971

Christian Meaning of Political Activity

46.   Is it not here that there appears a radical limitation to economics? Economic activity is necessary and, if it is at the service of man, it can be "a source of brotherhood and a sign of Providence."[28] It is the occasion of concrete exchanges between man, of rights recognized, of services rendered and of dignity affirmed in work. Though it is often a field of confrontation and domination, it can give rise to dialogue and foster cooperation. Yet it runs the risk of taking up too much strength and freedom.[29] This is why the need is felt to pass from economics to politics. It is true that in the term "politics" many confusions are possible and must be clarified, but each man feels that in the social and economic field, both national and international, the ultimate decision rests with political power.

Political power, which is the natural and necessary link for ensuring the cohesion of the social body, must have as its aim the achievement of the common good. While respecting the legitimate liberties of individuals, families and subsidiary groups, it acts in such a way as to create, effectively and for the well-being of all, the conditions required for attaining man's true and complete good, including his spiritual end. It acts within the limits of its competence, which can vary from people to people and from country to country. It always intervenes with care for justice and with devotion to the common good, for which it holds final responsibility. It does not, for all that, deprive individuals and intermediary bodies of the field of activity and responsibility which are proper to them and which lead them to collaborate in the attainment

Paul VI, *On the Occasion of the Eightieth Anniversary of* Rerum Novarum (*Octogesima Adveniens*), nos. 46-51 (May 14, 1971). See http://www.vatican.va/holy_father/paul_vi/apost_letters/documents/ hf_p-vi_apl_19710514_octogesima-adveniens_en.html (accessed May 9, 2005).

of this common good. In fact, "the true aim of all social activity should be to help individual members of the social body, but never to destroy or absorb them."[30] According to the vocation proper to it, the political power must know how to stand aside from particular interests in order to view its responsibility with regard to the good of all men, even going beyond national limits. To take politics seriously at its different levels—local, regional, national, and worldwide—is to affirm the duty of man, of every man, to recognize the concrete reality and the value of the freedom of choice that is offered to him to seek to bring about both the good of the city and of the nation and of mankind. Politics are a demanding manner—but not the only one—of living the Christian commitment to the service of others. Without of course solving every problem, it endeavors to apply solutions to the relationships men have with one another. The domain of politics is wide and comprehensive, but it is not exclusive. An attitude of encroachment which would tend to set up politics as an absolute value would bring serious danger. While recognizing the autonomy of the reality of politics, Christians who are invited to take up political activity should try to make their choices consistent with the Gospel and, in the framework of a legitimate plurality, to give both personal collective witness to the seriousness of their faith by effective and disinterested service of men.

Sharing in Responsibility

47. The passing to the political dimension also expresses a demand made by the man of today: a greater sharing in responsibility and in decision-making. This legitimate aspiration becomes more evident as the cultural level rises, as the sense of freedom develops, and as man becomes more aware of how, in a world facing an uncertain future, the choices of today already condition the life of tomorrow. In *Mater et Magistra*[31] Pope John XXIII stressed how much the admittance to responsibility is a basic demand of man's nature, a concrete exercise of his freedom, and a path to his development, and he showed how, in economic life and particularly in enterprise, this sharing in responsibilities should be ensured.[32] Today the field is wider, and extends to the social and political sphere in which a reasonable sharing in responsibility and in decisions must be established and strengthened. Admittedly, it is true that the choices proposed for a decision are more and more complex; the

considerations that must be borne in mind are numerous, and foreseeing of the consequences involves risk, even if new sciences strive to enlighten freedom at these important moments. However, although limits are sometimes called for, these obstacles must not slow down the giving of wider participation in working out decisions, making choices, and putting them into practice. In order to counterbalance increasing technocracy, modern forms of democracy must be devised, not only making it possible for each man to become informed and to express himself, but also by involving him in a shared responsibility.

Thus human groups will gradually begin to share and to live as communities. Thus freedom, which too often asserts itself as a claim for autonomy by opposing the freedom of others, will develop in its deepest human reality: to involve itself and to spend itself in building up active and lived solidarity. But, for the Christian, it is by losing himself in God who sets him free that man finds true freedom, renewed in the death and resurrection of the Lord.

CALL TO ACTION
Need to Become Involved in Action

48.   In the social sphere, the Church has always wished to assume a double function: first to enlighten minds in order to assist them to discover the truth and to find the right path to follow amid the different teachings that call for their attention; and secondly to take part in action and to spread, with a real care for service and effectiveness, the energies of the Gospel. Is it not in order to be faithful to this desire that the Church has sent on an apostolic mission among the workers priests who, by sharing fully the condition of the worker, are at that level the witnesses to the Church's solicitude and seeking?

It is to all Christians that we address a fresh and insistent call to action. In our encyclical on the Development of Peoples we urged that all should set themselves to the task: "Laymen should take up as their own proper task the renewal of the temporal order. If the role of the hierarchy is to teach and to interpret authentically the norms of morality to be followed in this matter, it belongs to the laity, without waiting passively for orders and directives, to take the initiatives freely and to infuse a Christian spirit into the mentality, customs, laws and structures of the community in which they live."[33] Let each one examine himself, to see what he has done up to now, and what he ought to do. It is not enough to recall principles, state intentions, point to crying injustice, and utter prophetic denunciations; these words will lack real weight unless they are accompanied for each individual by a livelier awareness of personal responsibility and by effective action. It is too easy to throw back on others responsibility for injustice, if at the same time one does not realize how each one shares in it personally, and how personal conversion is needed first. This basic humility will rid action of all inflexibility and sectarianism; it will also avoid discouragement in the face of a task which seems limitless in size. The Christian's hope comes primarily from the fact that he knows that the Lord is working with us in the world, continuing in his Body which is the Church—and, through the Church, in the whole of mankind—the Redemption which was accomplished on the Cross and which burst forth in victory on the morning of the Resurrection.[34] This hope springs also from the fact that the Christian knows that other men are at work, to undertake actions of justice and peace working for the same ends. For beneath an outward appearance of indifference, in the heart of every man there is a will to live in brotherhood and a thirst for justice and peace, which is to be expanded.

Each One to Determine

49.   Thus, amid the diversity of situations, functions and organizations, each one must determine, in his conscience, the actions which he is called to share in. Surrounded by various currents into which, besides legitimate aspirations, there insinuate themselves more ambiguous tendencies, the Christian must make a wise and vigilant choice and avoid involving himself in collaboration without conditions and contrary to the principles of a true humanism, even in the name of a genuinely left solidarity. If in fact he wishes to play a specific part as a Christian in accordance with his faith—a part that unbelievers themselves expect of him—he must take care in the midst of his active commitment to clarify his motives and to rise above the objectives aimed at, by taking a more all-embracing view which will avoid the danger of selfish particularism and oppressive totalitarianism.

Pluralism of Options

50.   In concrete situations, and taking account of solidarity in each person's life, one must recognize a legitimate variety of possible options. The same Christian faith can lead to different commitments.[35] The Church invites all Christians to take up a double task of inspiring and of innovating, in order to make structures evolve, so as to adapt them to the real needs of today. From Christians who at first sight seem to be in opposition, as a result of starting from differing options, she asks an effort at mutual understanding of the other's positions and motives; a loyal examination of one's behavior and its correctness will suggest to each one an attitude of more profound charity which, while recognizing the differences, believes nonetheless in the possibility of convergence and unity. "The bonds which unite the faithful are mightier than any-thing which divides them."[36]

It is true that many people, in the midst of modern structures and conditioning circumstances, are determined by their habits of thought and their functions, even apart from the safeguarding of material inter-ests. Others feel so deeply the solidarity of classes and cultures that they reach the point of sharing without reserve all the judgments and options of their surroundings.[37] Each one will take great care to exam-ine himself and to bring about that true freedom according to Christ which makes one receptive to the universal in the very midst of the most particular conditions.

"Awakening the People of God"

51.   It is in this regard too that Christian organizations, under their different forms, have a responsibility for collective action. Without put-ting themselves in the place of the institutions of civil society, they have to express, in their own way and rising above their particular nature, the concrete demands of the Christian faith for a just, and consequently nec-essary, transformation of society.[38]

Today more than ever the Word of God will be unable to be pro-claimed and heard unless it is accompanied by the witness of the power of the Holy Spirit, working within the action of Christian in the service of their brothers, at the points in which their existence and their future are at stake.

NOTES

28   *Populorum Progressio* 86: AAS 59 (1967), p. 299.

29   *Gaudium et Spes*, 63: AAS 58 (1966), p. 1085.

30   *Quadragesimo Anno*: AAS 23 (1931), p. 203; cf. *Mater et Magistra*: AAS 53 (1961), pp. 414, 428;
     Gaudium et Spes, 74-76: AAS 58 (1966), pp. 1095-1100.

31   AAS 53 (19fil), pp. 420-422.

32   *Gaudium et Spes*, 68, 75: AAS 58 (1966), pp. 1089-1090, 1097.

33   81: AAS 59 (1967); pp. 296-297.

34   Cf. Mt 28:30; Phil 2:8-11.

35   *Gaudium et Spes*, 43: AAS 58 (1966), p. 1061.

36   Ibid., 93: p. 1113.

37   Cf. 1 Thes 5:21.

38   *Lumen Gentium*, 31: AAS 57 (1965), pp. 37-38; *Apostolicam Actuositatem*, 5: AAS 58 (1966),
     p. 842.

On the Vocation and the Mission of the Lay Faithful in the Church and in the World (*Christifideles Laici*)

Pope John Paul II, 1988

INTRODUCTION

The Pressing Needs of the World Today: "Why do you stand here idle all day?"

3. The basic meaning of this Synod, and the most precious fruit desired as a result of it, is *the lay faithful's hearkening to the call of Christ the Lord to work in his vineyard*, to take an active, conscientious, and responsible part in the mission of the Church *in this great moment in history*, made especially dramatic by occurring on the threshold of the Third Millennium.

A new state of affairs today both in the Church and in social, economic, political, and cultural life calls with a particular urgency for the action of the lay faithful. If lack of commitment is always unacceptable, the present time renders it even more so. *It is not permissible for anyone to remain idle.*

We continue in our reading of the Gospel parable: "And about the eleventh hour he went out and found others standing; and he said to them, 'Why do you stand here idle all day?' They said to him, 'Because no one has hired us.' He said to them, 'You go into the vineyard too'" (Mt 20:6-7).

Since the work that awaits everyone in the vineyard of the Lord is so great, there is no place for idleness. With even greater urgency the "householder" repeats his invitation: "You go into my vineyard too."

John Paul II, *On the Vocation and the Mission of the Lay Faithful in the Church and in the World* (*Christifideles Laici*), nos. 3, 5, 38, 42, 59-60. (December 30, 1988). See http://www.vatican.va/holy_father/john_paul_ii/apost_exhortations/documents/hf_jp-ii_exh_30121988_christifideles-laici_en.html (accessed May 9, 2005).

The voice of the Lord clearly resounds in the depths of each of Christ's followers, who through faith and the sacraments of Christian initiation is made like to Jesus Christ, is incorporated as a living member in the Church, and has an active part in her mission of salvation. The voice of the Lord also comes to be heard through the historic events of the Church and humanity, as the Council reminds us: "The People of God believes that it is led by the Spirit of the Lord, who fills the whole world. Moved by this faith it tries to discern authentic signs of God's presence and purpose in the events, the needs, and the longings which it shares with other people of our time. For faith throws a new light on all things and makes known the full ideal to which God has called each individual, and thus guides the mind towards solutions which are fully human."[6]

It is necessary, then, to keep a watchful eye on this our world, with its problems and values, its unrest and hopes, its defeats and triumphs: a world whose economic, social, political, and cultural affairs pose problems and grave difficulties in light of the description provided by the Council in the Pastoral Constitution, *Gaudium et Spes*.[7] *This*, then, is the vineyard; *this* is the field in which the faithful are called to fulfill their mission. Jesus wants them, as he wants all his disciples, to be the "salt of the earth" and the "light of the world" (cf. Mt 5:13-14). But what is the *actual state of affairs of the "earth" and the "world,"* for which Christians ought to be "salt" and "light"?

The variety of situations and problems that exist in our world is indeed great and rapidly changing. For this reason it is all the more necessary to guard against generalizations and unwarranted simplifications. It is possible, however, to highlight *some trends that are emerging in present-day society.* The Gospel records that the weeds and the good grain grew together in the farmer's field. The same is true in history, where in everyday life there often exist contradictions in the exercise of human freedom, where there is found, side by side and at times closely intertwined, evil and good, injustice and justice, anguish and hope.

NOTES

6 Second Vatican Council, *Pastoral Constitution on the Church in the Modern World* (*Gaudium et Spes*), no. 11.

7 The Fathers of the Extraordinary Synod of 1985, after affirming "the great importance and timeliness of the Pastoral Constitution, *Gaudium et Spes*," continue: "Nevertheless, at the same time, they perceive that the signs of our times are in part different from those at the time of the Council, with its problems and major trials. In fact, hunger, oppression, injustice and war, suffering terrorism and forms of various kinds of violence are growing everywhere in the world today" (*Ecclesia sub Verbo Dei Mysteria Christi Celebrans pro salute Mundi. Relatio Finalis*, II, D, 1).

The Human Person: A Dignity Violated and Exalted

5. We furthermore call to mind the *violations* to which the human person is subjected. When the individual is not recognized and loved in the person's dignity as the living image of God (cf. Gen 1:26), the human being is exposed to more humiliating and degrading forms of "manipulation" that most assuredly reduce the individual to a slavery to those who are stronger. "Those who are stronger" can take a variety of names: an ideology, economic power, political and inhumane systems, scientific technocracy or the intrusiveness of the mass media. Once again we find ourselves before many persons, our sisters and brothers, whose fundamental rights are being violated, owing to their exceedingly great capacity for endurance and to the clear injustice of certain civil laws: the right to life and to integrity, the right to a house and to work, the right to a family and responsible parenthood, the right to participation in public and political life, the right to freedom of conscience and the practice of religion.

Who is able to count the number of babies unborn because they have been killed in their mothers' wombs, children abandoned and abused by their own parents, children who grow without affection and education? In some countries entire populations are deprived of housing and work, lacking the means absolutely essential for leading a life worthy of a human being, and are deprived even of those things necessary for their sustenance. There are great areas of poverty and of misery, both physical and moral, existing at this moment on the periphery of great cities. Entire groups of human beings have been seriously afflicted.

But the *sacredness of the human person* cannot be obliterated, no matter how often it is devalued and violated, because it has its unshakable foundation in God as Creator and Father. The sacredness of the person always keeps returning, again and again.

The sense of the dignity of the human person must be pondered and reaffirmed in stronger terms. A beneficial trend is advancing and permeating all peoples of the earth, making them ever more aware of the dignity of the individual: the person is not at all a "thing" or an "object" to be used, but primarily a responsible "subject," one endowed with conscience and freedom, called to live responsibly in society and history, and oriented towards spiritual and religious values.

It has been said that ours is the time of "humanism": paradoxically, some of its atheistic and secularistic forms arrive at a point where the human person is diminished and annihilated; other forms of humanism, instead, exalt the individual in such a manner that these forms become a veritable and real idolatry. There are still other forms, however, in line with the truth, which rightly acknowledge the greatness and misery of individuals and manifest, sustain, and foster the total dignity of the human person.

The sign and fruit of this trend towards humanism is the growing need for participation, which is undoubtedly one of the distinctive features of present-day humanity, a true "sign of the times" that is developing in various fields and in different ways: above all the growing need for participation regarding women and young people, not only in areas of family and academic life, but also in cultural, economic, social, and political areas. To be leading characters in this development, in some ways to be creators of a new, more humane culture, is a requirement both for the individual and for peoples as a whole.[10]

NOTE

10   Cf. *Instrumentum Laboris*, "The Vocation and Mission of the Lay Faithful in the Church and in the World Twenty Years after the Second Vatican Council," 5-10.

Respecting the Inviolable Right to Life

38.   In effect the acknowledgment of the personal dignity of every human being demands *the respect, the defense, and the promotion of the rights of the human person*. It is a question of inherent, universal, and inviolable rights. No one, no individual, no group, no authority, no State, can change—let alone eliminate—them because such rights find their source in God himself.

The inviolability of the person, which is a reflection of the absolute inviolability of God, finds its primary and fundamental expression in the *inviolability of human life*. Above all, the common outcry, which is justly made on behalf of human rights—for example, the right to health, to home, to work, to family, to culture—is false and illusory if *the right to life*, the most basic and fundamental right and the condition for all other personal rights, is not defended with maximum determination.

The Church has never yielded in the face of all the violations that the right to life of every human being has received, and continues to receive, both from individuals and from those in authority. The human being is entitled to such rights, *in every phase of development*, from conception until natural death; and *in every condition*, whether healthy or sick, whole or handicapped, rich or poor. The Second Vatican Council openly proclaimed: "All offences against life itself, such as every kind of murder, genocide, abortion, euthanasia and willful suicide; all violations of the integrity of the human person, such as mutilation, physical and mental torture, undue psychological pressures; all offences against human dignity, such as subhuman living conditions, arbitrary imprisonment, deportation, slavery, prostitution, the selling of women and children, degrading working conditions where men are treated as mere tools for profit rather than free and responsible persons; all these and the like are certainly criminal: they poison human society; and they do more harm to those who practice them than those who suffer from the injury. Moreover, they are a supreme dishonor to the Creator."[137]

If, indeed, everyone has the mission and responsibility of acknowledging the personal dignity of every human being and of defending the right to life, some lay faithful are given a particular title to this task: such as *parents, teachers, health workers, and the many who hold economic and political power.*

The Church today lives a fundamental aspect of her mission in lovingly and generously accepting every human being, especially those who are weak and sick. This is made all the more necessary as a "culture of death" threatens to take control. In fact, "the Church family believes that human life, even if weak and suffering, is always a wonderful gift of God's goodness. Against the pessimism and selfishness which casts a shadow over the world, the Church stands for life: in each human life she sees the splendor of that 'Yes,' that 'Amen,' which is Christ himself (cf. 2 Cor 1:19; Rev 3:14). To the 'No' which assails and afflicts the world, she replies with this living 'Yes,' this defending of the human person and the world from all who plot against life."[138] It is the responsibility of the lay faithful, who more directly through their vocation or their profession are involved in accepting life, to make the Church's "Yes" to human life concrete and efficacious.

The enormous development of *biological and medical science,* united to an amazing power *in technology,* today provides possibilities on the very frontier of human life which imply new responsibilities. In fact, today humanity is in the position not only of "observing" but even "exercising a control over" human life at its very beginning and in its first stages of development.

The *moral conscience* of humanity is not able to turn aside or remain indifferent in the face of these gigantic strides accomplished by a technology that is acquiring a continually more extensive and profound dominion over the working processes that govern procreation and the first phases of human life. Today as perhaps never before in history or in this field, *wisdom shows itself to be the only firm basis to salvation,* in that persons engaged in scientific research and in its application are always to act with intelligence and love, that is, respecting, even remaining in veneration of, the inviolable dignity of the personhood of every human being, from the first moment of life's existence. This occurs when science and technology are committed with licit means to the defense of life and the cure of disease in its beginnings, refusing on the contrary—even for the dignity of research itself—to perform operations that result in falsifying the genetic patrimony of the individual and of human generative power.[139]

The lay faithful, having responsibility in various capacities and at different levels of science as well as in the medical, social, legislative, and economic fields, *must courageously accept the "challenge" posed by new problems in bioethics.* The Synod Fathers used these words: "Christians ought to exercise their responsibilities as masters of science and technology, and not become their slaves. . . . In view of the moral challenges presented by enormous new technological power, endangering not only fundamental human rights but the very biological essence of the human species, it is of utmost importance that lay Christians with the help of the universal Church—take up the task of calling culture back to the principles of an authentic humanism, giving a dynamic and sure foundation to the promotion and defense of the rights of the human being in one's very essence, an essence which the preaching of the Gospel reveals to all."[140]

Today maximum vigilance must be exercised by everyone in the face of the phenomenon of the concentration of power and technology. In fact such a concentration has a tendency to manipulate not only the biological essence but the very content of people's consciences and life styles, thereby worsening the condition of entire peoples by discrimination and marginalization.

NOTES

137 Second Vatican Council, *Pastoral Constitution on the Church in the Modern World* (*Gaudium et Spes*), no. 27.

138 John Paul II, Apostolic Exhortation *Familiaris Consortio*, no. 30: AAS 74 (1982), 116.

139 Cf. Congregation for the Doctrine of the Faith, *Instruction on the Respect for Human Life in its Origin and the Dignity of Procreation: Responses to Some Questions in Bioethics* (*Donum Vitae*) (11 March 1987): AAS 80 (1988), 70-102.

140 John Paul II, Message for the Twenty-First World Day of Peace, "Religious Freedom: Condition for Peace" (8 December 1987): AAS 80 (1988), 278, 280.

Public Life: For Everyone and By Everyone

42.   A charity that loves and serves the person is never able to be separated from *justice*. Each in its own way demands the full, effective acknowledgment of the rights of the individual, to which society is ordered in all its structures and institutions.[149]

In order to achieve their task directed to the Christian animation of the temporal order, in the sense of serving persons and society, the lay faithful *are never to relinquish their participation in "public life,"* that is, in the many different economic, social, legislative, administrative, and cultural areas, which are intended to promote organically and institutionally the *common good*. The Synod Fathers have repeatedly affirmed that every person has a right and duty to participate in public life, albeit in a diversity and complementarity of forms, levels, tasks, and responsibilities. Charges of careerism, idolatry of power, egoism, and corruption that are oftentimes directed at persons in government, parliaments, the ruling classes, or political parties, as well as the common opinion that participating in politics is an absolute moral danger, do not in the least justify either skepticism or an absence on the part of Christians in public life.

On the contrary, the Second Vatican Council's words are particularly significant: "The Church regards as worthy of praise and consideration the work of those who, as a service to others, dedicate themselves to the public good of the state and undertake the burdens of this task."[150]

Public life on behalf of the person and society finds its *basic standard in the pursuit of the common good,* as the good of *everyone* and as the good of each person taken as a *whole*, which is guaranteed and offered in a fitting manner to people, both as individuals and in groups, for their free and responsible acceptance. "The political community"—we read in the Constitution *Gaudium et Spes*—exists for that common good in which "the community finds its full justification" and meaning, and from which it derives its basic, proper, and lawful arrangement. The common good embraces the sum total of all those conditions of social life by which individuals, families, and organizations can achieve more thoroughly their own fulfillment.[151] Furthermore, public life on behalf of the person and society finds *its continuous line of action* in *the defense and the promotion of justice,* understood to be a "virtue," an understanding which requires education, as well as a moral "force" that sustains the obligation to foster the rights and duties of each and everyone, based on the personal dignity of each human being.

The spirit of service is a fundamental element in the exercise of political power. This spirit of service, together with the necessary competence and efficiency, can make "virtuous" or "above criticism" the activity of persons in public life which is justly demanded by the rest of the people. To accomplish this requires a full-scale battle and a determination to overcome every temptation, such as the recourse to disloyalty and to falsehood, the waste of public funds for the advantage of a few and those with special interests, and the use of ambiguous and illicit means for acquiring, maintaining, and increasing power at any cost.

The lay faithful given a charge in public life certainly ought to respect the autonomy of earthly realities properly understood, as we read in the Constitution *Gaudium et Spes*: "It is of great importance, especially in a pluralistic society, to work out a proper vision of the relationship between the political community and the Church, and to distinguish clearly between the activities of Christians, acting individually or collectively, in their own name as citizens guided by the dictates of a Christian conscience, and their activity in communion with their Pastors in the name of the Church. The Church by reason of her role and competence, is not identified with any political community nor bound by ties to any political system. She is at once the sign and the safeguard of the transcendental dimension of the human person."[152] At the same time—and this is felt today as a pressing responsibility—the lay faithful must bear witness to those human and gospel values that are intimately connected with political activity itself, such as liberty and justice, solidarity, faithful and unselfish dedication for the good of all, a simple lifestyle, and a preferential love for the poor and the least. This demands that the lay faithful always be more animated by a real participation in the life of the Church and enlightened by her social doctrine. In this they can be supported and helped by the nearness of the Christian community and their Pastor.[153]

The manner and means for achieving a public life which has true human development as its goal is *solidarity*. This concerns the active and responsible *participation* of all in public life, from individual citizens to various groups, from labor unions to political parties. All of us, each and everyone, are the goal of public life as well as its leading participants. In this environment, as I wrote in the Encyclical *Sollicitudo Rei Socialis*, solidarity "is not a feeling of vague compassion or shallow distress at the misfortunes of so many people, both near and far. On the contrary, it is *a firm and persevering determination* to commit oneself to the *common good*, that is to say, to the good of all and of each individual because *we are all really responsible for all.*"[154]

Today political solidarity requires going beyond single nations or a single block of nations, to a consideration on a properly continental and world level.

The fruit of sound political activity, which is so much desired by everyone but always lacking in advancement, is *peace*. The lay faithful cannot remain indifferent or be strangers and inactive in the face of all that denies and compromises peace, namely, violence and war, torture and terrorism, concentration camps, militarization of public life, the arms race, and the nuclear threat. On the contrary, as disciples of Jesus Christ, "Prince of Peace" (Is 9:5) and "Our Peace" (Eph 2:14), the lay faithful ought to take upon themselves the task of being "peacemakers" (Mt 5:9), both through a conversion of "heart," justice, and charity, all of which are the undeniable foundation of peace.[155]

The lay faithful, in working together with all those that truly seek peace and themselves serving in specific organizations as well as national and international institutions, ought to promote an extensive work of education intended to defeat the ruling culture of egoism, hate, the vendetta, and hostility, and thereby to develop the culture of solidarity at every level. Such solidarity, in fact, "*is the way to peace and at the same time to development.*"[156] From this perspective the Synod Fathers have invited Christians to reject as unacceptable all forms of violence, to promote attitudes of dialogue and peace, and to commit themselves to establish a just international and social order.[157]

NOTES

149 For the relationship between justice and mercy, see John Paul II, Encyclical Letter *Dives in Misericordia*, 12: AAS 72 (1980), 1215-1217.

150 Second Vatican Council, *Pastoral Constitution on the Church in the Modern World* (*Gaudium et Spes*), no. 75.

151 Ibid., no. 74.

152 Ibid., no. 76.

153 Cf. *Propositio* 28.

154 John Paul II, Encyclical Letter *Sollicitudo Rei Socialis*, 38: AAS 80 (1988), 565-566.

155 Cf. John XXIII, Encyclical Letter *Pacem in Terris*: AAS 55 (1963), 265-266.

156 John Paul II, Encyclical Letter *Sollicitudo Rei Socialis*, 39: AAS 80 (1988), 568.

157 Cf. *Propositio* 26.

A Total Integrated Formation for Living an Integrated Life

59. In discovering and living their proper vocation and mission, the lay faithful must be formed according to the *union* which exists from their being *members of the Church and citizens of human society*.

There cannot be two parallel lives in their existence: on the one hand, the so-called "spiritual" life, with its values and demands; and on the other, the so-called "secular" life, that is, life in a family, at work, in social relationships, in the responsibilities of public life, and in culture. The branch, engrafted to the vine which is Christ, bears its fruit in every sphere of existence and activity. In fact, every area of the lay faithful's lives, as different as they are, enters into the plan of God, who desires that these very areas be the "places in time" where the love of Christ is revealed and realized for both the glory of the Father and service of others. Every activity, every situation, every precise responsibility—as, for example, skill and solidarity in work, love and dedication in the family and the education of children, service to society and public life, and the promotion of truth in the area of culture—are the occasions ordained by Providence for a "continuous exercise of faith, hope and charity."[211]

The Second Vatican Council has invited all the lay faithful to this *unity of life* by forcefully decrying the grave consequences in separating faith from life, and the gospel from culture: "The Council exhorts Christians, as citizens of one city and the other, to strive to perform their earthly duties faithfully in response to the spirit of the Gospel. They are mistaken who, knowing that we have here no abiding city but seek one which is to come, think that they may therefore shirk their earthly responsibilities; for they are forgetting that by faith itself they are more than ever obliged to measure up to these duties, each according to one's vocation. . . . This split between the faith which many profess and their daily lives deserves to be counted among the more serious errors of our age."[212]

Therefore, I have maintained that a faith that does not affect a person's culture is a faith "not fully embraced, not entirely thought out, not faithfully lived."[213]

Various Aspects of Formation

60.   The many interrelated aspects of a *totally integrated formation* of the lay faithful are situated within this unity of life.

There is no doubt that *spiritual* formation ought to occupy a privileged place in a person's life. Everyone is called to grow continually in intimate union with Jesus Christ, in conformity to the Father's will, in devotion to others in charity and justice. The Council writes: "This life of intimate union with Christ in the Church is nourished by spiritual helps available to all the faithful, especially by active participation in the liturgy. Lay people should so make use of these helps in such a way that, while properly fulfilling their secular duties in the ordinary conditions of life, they do not disassociate union with Christ from that life, but through the very performance of their tasks according to God's will, may they actually grow in it."[214]

The situation today points to an ever-increasing urgency for a *doctrinal* formation of the lay faithful, not simply in a better understanding which is natural to faith's dynamism but also in enabling them to "give a reason for their hoping" in view of the world and its grave and complex problems. Therefore, a systematic approach to *catechesis*, geared to age and the diverse situations of life, is an absolute necessity, as is a more decided Christian promotion of *culture*, in response to the perennial yet always new questions that concern individuals and society today.

This is especially true for the lay faithful who have responsibilities in various fields of society and public life. Above all, it is indispensable that they have a more exact knowledge—and this demands a more widespread and precise presentation—of the *Church's social doctrine*, as repeatedly stressed by the Synod Fathers in their presentations. They refer to the participation of the lay faithful in public life, in the following words: "But for the lay faithful to take up actively this noble purpose in political matters, it is not enough to exhort them. They must be offered a proper formation of a social conscience, especially in the Church's social teaching, which contains principles—of reflection, criteria for judging and practical directives (cf. Congregation for the Doctrine of the Faith, *Instruction on Christian Freedom and Liberation*, 72), and which must be present in general catechetical instruction and in specialized gatherings, as well as in schools and universities. Nevertheless, this social doctrine of the Church is dynamic; that is, adapted to circumstances of time and place. It is the right and duty of Pastors to propose moral principles even concerning the social order and of all Christians to apply them in defense of human rights. Nevertheless, active participation in political parties is reserved to the lay faithful."[215]

The cultivation of *human values* finds a place in the context of a totally integrated formation, bearing a particular significance for the missionary and apostolic activities of the lay faithful. In this regard the Council wrote: "(the lay faithful) should also hold in high esteem professional skill, family and civic spirit, and the virtues related to social behavior, namely, honesty, a spirit of justice, sincerity, courtesy, moral courage; without them there is no true Christian life."[216]

In bringing their lives into an organic synthesis, which is, at one and the same time, the manifestation of the unity of "who they are" in the Church and society as well as the condition for the effective fulfillment of their mission, the lay faithful are to be guided interiorly and sustained by the Holy Spirit, who is the Spirit of unity and fullness of life.

NOTES

211 Second Vatican Council, *Decree on the Apostolate of Lay People* (*Apostolicam Actuositatem*), no. 4.

212 Second Vatican Council, *Pastoral Constitution on the Church in the Modern World* (*Gaudium et Spes*), no. 43. Cf. also Second Vatican Council, *Decree on the Mission Activity of the Church* (*Ad Gentes*), no. 21; Paul VI, Apostolic Exhortation *On Evangelization in the Modern World* (*Evangelii Nuntiandi*), no. 20: AAS 68 (1976), 19.

213 John Paul II, Discourse to the Participants in the National Congress of Church Movements of Cultural Responsibility (MEIC) (16 January 1982), 2; *Insegnamenti*, V, I (1982), 131; Also Letter to Cardinal Agostino Casaroli, Secretary of State, establishing the Pontifical Council for Culture (20 May 1982: AAS 74 (1982), 685; Discourse to the Community of the University of Louvain (20 May 1985), 2; *Insegnamenti*, VIII, 1 (1985), 1591.

214 Second Vatican Council, *Decree on the Apostolate of Lay People* (*Apostolicam Actuositatem*), no. 4.

215 *Propositio* 22; cf. also John Paul II, Encyclical *Sollicitudo Rei Socialis*, 41: AAS 80 (1988), 570-572.

216 Second Vatican Council, *Decree on the Apostolate of Lay People* (*Apostolicam Actuositatem*), no. 4.

On the Hundredth Anniversary of Rerum Novarum (*Centesimus Annus*)

Pope John Paul II, 1991

46. The Church values the democratic system inasmuch as it ensures the participation of citizens in making political choices, guarantees to the governed the possibility both of electing and holding accountable those who govern them, and of replacing them through peaceful means when appropriate.[93] Thus she cannot encourage the formation of narrow ruling groups which usurp the power of the State for individual interests or for ideological ends.

Authentic democracy is possible only in a State ruled by law, and on the basis of a correct conception of the human person. It requires that the necessary conditions be present for the advancement both of the individual through education and formation in true ideals, and of the "subjectivity" of society through the creation of structures of participation and shared responsibility. Nowadays there is a tendency to claim that agnosticism and sceptical relativism are the philosophy and the basic attitude which correspond to democratic forms of political life. Those who are convinced that they know the truth and firmly adhere to it are considered unreliable from a democratic point of view, since they do not accept that truth is determined by the majority, or that it is subject to variation according to different political trends. It must be observed in this regard that if there is no ultimate truth to guide and direct political activity, then ideas and convictions can easily be manipulated for reasons of power. As history demonstrates, a democracy without values easily turns into open or thinly disguised totalitarianism.

John Paul II, *On the Hundredth Anniversary of* Rerum Novarum (*Centesimus Annus*), no. 46 (May 1, 1991). See http://www.vatican.va/edocs/ENG0214/__P7.HTM (accessed October 11, 2005).

Nor does the Church close her eyes to the danger of fanaticism or fundamentalism among those who, in the name of an ideology which purports to be scientific or religious, claim the right to impose on others their own concept of what is true and good. *Christian truth* is not of this kind. Since it is not an ideology, the Christian faith does not presume to imprison changing socio-political realities in a rigid schema, and it recognizes that human life is realized in history in conditions that are diverse and imperfect. Furthermore, in constantly reaffirming the transcendent dignity of the person, the Church's method is always that of respect for freedom.[94]

But freedom attains its full development only by accepting the truth. In a world without truth, freedom loses its foundation and man is exposed to the violence of passion and to manipulation, both open and hidden. The Christian upholds freedom and serves it, constantly offering to others the truth which he has known (cf. Jn 8:31-32), in accordance with the missionary nature of his vocation. While paying heed to every fragment of truth which he encounters in the life experience and in the culture of individuals and of nations, he will not fail to affirm in dialogue with others all that his faith and the correct use of reason have enabled him to understand.[95]

NOTES

93   Cf. Second Vatican Ecumenical Council, *Pastoral Constitution on the Church in the World of Today* (*Gaudium et Spes*), 29; Pius XII, Christmas Radio Message on December 24, 1944: AAS 37 (1945), 10-20.

94   Cf. Second Vatican Ecumenical Council, Declaration on Religious Freedom *Dignitatis Humanae*.

95   Cf. Encyclical Letter *Redemptoris Missio*, 11 : *L'OsservatoreRomano*, January 23, 1991.

On the Value and Inviolability of Human Life
(*Evangelium Vitae*)
Pope John Paul II, 1995

"What have you done?" (Gen 4:10):

The Eclipse of the Value of Life

10.   The Lord said to Cain: "What have you done? The voice of your brother's blood is crying to me from the ground" (Gen 4:10). The voice of the blood shed by men continues to cry out, from generation to generation, in ever new and different ways.

The Lord's question "What have you done?," which Cain cannot escape, is addressed also to the people of today, to make them realize the extent and gravity of the attacks against life which continue to mark human history; to make them discover what causes these attacks and feeds them; and to make them ponder seriously the consequences which derive from these attacks for the existence of individuals and peoples.

Some threats come from nature itself, but they are made worse by the culpable indifference and negligence of those who could in some cases remedy them. Others are the result of situations of violence, hatred, and conflicting interests, which lead people to attack others through murder, war, slaughter, and genocide.

And how can we fail to consider the violence against life done to millions of human beings, especially children, who are forced into poverty, malnutrition, and hunger because of an unjust distribution of resources between peoples and between social classes? And what of the violence inherent not only in wars as such but in the scandalous arms trade, which spawns the many armed conflicts which stain our world

John Paul II, *On the Value and Inviolability of Human Life* (*Evangelium Vitae*), nos. 10-12, 59, 70-73, 90 (March 25, 1995). See http://www.vatican.va/holy_father/john_paul_ii/encyclicals/documents/ hf_jp-ii_enc_25031995_evangelium-vitae_en.html (accessed May 9, 2005).

with blood? What of the spreading of death caused by reckless tampering with the world's ecological balance, by the criminal spread of drugs, or by the promotion of certain kinds of sexual activity which, besides being morally unacceptable, also involve grave risks to life? It is impossible to catalogue completely the vast array of threats to human life, so many are the forms, whether explicit or hidden, in which they appear today!

11. Here though we shall concentrate particular attention on another category of attacks, affecting life in its earliest and in its final stages, attacks which present new characteristics with respect to the past and which raise questions of extraordinary seriousness. It is not only that in generalized opinion these attacks tend no longer to be considered as "crimes"; paradoxically they assume the nature of "rights," to the point that the State is called upon to give them legal recognition and to make them available through the free services of health-care personnel. Such attacks strike human life at the time of its greatest frailty, when it lacks any means of self-defense. Even more serious is the fact that, most often, those attacks are carried out in the very heart of and with the complicity of the family—the family which by its nature is called to be the "sanctuary of life."

How did such a situation come about? Many different factors have to be taken into account. In the background there is the profound crisis of culture, which generates skepticism in relation to the very foundations of knowledge and ethics, and which makes it increasingly difficult to grasp clearly the meaning of what man is, the meaning of his rights and his duties. Then there are all kinds of existential and interpersonal difficulties, made worse by the complexity of a society in which individuals, couples, and families are often left alone with their problems. There are situations of acute poverty, anxiety, or frustration in which the struggle to make ends meet, the presence of unbearable pain, or instances of violence, especially against women, make the choice to defend and promote life so demanding as sometimes to reach the point of heroism.

All this explains, at least in part, how the value of life can today undergo a kind of "eclipse," even though conscience does not cease to point to it as a sacred and inviolable value, as is evident in the tendency to disguise certain crimes against life in its early or final stages by using innocuous medical terms which distract attention from the fact that what is involved is the right to life of an actual human person.

12.   In fact, while the climate of widespread moral uncertainty can in some way be explained by the multiplicity and gravity of today's social problems, and these can sometimes mitigate the subjective responsibility of individuals, it is no less true that we are confronted by an even larger reality, which can be described as a veritable structure of sin. This reality is characterized by the emergence of a culture which denies solidarity and in many cases takes the form of a veritable "culture of death." This culture is actively fostered by powerful cultural, economic, and political currents which encourage an idea of society excessively concerned with efficiency. Looking at the situation from this point of view, it is possible to speak in a certain sense of a war of the powerful against the weak: a life which would require greater acceptance, love, and care is considered useless, or held to be an intolerable burden, and is therefore rejected in one way or another. A person who, because of illness, handicap or, more simply, just by existing, compromises the well-being or lifestyle of those who are more favored tends to be looked upon as an enemy to be resisted or eliminated. In this way a kind of "conspiracy against life" is unleashed. This conspiracy involves not only individuals in their personal, family, or group relationships, but goes far beyond, to the point of damaging and distorting, at the international level, relations between peoples and States.

59.   As well as the mother, there are often other people too who decide upon the death of the child in the womb. In the first place, the father of the child may be to blame, not only when he directly pressures the woman to have an abortion, but also when he indirectly encourages such a decision on her part by leaving her alone to face the problems of pregnancy:[55] in this way the family is thus mortally wounded and profaned in its nature as a community of love and in its vocation to be the "sanctuary of life." Nor can one overlook the pressures which sometimes come from the wider family circle and from friends. Sometimes the woman is subjected to such strong pressure that she feels psychologically forced to have an abortion: certainly in this case moral responsibility lies particularly with those who have directly or indirectly obliged her to have an abortion. Doctors and nurses are also responsible,

when they place at the service of death skills which were acquired for promoting life.

But responsibility likewise falls on the legislators who have promoted and approved abortion laws, and, to the extent that they have a say in the matter, on the administrators of the health-care centers where abortions are performed. A general and no less serious responsibility lies with those who have encouraged the spread of an attitude of sexual permissiveness and a lack of esteem for motherhood, and with those who should have ensured—but did not—effective family and social policies in support of families, especially larger families and those with particular financial and educational needs. Finally, one cannot overlook the network of complicity which reaches out to include international institutions, foundations, and associations which systematically campaign for the legalization and spread of abortion in the world. In this sense abortion goes beyond the responsibility of individuals and beyond the harm done to them, and takes on a distinctly social dimension. It is a most serious wound inflicted on society and its culture by the very people who ought to be society's promoters and defenders. As I wrote in my *Letter to Families*, "we are facing an immense threat to life: not only to the life of individuals but also to that of civilization itself."[56] We are facing what can be called a "structure of sin" which opposes human life not yet born.

NOTES

55   Cf. John Paul II, Apostolic Letter *Mulieris Dignitatem* (15 August 1988), 14: AAS 80 (1988), 1686.
56   No. 21: AAS 86 (1994), 920.

70.   At the basis of all these tendencies lies the ethical relativism which characterizes much of present-day culture. There are those who consider such relativism an essential condition of democracy, inasmuch as it alone is held to guarantee tolerance, mutual respect between people, and acceptance of the decisions of the majority, whereas moral norms considered to be objective and binding are held to lead to authoritarianism and intolerance.

But it is precisely the issue of respect for life which shows what misunderstandings and contradictions, accompanied by terrible practical consequences, are concealed in this position.

It is true that history has known cases where crimes have been committed in the name of "truth." But equally grave crimes and radical denials of freedom have also been committed and are still being committed in the name of "ethical relativism." When a parliamentary or social majority decrees that it is legal, at least under certain conditions, to kill unborn human life, is it not really making a "tyrannical" decision with regard to the weakest and most defenseless of human beings? Everyone's conscience rightly rejects those crimes against humanity of which our century has had such sad experience. But would these crimes cease to be crimes if, instead of being committed by unscrupulous tyrants, they were legitimated by popular consensus?

Democracy cannot be idolized to the point of making it a substitute for morality or a panacea for immorality. Fundamentally, democracy is a "system" and as such is a means and not an end. Its "moral" value is not automatic, but depends on conformity to the moral law to which it, like every other form of human behavior, must be subject: in other words, its morality depends on the morality of the ends which it pursues and of the means which it employs. If today we see an almost universal consensus with regard to the value of democracy, this is to be considered a positive "sign of the times," as the Church's Magisterium has frequently noted.[88] But the value of democracy stands or falls with the values which it embodies and promotes. Of course, values such as the dignity of every human person, respect for inviolable and inalienable human rights, and the adoption of the "common good" as the end and criterion regulating political life are certainly fundamental and not to be ignored.

The basis of these values cannot be provisional and changeable "majority" opinions, but only the acknowledgment of an objective moral law which, as the "natural law" written in the human heart, is the obligatory point of reference for civil law itself. If, as a result of a tragic obscuring of the collective conscience, an attitude of skepticism were to succeed in bringing into question even the fundamental principles of the moral law, the democratic system itself would be shaken in its foundations, and would be reduced to a mere mechanism for regulating different and opposing interests on a purely empirical basis.[89]

Some might think that even this function, in the absence of anything better, should be valued for the sake of peace in society. While one acknowledges some element of truth in this point of view, it is easy to see that without an objective moral grounding, not even democracy is capable of ensuring a stable peace, especially since peace which is not built upon the values of the dignity of every individual and of solidarity between all people frequently proves to be illusory. Even in participatory systems of government, the regulation of interests often occurs to the advantage of the most powerful, since they are the ones most capable of maneuvering not only the levers of power but also of shaping the formation of consensus. In such a situation, democracy easily becomes an empty word.

71.   It is therefore urgently necessary, for the future of society and the development of a sound democracy, to rediscover those essential and innate human and moral values which flow from the very truth of the human being and express and safeguard the dignity of the person: values which no individual, no majority, and no State can ever create, modify, or destroy, but must only acknowledge, respect, and promote.

Consequently there is a need to recover the basic elements of a vision of the relationship between civil law and moral law, which are put forward by the Church, but which are also part of the patrimony of the great juridical traditions of humanity.

Certainly the purpose of civil law is different and more limited in scope than that of the moral law. But "in no sphere of life can the civil law take the place of conscience or dictate norms concerning things which are outside its competence,"[90] which is that of ensuring the common good of people through the recognition and defense of their fundamental rights, and the promotion of peace and of public morality.[91] The real purpose of civil law is to guarantee an ordered social coexistence in true justice, so that all may "lead a quiet and peaceable life, godly and respectful in every way" (1 Tim 2:2). Precisely for this reason, civil law must ensure that all members of society enjoy respect for certain fundamental rights which innately belong to the person, rights which every positive law must recognize and guarantee. First and fundamental among these is the inviolable right to life of every innocent human being. While public authority can sometimes choose not to put a stop to something which—were it prohibited—would cause more serious harm,[92] it can never presume to legitimize as a right of individuals— even if they are the majority of the members of society—an offence against other persons caused by the disregard of so fundamental a right as the right to life. The legal toleration of abortion or of euthanasia can in no way claim to be based on respect for the conscience of others, precisely because society has the right and the duty to protect itself against the abuses which can occur in the name of conscience and under the pretext of freedom.[93]

In the Encyclical *Pacem in Terris*, John XXIII pointed out that "it is generally accepted today that the common good is best safeguarded when personal rights and duties are guaranteed. The chief concern of civil authorities must therefore be to ensure that these rights are recognized, respected, coordinated, defended and promoted, and that each individual is enabled to perform his duties more easily. For 'to safeguard the inviolable rights of the human person, and to facilitate the performance of his duties, is the principal duty of every public authority.' Thus any government which refused to recognize human rights or acted in violation of them, would not only fail in its duty; its decrees would be wholly lacking in binding force."[94]

72. The doctrine on the necessary conformity of civil law with the moral law is in continuity with the whole tradition of the Church. This is clear once more from John XXIII's Encyclical: "Authority is a postulate of the moral order and derives from God. Consequently, laws and decrees enacted in contravention of the moral order, and hence of the divine will, can have no binding force in conscience . . . ; indeed, the passing of such laws undermines the very nature of authority and results in shameful abuse."[95] This is the clear teaching of St. Thomas Aquinas, who writes that "human law is law inasmuch as it is in conformity with right reason and thus derives from the eternal law. But when a law is contrary to reason, it is called an unjust law; but in this case it ceases to be a law and becomes instead an act of violence."[96] And again: "Every law made by man can be called a law insofar as it derives from the natural law. But if it is somehow opposed to the natural law, then it is not really a law but rather a corruption of the law."[97]

Now the first and most immediate application of this teaching concerns a human law which disregards the fundamental right and source of all other rights, which is the right to life, a right belonging to every individual. Consequently, laws which legitimize the direct killing of innocent human beings through abortion or euthanasia are in complete opposition to the inviolable right to life proper to every individual; they thus deny the equality of everyone before the law. It might be objected that such is not the case in euthanasia, when it is requested with full awareness by the person involved. But any State which made such a request legitimate and authorized it to be carried out would be legalizing a case of suicide-murder, contrary to the fundamental principles of absolute respect for life and of the protection of every innocent life. In this way the State contributes to lessening respect for life and opens the door to ways of acting which are destructive of trust in relations between people. Laws which authorize and promote abortion and euthanasia are therefore radically opposed not only to the good of the individual but also to the common good; as such they are completely lacking in authentic juridical validity. Disregard for the right to life, precisely because it leads to the killing of the person whom society exists to serve, is what most directly conflicts with the possibility of achieving the common good. Consequently, a civil law authorizing abortion or euthanasia ceases by that very fact to be a true, morally binding civil law.

73.   Abortion and euthanasia are thus crimes which no human law can claim to legitimize. There is no obligation in conscience to obey such laws; instead there is a grave and clear obligation to oppose them by conscientious objection. From the very beginnings of the Church, the apostolic preaching reminded Christians of their duty to obey legitimately constituted public authorities (cf. Rom 13:1-7; 1 Pet 2:13-14), but at the same time it firmly warned that "we must obey God rather than men" (Acts 5:29). In the Old Testament, precisely in regard to threats against life, we find a significant example of resistance to the unjust command of those in authority. After Pharaoh ordered the killing of all newborn males, the Hebrew midwives refused. "They did not do as the king of Egypt commanded them, but let the male children live" (Ex 1:17). But the ultimate reason for their action should be noted: "the midwives feared God" (ibid.). It is precisely from obedience to God—to whom alone is due that fear which is acknowledgment of his absolute sovereignty—that the strength and the courage to resist unjust human laws are born. It is the strength and the courage of those prepared even to be imprisoned or put to the sword, in the certainty that this is what makes for "the endurance and faith of the saints" (Rev 13:10).

In the case of an intrinsically unjust law, such as a law permitting abortion or euthanasia, it is therefore never licit to obey it, or to "take part in a propaganda campaign in favor of such a law, or vote for it."[98]

A particular problem of conscience can arise in cases where a legislative vote would be decisive for the passage of a more restrictive law, aimed at limiting the number of authorized abortions, in place of a more permissive law already passed or ready to be voted on. Such cases are not infrequent. It is a fact that while in some parts of the world there continue to be campaigns to introduce laws favoring abortion, often supported by powerful international organizations, in other nations— particularly those which have already experienced the bitter fruits of such permissive legislation—there are growing signs of a rethinking in this matter. In a case like the one just mentioned, when it is not possible to overturn or completely abrogate a pro-abortion law, an elected official, whose absolute personal opposition to procured abortion was well known, could licitly support proposals aimed at limiting the harm done by such a law and at lessening its negative consequences at the level of general opinion and public morality. This does not in fact represent an illicit cooperation with an unjust law, but rather a legitimate and proper attempt to limit its evil aspects.

NOTES

88 Cf. John Paul II, Encyclical Letter *Centesimus Annus* (1 May 1991), 46: AAS 83 (1991), 850; Pius XII, Christmas Radio Message (24 December 1944): AAS 37 (1945), 10-20.

89 Cf. John Paul II, Encyclical Letter *Veritatis Splendor* (6 August 1993), 97 and 99: AAS 85 (1993), 1209-1211.

90 Congregation for the Doctrine of the Faith, *Instruction on Respect for Human Life in its Origin and on the Dignity of Procreation (Donum Vitae)* (22 February 1987), III: AAS 80 (1988), 98.

91 Cf. Second Vatican Ecumenical Council, *Declaration on Religious Freedom Dignitatis Humanae*, 7.

92 Cf. St. Thomas Aquinas, *Summa Theologiae* I-II, q. 96, a. 2.

93 Cf. Second Vatican Ecumenical Council, *Declaration on Religious Freedom (Dignitatis Humanae)*, 7.

94 Encyclical Letter *Pacem in Terris* (11 April 1963), II: AAS 55 (1963), 273-274. The internal quote is from Pius XII, Radio Message of Pentecost 1941 (1 June 1941): AAS 33 (1941), 200. On this topic, the Encyclical cites: Pius XII, Encyclical Letter *Mit brennender Sorge* (14 March 1937): AAS 29 (1937): AAS 29 (1937), 159; Encyclical Letter *Divini Redemptoris* (19 March 1937), III: AAS 29 (1937), 79; Pius XII, Christmas Radio Message (24 December 1942): AAS 35 (1943), 9-24.

95 Encyclical Letter *Pacem in Terris* (11 April 1963), II: loc. cit., 271.

96 *Summa Theologiae* I-II, q. 93, a. 3, ad 2um.

97 Ibid., I-II, q. 95, a. 2. Aquinas quotes St. Augustine: "Non videtur esse lex, quae iusta non fuerit," *De Libero Arbitrio*, I, 5, 11: PL 32, 1227.

98 Congregation for the Doctrine of the Faith, *Declaration on Procured Abortion* (18 November 1974), no. 22: AAS 66 (1974), 744.

90.   Volunteer workers have a specific role to play: they make a valuable contribution to the service of life when they combine professional ability and generous, selfless love. The Gospel of life inspires them to lift their feelings of good will towards others to the heights of Christ's charity; to renew every day, amid hard work and weariness, their awareness of the dignity of every person; to search out people's needs; and, when necessary, to set out on new paths where needs are greater but care and support weaker.

If charity is to be realistic and effective, it demands that the Gospel of life be implemented also by means of certain forms of social activity and commitment in the political field, as a way of defending and promoting the value of life in our ever more complex and pluralistic societies. Individuals, families, groups, and associations, albeit for different reasons and in different ways, all have a responsibility for shaping society and developing cultural, economic, political, and legislative projects which, with respect for all and in keeping with democratic principles, will contribute to the building of a society in which the dignity of each person is recognized and protected and the lives of all are defended and enhanced.

This task is the particular responsibility of civil leaders. Called to serve the people and the common good, they have a duty to make courageous choices in support of life, especially through legislative measures. In a democratic system, where laws and decisions are made on the basis of the consensus of many, the sense of personal responsibility in the consciences of individuals invested with authority may be weakened. But no one can ever renounce this responsibility, especially when he or she has a legislative or decision-making mandate, which calls that person to answer to God, to his or her own conscience, and to the whole of society for choices which may be contrary to the common good. Although laws are not the only means of protecting human life, nevertheless they do play a very important and sometimes decisive role in influencing patterns of thought and behavior. I repeat once more that a law which violates an innocent person's natural right to life is unjust and, as such, is not valid as a law. For this reason I urgently appeal once more to all political leaders not to pass laws which, by disregarding the dignity of the person, undermine the very fabric of society.

The Church well knows that it is difficult to mount an effective legal defense of life in pluralistic democracies, because of the presence of strong cultural currents with differing outlooks. At the same time, certain that moral truth cannot fail to make its presence deeply felt in every conscience, the Church encourages political leaders, starting with those who are Christians, not to give in, but to make those choices which, taking into account what is realistically attainable, will lead to the re-establishment of a just order in the defense and promotion of the value of life. Here it must be noted that it is not enough to remove unjust laws. The underlying causes of attacks on life have to be eliminated, especially by ensuring proper support for families and motherhood. A family policy must be the basis and driving force of all social policies. For this reason there need to be set in place social and political initiatives capable of guaranteeing conditions of true freedom of choice in matters of parenthood. It is also necessary to rethink labor, urban, residential, and social service policies so as to harmonize working schedules with time available for the family, so that it becomes effectively possible to take care of children and the elderly.

Other Documents of the Universal Church

✣ ✣ ✣

Pastoral Constitution on the Church in the Modern World (*Gaudium et Spes*)

Second Vatican Council, 1965

Preface

1. The joys and the hopes, the griefs and the anxieties of the men of this age, especially those who are poor or in any way afflicted, these are the joys and hopes, the griefs and anxieties of the followers of Christ. Indeed, nothing genuinely human fails to raise an echo in their hearts. For theirs is a community composed of men. United in Christ, they are led by the Holy Spirit in their journey to the Kingdom of their Father and they have welcomed the news of salvation which is meant for every man. That is why this community realizes that it is truly linked with mankind and its history by the deepest of bonds.

PART I
CHAPTER 2: THE COMMUNITY OF MANKIND

25. Man's social nature makes it evident that the progress of the human person and the advance of society itself hinge on one another. For the beginning, the subject and the goal of all social institutions is and must be the human person which for its part and by its very nature stands completely in need of social life.[3] Since this social life is not something added on to man, through his dealings with others, through reciprocal duties, and through fraternal dialogue he develops all his gifts and is able to rise to his destiny.

Among those social ties which man needs for his development some, like the family and political community, relate with greater immediacy to his innermost nature; others originate rather from his free decision.

Second Vatican Council, *Pastoral Constitution on the Church in the Modern World* (*Gaudium et Spes*), nos. 1, 25-28, 43, 73-76 (December 7, 1965). See http://www.vatican.va/archive/hist_councils/ii_vatican_council/documents/vat-ii_cons_19651207_gaudium-et-spes_en.html (accessed May 10, 2005).

In our era, for various reasons, reciprocal ties and mutual dependencies increase day by day and give rise to a variety of associations and organizations, both public and private. This development, which is called socialization, while certainly not without its dangers, brings with it many advantages with respect to consolidating and increasing the qualities of the human person, and safeguarding his rights.[4]

But if by this social life the human person is greatly aided in responding to his destiny, even in its religious dimensions, it cannot be denied that men are often diverted from doing good and spurred toward and by the social circumstances in which they live and are immersed from their birth. To be sure, the disturbances which so frequently occur in the social order result in part from the natural tensions of economic, political, and social forms. But at a deeper level they flow from man's pride and selfishness, which contaminate even the social sphere. When the structure of affairs is flawed by the consequences of sin, man, already born with a bent toward evil, finds there new inducements to sin, which cannot be overcome without strenuous efforts and the assistance of grace.

26.   Every day human interdependence grows more tightly drawn and spreads by degrees over the whole world. As a result the common good, that is, the sum of those conditions of social life which allow social groups and their individual members relatively thorough and ready access to their own fulfillment, today takes on an increasingly universal complexion and consequently involves rights and duties with respect to the whole human race. Every social group must take account of the needs and legitimate aspirations of other groups, and even of the general welfare of the entire human family.[5]

At the same time, however, there is a growing awareness of the exalted dignity proper to the human person, since he stands above all things, and his rights and duties are universal and inviolable. Therefore, there must be made available to all men everything necessary for leading a life truly human, such as food, clothing, and shelter; the right to choose a state of life freely and to found a family; the right to education, to employment, to a good reputation, to respect, to appropriate information, to activity in accord with the upright norm of one's own conscience, to protection of privacy and rightful freedom, even in matters religious.

Hence, the social order and its development must invariably work to the benefit of the human person if the disposition of affairs is to be subordinate to the personal realm and not contrariwise, as the Lord indicated when he said that the Sabbath was made for man, and not man for the Sabbath.[6]

This social order requires constant improvement. It must be founded on truth, built on justice, and animated by love; in freedom it should grow every day toward a more humane balance.[7] An improvement in attitudes and abundant changes in society will have to take place if these objectives are to be gained.

God's Spirit, who with a marvelous providence directs the unfolding of time and renews the face of the earth, is not absent from this development. The ferment of the Gospel too has aroused and continues to arouse in man's heart the irresistible requirements of his dignity.

27. Coming down to practical and particularly urgent consequences, this council lays stress on reverence for man; everyone must consider his every neighbor without exception as another self, taking into account first of all his life and the means necessary to living it with dignity,[8] so as not to imitate the rich man who had no concern for the poor man Lazarus.[9]

In our times a special obligation binds us to make ourselves the neighbor of every person without exception, and of actively helping him when he comes across our path, whether he be an old person abandoned by all, a foreign laborer unjustly looked down upon, a refugee, a child born of an unlawful union and wrongly suffering for a sin he did not commit, or a hungry person who disturbs our conscience by recalling the voice of the Lord, "As long as you did it for one of these the least of my brethren, you did it for me" (Mt 25:40).

Furthermore, whatever is opposed to life itself, such as any type of murder, genocide, abortion, euthanasia, or willful self-destruction, whatever violates the integrity of the human person, such as mutilation, torments inflicted on body or mind, attempts to coerce the will itself; whatever insults human dignity, such as subhuman living conditions, arbitrary imprisonment, deportation, slavery, prostitution, the selling of women and children; as well as disgraceful working conditions, where men are treated as mere tools for profit, rather than as free and responsible persons; all these things and others of their like are infamies indeed. They poison human society, but they do more harm to those who practice them than those who suffer from the injury. Moreover, they are supreme dishonor to the Creator.

28.   Respect and love ought to be extended also to those who think or act differently than we do in social, political, and even religious matters. In fact, the more deeply we come to understand their ways of thinking through such courtesy and love, the more easily will we be able to enter into dialogue with them.

This love and good will, to be sure, must in no way render us indifferent to truth and goodness. Indeed love itself impels the disciples of Christ to speak the saving truth to all men. But it is necessary to distinguish between error, which always merits repudiation, and the person in error, who never loses the dignity of being a person even when he is flawed by false or inadequate religious notions.[10] God alone is the judge and searcher of hearts; for that reason he forbids us to make judgments about the internal guilt of anyone.[11]

The teaching of Christ even requires that we forgive injuries,[12] and extends the law of love to include every enemy, according to the command of the New Law: "You have heard that it was said: Thou shalt love thy neighbor and hate thy enemy. But I say to you: love your enemies, do good to those who hate you, and pray for those who persecute and calumniate you" (Mt 5:43-44).

NOTES

3   Cf. St. Thomas, 1 *Ethica Lect.* 1.
4   Cf. John XXIII, Encyclical Letter *Mater et Magistra*: AAS 53 (1961), p. 418. Cf. also Pius XI, Encyclical Letter *Quadragesimo Anno*: AAS 23 (1931), p. 222 ff.
5   Cf. John XXIII, Encyclical Letter *Mater et Magistra*: AAS 53 (1961).
6   Cf. Mk 2:27.
7   Cf. John XXIII, Encyclical Letter *Pacem in Terris*: AAS 55 (1963), p. 266.
8   Cf. Jas 2:15-16.
9   Cf. Lk 16:19-31.
10   Cf. John XXIII, Encyclical Letter *Pacem in Terris*: AAS 55 (1963), pp. 299-300.
11   Cf. Lk 6:37-38; Mt 7:1-2; Rom 2:1-11; 14:10-12.
12   Cf. Mt 5:43-47.

CHAPTER 4: THE ROLE OF THE
CHURCH IN THE MODERN WORLD

43. This council exhorts Christians, as citizens of two cities, to strive to discharge their earthly duties conscientiously and in response to the Gospel spirit. They are mistaken who, knowing that we have here no abiding city but seek one which is to come,[13] think that they may therefore shirk their earthly responsibilities. For they are forgetting that by the faith itself they are more obliged than ever to measure up to these duties, each according to his proper vocation.[14] Nor, on the contrary, are they any less wide of the mark who think that religion consists in acts of worship alone and in the discharge of certain moral obligations, and who imagine they can plunge themselves into earthly affairs in such a way as to imply that these are altogether divorced from the religious life. This split between the faith which many profess and their daily lives deserves to be counted among the more serious errors of our age. Long since, the Prophets of the Old Testament fought vehemently against this scandal[15] and even more so did Jesus Christ himself in the New Testament threaten it with grave punishments.[16] Therefore, let there be no false opposition between professional and social activities on the one part, and religious life on the other. The Christian who neglects his temporal duties neglects his duties toward his neighbor and even God, and jeopardizes his eternal salvation. Christians should rather rejoice that, following the example of Christ who worked as an artisan, they are free to give proper exercise to all their earthly activities and to their humane, domestic, professional, social, and technical enterprises by gathering them into one vital synthesis with religious values, under whose supreme direction all things are harmonized unto God's glory.

Secular duties and activities belong properly although not exclusively to laymen. Therefore acting as citizens in the world, whether individually or socially, they will keep the laws proper to each discipline, and labor to equip themselves with a genuine expertise in their various fields. They will gladly work with men seeking the same goals. Acknowledging the demands of faith and endowed with its force, they will unhesitatingly devise new enterprises, where they are appropriate, and put them into action. Laymen should also know that it is generally the function of their well-formed Christian conscience to see that the divine law is inscribed in the life of the earthly city; from priests they may look for spiritual light and nourishment. Let the layman not imagine that his pastors are always such experts, that to every problem which arises, however complicated, they can readily give him a concrete solution, or even that such is their mission. Rather, enlightened by Christian wisdom and giving close attention to the teaching authority of the Church,[17] let the layman take on his own distinctive role.

Often enough the Christian view of things will itself suggest some specific solution in certain circumstances. Yet it happens rather frequently, and legitimately so, that with equal sincerity some of the faithful will disagree with others on a given matter. Even against the intentions of their proponents, however, solutions proposed on one side or another may be easily confused by many people with the Gospel message. Hence it is necessary for people to remember that no one is allowed in the aforementioned situations to appropriate the Church's authority for his opinion. They should always try to enlighten one another through honest discussion, preserving mutual charity and caring above all for the common good.

Since they have an active role to play in the whole life of the Church, laymen are not only bound to penetrate the world with a Christian spirit, but are also called to be witnesses to Christ in all things in the midst of human society.

Bishops, to whom is assigned the task of ruling the Church of God, should, together with their priests, so preach the news of Christ that all the earthly activities of the faithful will be bathed in the light of the Gospel. All pastors should remember too that by their daily conduct and concern[18] they are revealing the face of the Church to the world, and men will judge the power and truth of the Christian message thereby. By their lives and speech, in union with Religious and their faithful, may they demonstrate that even now the Church, by her presence alone and by all the gifts which she contains, is an unspent fountain of those virtues which the modern world needs the most.

By unremitting study they should fit themselves to do their part in establishing dialogue with the world and with men of all shades of opinion. Above all let them take to heart the words which this council has spoken: "Since humanity today increasingly moves toward civil, economic and social unity, it is more than ever necessary that priests, with joint concern and energy, and under the guidance of the bishops and the supreme pontiff, erase every cause of division, so that the whole human race may be led to the unity of God's family."[19]

Although by the power of the Holy Spirit the Church will remain the faithful spouse of her Lord and will never cease to be the sign of salvation on earth, still she is very well aware that among her members,[20] both clerical and lay, some have been unfaithful to the Spirit of God during the course of many centuries; in the present age, too, it does not escape the Church how great a distance lies between the message she offers and the human failings of those to whom the Gospel is entrusted. Whatever be the judgment of history on these defects, we ought to be conscious of them, and struggle against them energetically, lest they inflict harm on spread of the Gospel. The Church also realizes that in working out her relationship with the world she always has great need of the ripening which comes with the experience of the centuries. Led by the Holy Spirit, Mother Church unceasingly exhorts her sons "to purify and renew themselves so that the sign of Christ can shine more brightly on the face of the Church."[21]

NOTES

13   Cf. Heb 13:14.
14   Cf. 2 Thes 3:6-13; Eph 4:28.
15   Cf. Is 58:1-12.
16   Cf. Mt 23:3-23; Mk 7:10-13.
17   Cf. John XXIII, Encyclical Letter *Mater et Magistra*, IV: AAS 53 (1961), pp. 456-457; cf. I: AAS loc. cit., pp. 407, 410-11.
18   Cf. *Dogmatic Constitution on the Church*, Chapter III, no. 28: AAS 57 (1965), p. 35.
19   Ibid., no. 28: AAS loc. cit., pp. 35-36.
20   Cf. St. Ambrose, *De virginitate*, Chapter VIII, no. 48: ML 16, 278.
21   Cf. *Dogmatic Constitution on the Church*, Chapter 11, no. 15: AAS 57 (1965), p. 17.

PART II
CHAPTER 4: THE LIFE OF THE POLITICAL COMMUNITY

73.   In our day, profound changes are apparent also in the structure and institutions of peoples. These result from their cultural, economic, and social evolution. Such changes have a great influence on the life of the political community, especially regarding the rights and duties of all in the exercise of civil freedom and in the attainment of the common good, and in organizing the relations of citizens among themselves and with respect to public authority.

The present keener sense of human dignity has given rise in many parts of the world to attempts to bring about a politico-juridical order which will give better protection to the rights of the person in public life. These include the right freely to meet and form associations, the right to express one's own opinion and to profess one's religion both publicly and privately. The protection of the rights of a person is indeed a necessary condition so that citizens, individually or collectively, can take an active part in the life and government of the state.

Along with cultural, economic, and social development, there is a growing desire among many people to play a greater part in organizing the life of the political community. In the conscience of many arises an increasing concern that the rights of minorities be recognized, without any neglect for their duties toward the political community. In addition, there is a steadily growing respect for men of other opinions or other religions. At the same time, there is wider cooperation to guarantee the actual exercise of personal rights to all citizens, and not only to a few privileged individuals.

However, those political systems, prevailing in some parts of the world, are to be reproved which hamper civic or religious freedom, victimize large numbers through avarice and political crimes, and divert the exercise of authority from the service of the common good to the interests of one or another faction or of the rulers themselves.

There is no better way to establish political life on a truly human basis than by fostering an inward sense of justice and kindliness, and of service to the common good, and by strengthening basic convictions as to the true nature of the political community and the aim, right exercise, and sphere of action of public authority.

74. Men, families, and the various groups which make up the civil community are aware that they cannot achieve a truly human life by their own unaided efforts. They see the need for a wider community, within which each one makes his specific contribution every day toward an ever broader realization of the common good.[1] For this purpose they set up a political community according to various forms. The political community exists, consequently, for the sake of the common good, in which it finds its full justification and significance, and the source of its inherent legitimacy. Indeed, the common good embraces the sum of those conditions of the social life whereby men, families, and associations more adequately and readily may attain their own perfection.[2]

Yet the people who come together in the political community are many and diverse, and they have every right to prefer divergent solutions. If the political community is not to be torn apart while everyone follows his own opinion, there must be an authority to direct the energies of all citizens toward the common good, not in a mechanical or despotic fashion, but by acting above all as a moral force which appeals to each one's freedom and sense of responsibility.

It is clear, therefore, that the political community and public authority are founded on human nature and hence belong to the order designed by God, even though the choice of a political regime and the appointment of rulers are left to the free will of citizens.[3]

It follows also that political authority, both in the community as such and in the representative bodies of the state, must always be exercised within the limits of the moral order and directed toward the common good—with a dynamic concept of that good—according to the juridical order legitimately established or due to be established. When authority is so exercised, citizens are bound in conscience to obey.[4] Accordingly, the responsibility, dignity, and importance of leaders are indeed clear.

But where citizens are oppressed by a public authority overstepping its competence, they should not protest against those things which are objectively required for the common good; but it is legitimate for them to defend their own rights and the rights of their fellow citizens against the abuse of this authority, while keeping within those limits drawn by the natural law and the Gospels.

According to the character of different peoples and their historic development, the political community can, however, adopt a variety of concrete solutions in its structures and the organization of public authority. For the benefit of the whole human family, these solutions must always contribute to the formation of a type of man who will be cultivated, peace-loving, and well-disposed towards all his fellow men.

75.   It is in full conformity with human nature that there should be juridico-political structures providing all citizens in an ever better fashion and without any discrimination the practical possibility of freely and actively taking part in the establishment of the juridical foundations of the political community and in the direction of public affairs, in fixing the terms of reference of the various public bodies, and in the election of political leaders.[5] All citizens, therefore, should be mindful of the

right and also the duty to use their free vote to further the common good. The Church praises and esteems the work of those who for the good of men devote themselves to the service of the state and take on the burdens of this office.

If the citizens' responsible cooperation is to produce the good results which may be expected in the normal course of political life, there must be a statute of positive law providing for a suitable division of the functions and bodies of authority and an efficient and independent system for the protection of rights. The rights of all persons, families, and groups, and their practical application, must be recognized, respected, and furthered, together with the duties binding on all citizen.[6] Among the latter, it will be well to recall the duty of rendering the political community such material and personal service as are required by the common good. Rulers must be careful not to hamper the development of family, social, or cultural groups, nor that of intermediate bodies or organizations, and not to deprive them of opportunities for legitimate and constructive activity; they should willingly seek rather to promote the orderly pursuit of such activity. Citizens, for their part, either individually or collectively, must be careful not to attribute excessive power to public authority, not to make exaggerated and untimely demands upon it in their own interests, lessening in this way the responsible role of persons, families, and social groups.

The complex circumstances of our day make it necessary for public authority to intervene more often in social, economic, and cultural matters in order to bring about favorable conditions which will give more effective help to citizens and groups in their free pursuit of man's total well-being. The relations, however, between socialization and the autonomy and development of the person can be understood in different ways according to various regions and the evolution of peoples. But when the exercise of rights is restricted temporarily for the common good, freedom should be restored immediately upon change of circumstances. Moreover, it is inhuman for public authority to fall back on dictatorial systems or totalitarian methods which violate the rights of the person or social groups.

Citizens must cultivate a generous and loyal spirit of patriotism, but without being narrow-minded. This means that they will always direct their attention to the good of the whole human family, united by the different ties which bind together races, people, and nations.

All Christians must be aware of their own specific vocation within the political community. It is for them to give an example by their sense of responsibility and their service of the common good. In this way they are to demonstrate concretely how authority can be compatible with freedom, personal initiative with the solidarity of the whole social organism, and the advantages of unity with fruitful diversity. They must recognize the legitimacy of different opinions with regard to temporal solutions, and respect citizens, who, even as a group, defend their points of view by honest methods. Political parties, for their part, must promote those things which in their judgment are required for the common good; it is never allowable to give their interests priority over the common good.

Great care must be taken about civic and political formation, which is of the utmost necessity today for the population as a whole, and especially for youth, so that all citizens can play their part in the life of the political community. Those who are suited or can become suited should prepare themselves for the difficult, but at the same time, the very noble art of politics,[8] and should seek to practice this art without regard for their own interests or for material advantages. With integrity and wisdom, they must take action against any form of injustice and tyranny, against arbitrary domination by an individual or a political party and any intolerance. They should dedicate themselves to the service of all with sincerity and fairness, indeed, with the charity and fortitude demanded by political life.

76. It is very important, especially where a pluralistic society prevails, that there be a correct notion of the relationship between the political community and the Church, and a clear distinction between the tasks which Christians undertake, individually or as a group, on their own responsibility as citizens guided by the dictates of a Christian conscience, and the activities which, in union with their pastors, they carry out in the name of the Church.

The Church, by reason of her role and competence, is not identified in any way with the political community nor bound to any political system. She is at once a sign and a safeguard of the transcendent character of the human person.

The Church and the political community in their own fields are autonomous and independent from each other. Yet both, under different titles, are devoted to the personal and social vocation of the same men. The more that both foster sounder cooperation between themselves with due consideration for the circumstances of time and place, the more effectively will their service be exercised for the good of all. For man's horizons are not limited only to the temporal order; while living in the context of human history, he preserves intact his eternal vocation. The Church, for her part, founded on the love of the Redeemer, contributes toward the reign of justice and charity within the borders of a nation and between nations. By preaching the truths of the Gospel, and bringing to bear on all fields of human endeavor the light of her doctrine and of a Christian witness, she respects and fosters the political freedom and responsibility of citizens.

The Apostles, their successors, and those who cooperate with them are sent to announce to mankind Christ, the Savior. Their apostolate is based on the power of God, who very often shows forth the strength of the Gospel on the weakness of its witnesses. All those dedicated to the ministry of God's Word must use the ways and means proper to the Gospel which in a great many respects differ from the means proper to the earthly city.

There are, indeed, close links between earthly things and those elements of man's condition which transcend the world. The Church herself makes use of temporal things insofar as her own mission requires it. She, for her part, does not place her trust in the privileges offered by civil authority. She will even give up the exercise of certain rights which have been legitimately acquired, if it becomes clear that their use will cast doubt on the sincerity of her witness or that new ways of life demand new methods. It is only right, however, that at all times and in all places, the Church should have true freedom to preach the faith, to teach her social doctrine, to exercise her role freely among men, and also to pass moral judgment in those matters which regard public order when the fundamental rights of a person or the salvation of souls require it. In this, she should make use of all the means—but only those—which accord with the Gospel and which correspond to the general good with due regard to the diverse circumstances of time and place.

While faithfully adhering to the Gospel and fulfilling her mission to the world, the Church, whose duty it is to foster and elevate[9] all that is found to be true, good, and beautiful in the human community, strengthens peace among men for the glory of God.[10]

NOTES

1   Cf. John XXIII, Encyclical *Letter Mater et Magistra*: AAS 53 (1961), p. 417.

2   Cf. John XXIII, ibid.

3   Cf. Rom 13:1-5.

4   Cf. Rom 13:5.

5   Cf. Pius XII, radio message, Dec. 24, 1942: AAS 35 (1943), pp. 9-24; Dec. 24, 1944: AAS 37 (1945), pp. 11-17; John XXIII, Encyclical Letter *Pacem in Terris*: AAS 55 (1963), pp. 263, 271, 277-278.

6   CF. Pius XII, radio message, June 7, 1941: AAS 33 (1941), p. 200; John XXIII, Encyclical Letter *Pacem in Terris*: 1c., pp. 273-274.

8   Pius XI, Allocution "Ai dirigenti della Federazione Universitaria Catolica," *Discorsi di Pio XI* (ed. Bertetto), Turin, vol. 1 (1960), p. 743.

9   Cf. Second Vatican Council, *Dogmatic Constitution on the Church*, no. 13: AAS 57 (1965), p. 17.

10   Cf. Lk 2:14.

Instruction on Respect for Human Life in Its Origin and on the Dignity of Procreation: Replies to Certain Questions of the Day (*Donum Vitae*)

Congregation for the Doctrine of the Faith, 1987

PART III
MORAL AND CIVIL LAW

The Values and Moral Obligations That Civil Legislation Must Respect and Sanction in This Matter

The intervention of the public authority must be inspired by the rational principles which regulate the relationships between civil law and moral law. The task of the civil law is to insure the common good of people through the recognition of and the defense of fundamental rights and through the promotion of peace and of public morality.[60] In no sphere of life can the civil law take the place of conscience or dictate norms concerning things which are outside its competence. It must sometimes tolerate, for the sake of public order, things which it cannot forbid without a greater evil resulting. However, the inalienable rights of their persons must be recognized and respected by civil society and the political authority. These human rights depend neither on single individuals nor on parents; nor do they represent a concession made by society and the state: they pertain to human nature and are inherent in the person by virtue of the creative act from which the person took his or her origin.

Congregation for the Doctrine of the Faith, *The Gift of Life* (*Donum Vitae*). *Instruction on Respect for Human Life in its Origin and on the Dignity of Procreation: Replies to Certain Questions of the Day* (February 22, 1987). See http://www.usccb.org/prolife/tdocs/donumvitae.htm (accessed May 10, 2005).

The civil legislation of many states confers an undue legitimation upon certain practices in the eyes of many today; it is seen to be incapable of guaranteeing that morality which is in conformity with the natural exigencies of the human person and with the "unwritten laws" etched by the Creator upon the human heart. All men of good will must commit themselves, particularly within their professional field and in the exercise of their civil rights, to ensuring the reform of morally unacceptable civil laws and the correction of illicit practices. In addition, "conscientious objection" vis-à-vis such laws must be supported and recognized. A movement of passive resistance to the legitimation of practices contrary to human life and dignity is beginning to make an ever sharper impression upon the moral conscience of many, especially among specialists in the biomedical sciences. (emphasis in original)

Congregation for the Doctrine of the Faith, *Instruction on Respect for Human Life in Its Origin and on the Dignity of Procreation: Replies to Certain Questions of the Day* (*Donum Vitae*) (Rome, February 22, 1987).

NOTE

60   Cf. Second Vatican Council, *Declaration on Religious Liberty* (*Dignitatis Humanae*) (December 7, 1965), no. 7.

Catechism of the Catholic Church

Libreria Editrice Vaticana, 1994

SECTION ONE:
MAN'S VOCATION: LIFE IN THE SPIRIT

Chapter One: The Dignity of the Human Person
Article 6: Moral Conscience

1776. "Deep within his conscience man discovers a law which he has not laid upon himself but which he must obey. Its voice, ever calling him to love and to do what is good and to avoid evil, sounds in his heart at the right moment. . . . For man has in his heart a law inscribed by God. . . . His conscience is man's most secret core and his sanctuary. There he is alone with God whose voice echoes in his depths."[47]

I. The Judgment of Conscience

1777. Moral conscience,[48] present at the heart of the person, enjoins him at the appropriate moment to do good and to avoid evil. It also judges particular choices, approving those that are good and denouncing those that are evil.[49] It bears witness to the authority of truth in reference to the supreme Good to which the human person is drawn, and it welcomes the commandments. When he listens to his conscience, the prudent man can hear God speaking.

1778. Conscience is a judgment of reason whereby the human person recognizes the moral quality of a concrete act that he is going to perform, is in the process of performing, or has already completed. In all he

Catechism of the Catholic Church, 2nd ed., nos. 1776-1794, 1897-1917, 2030-2046, 2234-2246, 2258-2317, 2401-2449. Washington, DC: United States Conference of Catholic Bishops–Libreria Editrice Vaticana, 2000.

says and does, man is obliged to follow faithfully what he knows to be just and right. It is by the judgment of his conscience that man perceives and recognizes the prescriptions of the divine law:

> Conscience is a law of the mind; yet [Christians] would not grant that it is nothing more; I mean that it was not a dictate, nor conveyed the notion of responsibility, of duty, of a threat and a promise. . . . [Conscience] is a messenger of him, who, both in nature and in grace, speaks to us behind a veil, and teaches and rules us by his representatives. Conscience is the aboriginal Vicar of Christ.[50]

1779. It is important for every person to be sufficiently present to himself in order to hear and follow the voice of his conscience. This requirement of *interiority* is all the more necessary as life often distracts us from any reflection, self-examination or introspection:

> Return to your conscience, question it. . . . Turn inward, brethren, and in everything you do, see God as your witness.[51]

1780. The dignity of the human person implies and requires *uprightness of moral conscience*. Conscience includes the perception of the principles of morality (*synderesis*); their application in the given circumstances by practical discernment of reasons and goods; and finally judgment about concrete acts yet to be performed or already performed. The truth about the moral good, stated in the law of reason, is recognized practically and concretely by the *prudent judgment* of conscience. We call that man prudent who chooses in conformity with this judgment.

1781. Conscience enables one to assume *responsibility* for the acts performed. If man commits evil, the just judgment of conscience can remain within him as the witness to the universal truth of the good, at the same time as the evil of his particular choice. The verdict of the judgment of conscience remains a pledge of hope and mercy. In attesting to the fault committed, it calls to mind the forgiveness that must be asked, the good that must still be practiced, and the virtue that must be constantly cultivated with the grace of God:

We shall . . . reassure our hearts before him whenever our hearts condemn us; for God is greater than our hearts, and he knows everything.[52]

1782. Man has the right to act in conscience and in freedom so as personally to make moral decisions. "He must not be forced to act contrary to his conscience. Nor must he be prevented from acting according to his conscience, especially in religious matters."[53]

II. The Formation of Conscience

1783. Conscience must be informed and moral judgment enlightened. A well-formed conscience is upright and truthful. It formulates its judgments according to reason, in conformity with the true good willed by the wisdom of the Creator. The education of conscience is indispensable for human beings who are subjected to negative influences and tempted by sin to prefer their own judgment and to reject authoritative teachings.

1784. The education of the conscience is a lifelong task. From the earliest years, it awakens the child to the knowledge and practice of the interior law recognized by conscience. Prudent education teaches virtue; it prevents or cures fear, selfishness and pride, resentment arising from guilt, and feelings of complacency, born of human weakness and faults. The education of the conscience guarantees freedom and engenders peace of heart.

1785. In the formation of conscience the Word of God is the light for our path;[54] we must assimilate it in faith and prayer and put it into practice. We must also examine our conscience before the Lord's Cross. We are assisted by the gifts of the Holy Spirit, aided by the witness or advice of others and guided by the authoritative teaching of the Church.[55]

III. To Choose in Accord with Conscience

1786. Faced with a moral choice, conscience can make either a right judgment in accordance with reason and the divine law or, on the contrary, an erroneous judgment that departs from them.

1787. Man is sometimes confronted by situations that make moral judgments less assured and decision difficult. But he must always seriously seek what is right and good and discern the will of God expressed in divine law.

1788. To this purpose, man strives to interpret the data of experience and the signs of the times assisted by the virtue of prudence, by the advice of competent people, and by the help of the Holy Spirit and his gifts.

1789. Some rules apply in every case:

- One may never do evil so that good may result from it;
- The Golden Rule: "Whatever you wish that men would do to you, do so to them."[56]
- Charity always proceeds by way of respect for one's neighbor and his conscience: "Thus sinning against your brethren and wounding their conscience . . . you sin against Christ."[57] Therefore "it is right not to . . . do anything that makes your brother stumble."[58]

IV. Erroneous Judgment

1790. A human being must always obey the certain judgment of his conscience. If he were deliberately to act against it, he would condemn himself. Yet it can happen that moral conscience remains in ignorance and makes erroneous judgments about acts to be performed or already committed.

1791. This ignorance can often be imputed to personal responsibility. This is the case when a man "takes little trouble to find out what is true and good, or when conscience is by degrees almost blinded through the habit of committing sin."[59] In such cases, the person is culpable for the evil he commits.

1792. Ignorance of Christ and his Gospel, bad example given by others, enslavement to one's passions, assertion of a mistaken notion of autonomy of conscience, rejection of the Church's authority and her teaching, lack of conversion and of charity: these can be at the source of errors of judgment in moral conduct.

1793. If—on the contrary—the ignorance is invincible, or the moral subject is not responsible for his erroneous judgment, the evil committed by the person cannot be imputed to him. It remains no less an evil, a privation, a disorder. One must therefore work to correct the errors of moral conscience.

1794. A good and pure conscience is enlightened by true faith, for charity proceeds at the same time "from a pure heart and a good conscience and sincere faith."[60]

The more a correct conscience prevails, the more do persons and groups turn aside from blind choice and try to be guided by objective standards of moral conduct.[61]

NOTES

47   GS 16.
48   Cf. Rom 2:14-16.
49   Cf. Rom 1:32.
50   John Henry Cardinal Newman, "Letter to the Duke of Norfolk," V, in *Certain Difficulties Felt by Anglicans in Catholic Teaching* II (London: Longmans Green, 1885), 248.
51   St. Augustine, *In ep Jo.* 8, 9: PL 35, 2041.
52   1 Jn 3:19-20.
53   DH 3 § 2.
54   Cf. Ps 119:105.
55   Cf. DH 14.
56   Mt 7:12; cf. Lk 6:31; Tob 4:15.
57   1 Cor 8:12.
58   Rom 14:21.
59   GS 16.
60   1 Tim 5; cf. 3:9; 2 Tim 3; 1 Pet 3:21; Acts 24:16.
61   GS 16.

Chapter Two: The Human Community
Article 2: Participation in Social Life

I. Authority

1897. "Human society can be neither well-ordered nor prosperous unless it has some people invested with legitimate authority to preserve its institutions and to devote themselves as far as is necessary to work and care for the good of all."[15]

By "authority" one means the quality by virtue of which persons or institutions make laws and give orders to men and expect obedience from them.

1898. Every human community needs an authority to govern it.[16] The foundation of such authority lies in human nature. It is necessary for the unity of the state. Its role is to ensure as far as possible the common good of the society.

1899. The authority required by the moral order derives from God: "Let every person be subject to the governing authorities. For there is no authority except from God, and those that exist have been instituted by God. Therefore he who resists the authorities resists what God has appointed, and those who resist will incur judgment."[17]

1900. The duty of obedience requires all to give due honor to authority and to treat those who are charged to exercise it with respect, and, insofar as it is deserved, with gratitude and good will.

> Pope St. Clement of Rome provides the Church's most ancient prayer for political authorities:[18] "Grant to them, Lord, health, peace, concord, and stability, so that they may exercise without offense the sovereignty that you have given them. Master, heavenly King of the ages, you give glory, honor, and power over the things of earth to the sons of men. Direct, Lord, their counsel, following what is pleasing and acceptable in your sight, so that by exercising with devotion and in peace and gentleness the power that you have given to them, they may find favor with you."[19]

1901. If authority belongs to the order established by God, "the choice of the political regime and the appointment of rulers are left to the free decision of the citizens."[20]

The diversity of political regimes is morally acceptable, provided they serve the legitimate good of the communities that adopt them. Regimes whose nature is contrary to the natural law, to the public order, and to the fundamental rights of persons cannot achieve the common good of the nations on which they have been imposed.

1902. Authority does not derive its moral legitimacy from itself. It must not behave in a despotic manner, but must act for the common good as a "moral force based on freedom and a sense of responsibility":[21]

> A human law has the character of law to the extent that it accords with right reason, and thus derives from the eternal law. Insofar as it falls short of right reason it is said to be an unjust law, and thus has not so much the nature of law as of a kind of violence.[22]

1903. Authority is exercised legitimately only when it seeks the common good of the group concerned and if it employs morally licit means to attain it. If rulers were to enact unjust laws or take measures contrary to the moral order, such arrangements would not be binding in conscience. In such a case, "authority breaks down completely and results in shameful abuse."[23]

1904. "It is preferable that each power be balanced by other powers and by other spheres of responsibility which keep it within proper bounds. This is the principle of the 'rule of law,' in which the law is sovereign and not the arbitrary will of men."[24]

II. The Common Good

1905. In keeping with the social nature of man, the good of each individual is necessarily related to the common good, which in turn can be defined only in reference to the human person:

> Do not live entirely isolated, having retreated into yourselves, as if you were already justified, but gather instead to seek the common good together.[25]

1906. By common good is to be understood "the sum total of social conditions which allow people, either as groups or as individuals, to reach their fulfillment more fully and more easily."[26] The common good concerns the life of all. It calls for prudence from each, and even more from those who exercise the office of authority. It consists of *three essential elements*:

1907. First, the common good presupposes *respect for the person* as such. In the name of the common good, public authorities are bound to respect the fundamental and inalienable rights of the human person. Society should permit each of its members to fulfill his vocation. In particular, the common good resides in the conditions for the exercise of the natural freedoms indispensable for the development of the human vocation, such as "the right to act according to a sound norm of conscience and to safeguard . . . privacy, and rightful freedom also in matters of religion."[27]

1908. Second, the common good requires the *social well-being* and *development* of the group itself. Development is the epitome of all social duties. Certainly, it is the proper function of authority to arbitrate, in the name of the common good, between various particular interests; but it should make accessible to each what is needed to lead a truly human life: food, clothing, health, work, education and culture, suitable information, the right to establish a family, and so on.[28]

1909. Finally, the common good requires *peace*, that is, the stability and *security* of a just order. It presupposes that authority should ensure by morally acceptable means the security of society and its members. It is the basis of the right to legitimate personal and collective defense.

1910. Each human community possesses a common good which permits it to be recognized as such; it is in the *political community* that its most complete realization is found. It is the role of the state to defend and promote the common good of civil society, its citizens, and intermediate bodies.

1911. Human interdependence is increasing and gradually spreading throughout the world. The unity of the human family, embracing people who enjoy equal natural dignity, implies a *universal common good*. This good calls for an organization of the community of nations able to "provide for the different needs of men; this will involve the sphere of social life to which belong questions of food, hygiene, education, . . . and certain situations arising here and there, as for example . . . alleviating the miseries of refugees dispersed throughout the world, and assisting migrants and their families."[29]

1912. The common good is always oriented towards the progress of persons: "The order of things must be subordinate to the order of persons, and not the other way around."[30] This order is founded on truth, built up in justice, and animated by love.

III. Responsibility and Participation

1913. "Participation" is the voluntary and generous engagement of a person in social interchange. It is necessary that all participate, each according to his position and role, in promoting the common good. This obligation is inherent in the dignity of the human person.

1914. Participation is achieved first of all by taking charge of the areas for which one *assumes personal responsibility*: by the care taken for the education of his family, by conscientious work, and so forth, man participates in the good of others and of society.[31]

1915. As far as possible citizens should take an active part in *public life*. The manner of this participation may vary from one country or culture to another. "One must pay tribute to those nations whose systems permit the largest possible number of the citizens to take part in public life in a climate of genuine freedom."[32]

1916. As with any ethical obligation, the participation of all in realizing the common good calls for a continually renewed *conversion* of the social partners. Fraud and other subterfuges, by which some people evade the constraints of the law and the prescriptions of societal obligation, must be firmly condemned because they are incompatible with the requirements of justice. Much care should be taken to promote institutions that improve the conditions of human life.[33]

1917. It is incumbent on those who exercise authority to strengthen the values that inspire the confidence of the members of the group and encourage them to put themselves at the service of others. Participation begins with education and culture. "One is entitled to think that the future of humanity is in the hands of those who are capable of providing the generations to come with reasons for life and optimism."[34]

NOTES

15 John XXIII, PT 46.

16 Cf. Leo XIII, *Immortale Dei; Diuturnum illud.*

17 Rom 13:1-2; cf. 1 Pet 2:13-17.

18 Cf. as early as 1 Tim 2:1-2.

19 St. Clement of Rome, *Ad Cor.* 61: SCh 167, 198-200.

20 GS 74 §3.

21 GS 74 §2.

22 St. Thomas Aquinas, *STh* I-II, 93, 3, ad 2.

23 John XXIII, PT 51.

24 CA 44.

25 *Ep. Barnabae*, 4, 10: PG 2, 734.

26 GS 26 §1; cf. GS 74 §1.

27 GS 26 §2.

28 Cf. GS 26 §2.

29 GS 84 §2.

30 GS 26 §3.

31 Cf. CA 43.

32 GS 31 §3.

33 Cf. GS 30 §1.

34 GS 31 §3.

Chapter Three: God's Salvation: Law and Grace
Article 3: The Church, Mother and Teacher

2030. It is in the Church, in communion with all the baptized, that the Christian fulfills his vocation. From the Church he receives the Word of God containing the teachings of "the law of Christ."[72] From the Church he receives the grace of the sacraments that sustains him on the "way." From the Church he learns *the example of holiness* and recognizes its model and source in the all-holy Virgin Mary; he discerns it in the authentic witness of those who live it; he discovers it in the spiritual tradition and long history of the saints who have gone before him and whom the liturgy celebrates in the rhythms of the sanctoral cycle.

2031. *The moral life is spiritual worship.* We "present [our] bodies as a living sacrifice, holy and acceptable to God,"[73] within the Body of Christ that we form and in communion with the offering of his Eucharist. In the liturgy and the celebration of the sacraments, prayer and teaching are conjoined with the grace of Christ to enlighten and nourish Christian activity. As does the whole of the Christian life, the moral life finds its source and summit in the Eucharistic sacrifice.

I. Moral Life and the Magisterium of the Church

2032. The Church, the "pillar and bulwark of the truth," "has received this solemn command of Christ from the apostles to announce the saving truth."[74] "To the Church belongs the right always and everywhere to announce moral principles, including those pertaining to the social order, and to make judgments on any human affairs to the extent that they are required by the fundamental rights of the human person or the salvation of souls."[75]

2033. The *Magisterium of the Pastors of the Church* in moral matters is ordinarily exercised in catechesis and preaching, with the help of the works of theologians and spiritual authors. Thus from generation to generation, under the aegis and vigilance of the pastors, the "deposit" of Christian moral teaching has been handed on, a deposit composed of a characteristic body of rules, commandments, and virtues proceeding from faith in Christ and animated by charity. Alongside the Creed and the Our Father, the basis for this catechesis has traditionally been the Decalogue, which sets out the principles of moral life valid for all men.

2034. The Roman Pontiff and the bishops are "authentic teachers, that is, teachers endowed with the authority of Christ, who preach the faith to the people entrusted to them, the faith to be believed and put into practice."[76] The *ordinary* and universal Magisterium of the Pope and the bishops in communion with him teach the faithful the truth to believe, the charity to practice, the beatitude to hope for.

2035. The supreme degree of participation in the authority of Christ is ensured by the charism of infallibility. This *infallibility* extends as far as does the deposit of divine Revelation; it also extends to all those elements of doctrine, including morals, without which the saving truths of the faith cannot be preserved, explained, or observed.[77]

2036. The authority of the Magisterium extends also to the specific precepts of the *natural law,* because their observance, demanded by the Creator, is necessary for salvation. In recalling the prescriptions of the natural law, the Magisterium of the Church exercises an essential part of its prophetic office of proclaiming to men what they truly are and reminding them of what they should be before God.[78]

2037. The law of God entrusted to the Church is taught to the faithful as the way of life and truth. The faithful therefore have the *right* to be instructed in the divine saving precepts that purify judgment and, with grace, heal wounded human reason.[79] They have the duty of observing the constitutions and decrees conveyed by the legitimate authority of the Church. Even if they concern disciplinary matters, these determinations call for docility in charity.

2038. In the work of teaching and applying Christian morality, the Church needs the dedication of pastors, the knowledge of theologians, and the contribution of all Christians and men of good will. Faith and the practice of the Gospel provide each person with an experience of life "in Christ," who enlightens him and makes him able to evaluate the divine and human realities according to the Spirit of God.[80] Thus the Holy Spirit can use the humblest to enlighten the learned and those in the highest positions.

2039. Ministries should be exercised in a spirit of fraternal service and dedication to the Church, in the name of the Lord.[81] At the same time the conscience of each person should avoid confining itself to individualistic considerations in its moral judgments of the person's own acts. As far as possible conscience should take account of the good of all, as expressed in the moral law, natural and revealed, and consequently in the law of the Church and in the authoritative teaching of the Magisterium on moral questions. Personal conscience and reason should not be set in opposition to the moral law or the Magisterium of the Church.
2040. Thus a true *filial spirit toward the Church* can develop among Christians. It is the normal flowering of the baptismal grace which has begotten us in the womb of the Church and made us members of the Body of Christ. In her motherly care, the Church grants us the mercy of God which prevails over all our sins and is especially at work in the sacrament of reconciliation. With a mother's foresight, she also lavishes

on us day after day in her liturgy the nourishment of the Word and Eucharist of the Lord.

II. The Precepts of the Church

2041. The precepts of the Church are set in the context of a moral life bound to and nourished by liturgical life. The obligatory character of these positive laws decreed by the pastoral authorities is meant to guarantee to the faithful the very necessary minimum in the spirit of prayer and moral effort, in the growth in love of God and neighbor:

2042. The first precept ("You shall attend Mass on Sundays and holy days of obligation and rest from servile labor") requires the faithful to sanctify the day commemorating the Resurrection of the Lord as well as the principal liturgical feasts honoring the Mysteries of the Lord, the Blessed Virgin Mary and the saints; in the first place, by participating in the Eucharistic Celebration, in which the Christian community is gathered, and by resting from those works and activities which could impede such a sanctification of these days.[82]

The second precept ("You shall confess your sins at least once a year") ensures preparation for the Eucharist by the reception of the sacrament of reconciliation, which continues Baptism's work of conversion and forgiveness.[83]

The third precept ("You shall receive the sacrament of the Eucharist at least [once] during the Easter season") guarantees as a minimum the reception of the Lord's Body and Blood in connection with the Paschal feasts, the origin and center of the Christian liturgy.[84]

2043. The fourth precept ("You shall observe the days of fasting and abstinence established by the Church") ensures the times of ascesis and penance which prepare us for the liturgical feasts and help us acquire mastery over our instincts and freedom of heart.[85]

The fifth precept ("You shall help to provide for the needs of the Church") means that the faithful are obliged to assist with the material needs of the Church, each according to his own ability.[86]

The faithful also have the duty of providing for the material needs of the Church, each according to his abilities.[87]

III. Moral Life and Missionary Witness

2044. The fidelity of the baptized is a primordial condition for the proclamation of the Gospel and for the *Church's mission in the world*. In order that the message of salvation can show the power of its truth and radiance before men, it must be authenticated by the witness of the life of Christians. "The witness of a Christian life and good works done in a supernatural spirit have great power to draw men to the faith and to God."[88]

2045. Because they are members of the Body whose Head is Christ,[89] Christians contribute to *building up the Church* by the constancy of their convictions and their moral lives. The Church increases, grows, and develops through the holiness of her faithful, until "we all attain to the unity of the faith and of the knowledge of the Son of God, to mature manhood, to the measure of the stature of the fullness of Christ."[90]

2046. By living with the mind of Christ, Christians hasten the coming of the Reign of God, "a kingdom of justice, love, and peace."[91] They do not, for all that, abandon their earthly tasks; faithful to their master, they fulfill them with uprightness, patience, and love.

NOTES

72   Gal 6:2.
73   Rom 12:1.
74   1 Tim 3:15; LG 17.
75   CIC, can. 747 §2.
76   LG 25.
77   Cf. LG 25; CDF, declaration, *Mysterium Ecclesiae* 3.
78   Cf. DH 14.
79   Cf. CIC, can. 213.
80   Cf. 1 Cor 2:10-15.
81   Cf. Rom 12:8, 11.
82   Cf. CIC, cann. 1246-1248; CCEO, can. 880 §3, 881 §§1, 2, 4.
83   Cf. CIC, can. 989; CCEO, can. 719.
84   Cf. CIC, can. 920; CCEO, cann. 708; 881 §3.
85   Cf. CIC, cann. 1249-1251: CCEO can. 882.
86   Cf. CIC, can. 222; CCEO, can. 25; Furthermore, episcopal conferences can establish other ecclesiastical precepts for their own territories (cf. CIC, can. 455).
87   Cf. CIC, can. 222.
88   AA 6 §2.
89   Cf. Eph 1:22.
90   Eph 4:13; cf. LG 39.
91   *Roman Missal*, Preface of Christ the King.

SECTION TWO:
THE TEN COMMANDMENTS

Chapter Two: "You Shall Love Your Neighbor as Yourself." Article 4, Section 5: The Authorities in Civil Society

2234. God's fourth commandment also enjoins us to honor all who for our good have received authority in society from God. It clarifies the duties of those who exercise authority as well as those who benefit from it.

Duties of Civil Authorities

2235. Those who exercise authority should do so as a service. "Whoever would be great among you must be your servant."[41] The exercise of authority is measured morally in terms of its divine origin, its reasonable nature, and its specific object. No one can command or establish what is contrary to the dignity of persons and the natural law.

2236. The exercise of authority is meant to give outward expression to a just hierarchy of values in order to facilitate the exercise of freedom and responsibility by all. Those in authority should practice distributive justice wisely, taking account of the needs and contribution of each, with a view to harmony and peace. They should take care that the regulations and measures they adopt are not a source of temptation by setting personal interest against that of the community.[42]

2237. *Political authorities* are obliged to respect the fundamental rights of the human person. They will dispense justice humanely by respecting the rights of everyone, especially of families and the disadvantaged.

The political rights attached to citizenship can and should be granted according to the requirements of the common good. They cannot be suspended by public authorities without legitimate and proportionate reasons. Political rights are meant to be exercised for the common good of the nation and the human community.

The Duties of Citizens

2238. Those subject to authority should regard those in authority as representatives of God, who has made them stewards of his gifts:[43] "Be subject for the Lord's sake to every human institution. . . . Live as free men, yet without using your freedom as a pretext for evil; but live as servants of God."[44] Their loyal collaboration includes the right, and at times the duty, to voice their just criticisms of that which seems harmful to the dignity of persons and to the good of the community.

2239. It is the *duty of citizens* to contribute along with the civil authorities to the good of society in a spirit of truth, justice, solidarity, and freedom. The love and service of *one's country* follow from the duty of gratitude and belong to the order of charity. Submission to legitimate authorities and service of the common good require citizens to fulfill their roles in the life of the political community.

2240. Submission to authority and co-responsibility for the common good make it morally obligatory to pay taxes, to exercise the right to vote, and to defend one's country:

> Pay to all of them their dues, taxes to whom taxes are due, revenue to whom revenue is due, respect to whom respect is due, honor to whom honor is due.[45]

> [Christians] reside in their own nations, but as resident aliens. They participate in all things as citizens and endure all things as foreigners. . . . They obey the established laws and their way of life surpasses the laws. . . . So noble is the position to which God has assigned them that they are not allowed to desert it.[46]

> The Apostle exhorts us to offer prayers and thanksgiving for kings and all who exercise authority, "that we may lead a quiet and peaceable life, godly and respectful in every way."[47]

2241. The more prosperous nations are obliged, to the extent they are able, to welcome the *foreigner* in search of the security and the means of livelihood which he cannot find in his country of origin. Public authorities should see to it that the natural right is respected that places a guest under the protection of those who receive him.

Political authorities, for the sake of the common good for which they are responsible, may make the exercise of the right to immigrate subject to various juridical conditions, especially with regard to the immigrants' duties toward their country of adoption. Immigrants are obliged to respect with gratitude the material and spiritual heritage of the country that receives them, to obey its laws and to assist in carrying civic burdens.

2242. The citizen is obliged in conscience not to follow the directives of civil authorities when they are contrary to the demands of the moral order, to the fundamental rights of persons or the teachings of the Gospel. *Refusing obedience* to civil authorities, when their demands are contrary to those of an upright conscience, finds its justification in the distinction between serving God and serving the political community. "Render therefore to Caesar the things that are Caesar's, and to God the things that are God's."[48] "We must obey God rather than men":[49]

> When citizens are under the oppression of a public authority which oversteps its competence, they should still not refuse to give or to do what is objectively demanded of them by the common good; but it is legitimate for them to defend their own rights and those of their fellow citizens against the abuse of this authority within the limits of the natural law and the Law of the Gospel.[50]

2243. Armed *resistance* to oppression by political authority is not legitimate, unless all the following conditions are met: (1) there is certain, grave, and prolonged violation of fundamental rights; (2) all other means of redress have been exhausted; (3) such resistance will not provoke worse disorders; (4) there is well-founded hope of success; and (5) it is impossible reasonably to foresee any better solution.

The Political Community and the Church

2244. Every institution is inspired, at least implicitly, by a vision of man and his destiny, from which it derives the point of reference for its judgment, its hierarchy of values, its line of conduct. Most societies have formed their institutions in the recognition of a certain preeminence of man over things. Only the divinely revealed religion has clearly recognized man's origin and destiny in God, the Creator and Redeemer. The Church invites political authorities to measure their judgments and decisions against this inspired truth about God and man:

> Societies not recognizing this vision or rejecting it in the name of their independence from God are brought to seek their criteria and goal in themselves or to borrow them from some ideology. Since they do not admit that one can defend an objective criterion of good and evil, they arrogate to themselves an explicit or implicit totalitarian power over man and his destiny, as history shows.[51]

2245. The Church, because of her commission and competence, is not to be confused in any way with the political community. She is both the sign and the safeguard of the transcendent character of the human person. "The Church respects and encourages the political freedom and responsibility of the citizen."[52]

2246. It is a part of the Church's mission "to pass moral judgments even in matters related to politics, whenever the fundamental rights of man or the salvation of souls requires it. The means, the only means, she may use are those which are in accord with the Gospel and the welfare of all men according to the diversity of times and circumstances."[53]

NOTES

41   Mt 20:26.
42   Cf. CA 25.
43   Cf. Rom 13:1-2.
44   1 Pet 2:13, 16.
45   Rom 13:7.
46   *Ad Diognetum* 5, 5 and 10; 6, 10: PG 2, 1173 and 1176.
47   1 Tim 2:2.
48   Mt 22:21.
49   Acts 5:29.
50   GS 74 §5.
51   Cf. CA 45, 46.
52   GS 76 §3.
53   GS 76 §5.

Article 5: The Fifth Commandment
(nos. 2258-2317)

You shall not kill.[54]

You have heard that it was said to the men of old, "You shall not kill: and whoever kills shall be liable to judgment." But I say to you that every one who is angry with his brother shall be liable to judgment.[55]

2258. *"Human life is sacred* because from its beginning it involves the creative action of God and it remains for ever in a special relationship with the Creator, who is its sole end. God alone is the Lord of life from its beginning until its end: no one can under any circumstance claim for himself the right directly to destroy an innocent human being."[56]

I. RESPECT FOR HUMAN LIFE

The Witness of Sacred History

2259. In the account of Abel's murder by his brother Cain,[57] Scripture reveals the presence of anger and envy in man, consequences of original sin, from the beginning of human history. Man has become the enemy of his fellow man. God declares the wickedness of this fratricide: "What have you done? The voice of your brother's blood is crying to me from the ground. And now you are cursed from the ground, which has opened its mouth to receive your brother's blood from your hand."[58]

2260. The covenant between God and mankind is interwoven with reminders of God's gift of human life and man's murderous violence:

For your lifeblood I will surely require a reckoning. . . . Whoever sheds the blood of man, by man shall his blood be shed; for God made man in his own image.[59]

The Old Testament always considered blood a sacred sign of life.[60] This teaching remains necessary for all time.

2261. Scripture specifies the prohibition contained in the fifth commandment: "Do not slay the innocent and the righteous."[61] The deliberate murder of an innocent person is gravely contrary to the dignity of the human being, to the golden rule, and to the holiness of the Creator. The law forbidding it is universally valid: it obliges each and everyone, always and everywhere.

2262. In the Sermon on the Mount, the Lord recalls the commandment, "You shall not kill,"[62] and adds to it the proscription of anger, hatred, and vengeance. Going further, Christ asks his disciples to turn the other cheek, to love their enemies.[63] He did not defend himself and told Peter to leave his sword in its sheath.[64]

Legitimate Defense

2263. The legitimate defense of persons and societies is not an exception to the prohibition against the murder of the innocent that constitutes intentional killing. "The act of self-defense can have a double effect: the preservation of one's own life; and the killing of the aggressor. . . . The one is intended, the other is not."[65]

2264. Love toward oneself remains a fundamental principle of morality. Therefore it is legitimate to insist on respect for one's own right to life. Someone who defends his life is not guilty of murder even if he is forced to deal his aggressor a lethal blow:

> If a man in self-defense uses more than necessary violence, it will be unlawful: whereas if he repels force with moderation, his defense will be lawful. . . . Nor is it necessary for salvation that a man omit the act of moderate self-defense to avoid killing the other man, since one is bound to take more care of one's own life than of another's.[66]

2265. Legitimate defense can be not only a right but a grave duty for one who is responsible for the lives of others. The defense of the common good requires that an unjust aggressor be rendered unable to cause harm. For this reason, those who legitimately hold authority also have the right to use arms to repel aggressors against the civil community entrusted to their responsibility.

2266. The efforts of the state to curb the spread of behavior harmful to people's rights and to the basic rules of civil society correspond to the requirement of safeguarding the common good. Legitimate public authority has the right and duty to inflict punishment proportionate to the gravity of the offense. Punishment has the primary aim of redressing the disorder introduced by the offense. When it is willingly accepted by the guilty party, it assumes the value of expiation. Punishment then, in addition to defending public order and protecting people's safety, has a medicinal purpose: as far as possible, it must contribute to the correction of the guilty party.[67]

2267. Assuming that the guilty party's identity and responsibility have been fully determined, the traditional teaching of the Church does not exclude recourse to the death penalty, if this is the only possible way of effectively defending human lives against the unjust aggressor.

If, however, non-lethal means are sufficient to defend and protect people's safety from the aggressor, authority will limit itself to such means, as these are more in keeping with the concrete conditions of the common good and are more in conformity to the dignity of the human person.

Today, in fact, as a consequence of the possibilities which the state has for effectively preventing crime, by rendering one who has committed an offense incapable of doing harm—without definitely taking away from him the possibility of redeeming himself—the cases in which the execution of the offender is an absolute necessity are very rare, if not practically nonexistent.[68]

Intentional Homicide

2268. The fifth commandment forbids *direct and intentional killing* as gravely sinful. The murderer and those who cooperate voluntarily in murder commit a sin that cries out to heaven for vengeance.[69]

Infanticide,[70] fratricide, parricide, and the murder of a spouse are especially grave crimes by reason of the natural bonds which they break. Concern for eugenics or public health cannot justify any murder, even if commanded by public authority.

2269. The fifth commandment forbids doing anything with the intention of *indirectly* bringing about a person's death. The moral law prohibits exposing someone to mortal danger without grave reason, as well as refusing assistance to a person in danger.

The acceptance by human society of murderous famines, without efforts to remedy them, is a scandalous injustice and a grave offense. Those whose usurious and avaricious dealings lead to the hunger and death of their brethren in the human family indirectly commit homicide, which is imputable to them.[71]

Unintentional killing is not morally imputable. But one is not exonerated from grave offense if, without proportionate reasons, he has acted in a way that brings about someone's death, even without the intention to do so.

Abortion

2270. Human life must be respected and protected absolutely from the moment of conception. From the first moment of his existence, a human being must be recognized as having the rights of a person—among which is the inviolable right of every innocent being to life.[72]

> Before I formed you in the womb I knew you, and before you were born I consecrated you.[73]

> My frame was not hidden from you, when I was being made in secret, intricately wrought in the depths of the earth.[74]

2271. Since the first century the Church has affirmed the moral evil of every procured abortion. This teaching has not changed and remains unchangeable. Direct abortion, that is to say, abortion willed either as an end or a means, is gravely contrary to the moral law:

> You shall not kill the embryo by abortion and shall not cause the newborn to perish.[75]

> God, the Lord of life, has entrusted to men the noble mission of safeguarding life, and men must carry it out in a manner worthy of themselves. Life must be protected with the utmost care from the moment of conception: abortion and infanticide are abominable crimes.[76]

2272. Formal cooperation in an abortion constitutes a grave offense. The Church attaches the canonical penalty of excommunication to this crime against human life. "A person who procures a completed abortion incurs excommunication *latae sententiae*,"[77] "by the very commission of the offense,"[78] and subject to the conditions provided by Canon Law.[79] The Church does not thereby intend to restrict the scope of mercy. Rather, she makes clear the gravity of the crime committed, the irreparable harm done to the innocent who is put to death, as well as to the parents and the whole of society.

2273. The inalienable right to life of every innocent human individual is a *constitutive element of a civil society and its legislation*:

"The inalienable rights of the person must be recognized and respected by civil society and the political authority. These human rights depend neither on single individuals nor on parents; nor do they represent a concession made by society and the state; they belong to human nature and are inherent in the person by virtue of the creative act from which the person took his origin. Among such fundamental rights one should mention in this regard every human being's right to life and physical integrity from the moment of conception until death."[80]

"The moment a positive law deprives a category of human beings of the protection which civil legislation ought to accord them, the state is denying the equality of all before the law. When the state does not place its power at the service of the rights of each citizen, and in particular of the more vulnerable, the very foundations of a state based on law are undermined. . . . As a consequence of the respect and protection which must be ensured for the unborn child from the moment of conception, the law must provide appropriate penal sanctions for every deliberate violation of the child's rights."[81]

2274. Since it must be treated from conception as a person, the embryo must be defended in its integrity, cared for, and healed, as far as possible, like any other human being.

Prenatal diagnosis is morally licit "if it respects the life and integrity of the embryo and the human fetus and is directed toward its safe guarding or healing as an individual. . . . It is gravely opposed to the moral law when this is done with the thought of possibly inducing an abortion, depending upon the results: a diagnosis must not be the equivalent of a death sentence."[82]

2275. "One must hold as licit procedures carried out on the human embryo which respect the life and integrity of the embryo and do not involve disproportionate risks for it, but are directed toward its healing the improvement of its condition of health, or its individual survival."[83]

"It is immoral to produce human embryos intended for exploitation as disposable biological material."[84]

"Certain attempts to *influence chromosomic or genetic inheritance* are not therapeutic but are aimed at producing human beings selected according to sex or other predetermined qualities. Such manipulations are contrary to the personal dignity of the human being and his integrity and identity"[85] which are unique and unrepeatable.

Euthanasia

2276. Those whose lives are diminished or weakened deserve special respect. Sick or handicapped persons should be helped to lead lives as normal as possible.

2277. Whatever its motives and means, direct euthanasia consists in putting an end to the lives of handicapped, sick, or dying persons. It is morally unacceptable.

Thus an act or omission which, of itself or by intention, causes death in order to eliminate suffering constitutes a murder gravely contrary to the dignity of the human person and to the respect due to the living God, his Creator. The error of judgment into which one can fall in good faith does not change the nature of this murderous act, which must always be forbidden and excluded.

2278. Discontinuing medical procedures that are burdensome, dangerous, extraordinary, or disproportionate to the expected outcome can be legitimate; it is the refusal of "over-zealous" treatment. Here one does not will to cause death; one's inability to impede it is merely accepted. The decisions should be made by the patient if he is competent and able or, if not, by those legally entitled to act for the patient, whose reasonable will and legitimate interests must always be respected.

2279. Even if death is thought imminent, the ordinary care owed to a sick person cannot be legitimately interrupted. The use of painkillers to alleviate the sufferings of the dying, even at the risk of shortening their days, can be morally in conformity with human dignity if death is not willed as either an end or a means, but only foreseen and tolerated as inevitable. Palliative care is a special form of disinterested charity. As such it should be encouraged.

Suicide

2280. Everyone is responsible for his life before God who has given it to him. It is God who remains the sovereign Master of life. We are obliged to accept life gratefully and preserve it for his honor and the salvation of our souls. We are stewards, not owners, of the life God has entrusted to us. It is not ours to dispose of.

2281. Suicide contradicts the natural inclination of the human being to preserve and perpetuate his life. It is gravely contrary to the just love of self. It likewise offends love of neighbor because it unjustly breaks the ties of solidarity with family, nation, and other human societies to which we continue to have obligations. Suicide is contrary to love for the living God.

2282. If suicide is committed with the intention of setting an example, especially to the young, it also takes on the gravity of scandal. Voluntary co-operation in suicide is contrary to the moral law.

Grave psychological disturbances, anguish, or grave fear of hardship, suffering, or torture can diminish the responsibility of the one committing suicide.

2283. We should not despair of the eternal salvation of persons who have taken their own lives. By ways known to him alone, God can provide the opportunity for salutary repentance. The Church prays for persons who have taken their own lives.

II. RESPECT FOR THE DIGNITY OF PERSONS

Respect for the Souls of Others: Scandal

2284. Scandal is an attitude or behavior which leads another to do evil. The person who gives scandal becomes his neighbor's tempter. He damages virtue and integrity; he may even draw his brother into spiritual death. Scandal is a grave offense if by deed or omission another is deliberately led into a grave offense.

2285. Scandal takes on a particular gravity by reason of the authority of those who cause it or the weakness of those who are scandalized. It prompted our Lord to utter this curse:

"Whoever causes one of these little ones who believe in me to sin, it would be better for him to have a great millstone fastened round his neck and to be drowned in the depth of the sea."[86] Scandal is grave when given by those who by nature or office are obliged to teach and educate others. Jesus reproaches the scribes and Pharisees on this account: he likens them to wolves in sheep's clothing.[87]

2286. Scandal can be provoked by laws or institutions, by fashion or opinion.

Therefore, they are guilty of scandal who establish laws or social structures leading to the decline of morals and the corruption of religious practice, or to "social conditions that, intentionally or not, make Christian conduct and obedience to the Commandments difficult and practically impossible."[88] This is also true of business leaders who make rules encouraging fraud, teachers who provoke their children to anger,[89] or manipulators of public opinion who turn it away from moral values.

2287. Anyone who uses the power at his disposal in such a way that it leads others to do wrong becomes guilty of scandal and responsible for the evil that he has directly or indirectly encouraged. "Temptations to sin are sure to come; but woe to him by whom they come!"[90]

Respect for Health

2288. Life and physical health are precious gifts entrusted to us by God. We must take reasonable care of them, taking into account the needs of others and the common good.

Concern for the health of its citizens requires that society help in the attainment of living conditions that allow them to grow and reach maturity: food and clothing, housing, health care, basic education, employment, and social assistance.

2289. If morality requires respect for the life of the body, it does not make it an absolute value. It rejects a neo-pagan notion that tends to promote the *cult of the body*, to sacrifice everything for its sake, to idolize physical perfection and success at sports. By its selective preference of the strong over the weak, such a conception can lead to the perversion of human relationships.

2290. The virtue of temperance disposes us to *avoid every kind of excess*: the abuse of food, alcohol, tobacco, or medicine. Those incur grave guilt who, by drunkenness or a love of speed, endanger their own and others' safety on the road, at sea, or in the air.

2291. *The use of drugs* inflicts very grave damage on human health and life. Their use, except on strictly therapeutic grounds, is a grave offense. Clandestine production of and trafficking in drugs are scandalous practices. They constitute direct cooperation in evil, since they encourage people to practices gravely contrary to the moral law.

Respect for the Person and Scientific Research

2292. Scientific, medical, or psychological experiments on human individuals or groups can contribute to healing the sick and the advancement of public health.

2293. Basic scientific research, as well as applied research, is a significant expression of man's dominion over creation. Science and technology are precious resources when placed at the service of man and promote his integral development for the benefit of all.

By themselves however they cannot disclose the meaning of existence and of human progress. Science and technology are ordered to man, from whom they take their origin and development; hence they find in the person and in his moral values both evidence of their purpose and awareness of their limits.

2294. It is an illusion to claim moral neutrality in scientific research and its applications. On the other hand, guiding principles cannot be inferred from simple technical efficiency, or from the usefulness accruing to some at the expense of others or, even worse, from prevailing ideologies. Science and technology by their very nature require unconditional respect for fundamental moral criteria. They must be at the service of the human person, of his inalienable rights, of his true and integral good, in conformity with the plan and the will of God.

2295. Research or experimentation on the human being cannot legitimate acts that are in themselves contrary to the dignity of persons and to the moral law. The subjects' potential consent does not justify such acts. Experimentation on human beings is not morally legitimate if it exposes the subject's life or physical and psychological integrity to disproportionate or avoidable risks. Experimentation on human beings does not conform to the dignity of the person if it takes place without the informed consent of the subject or those who legitimately speak for him.

2296. *Organ transplants* are in conformity with the moral law if the physical and psychological dangers and risks to the donor are proportionate to the good sought for the recipient. Organ donation after death is a noble and meritorious act and is to be encouraged as a expression of generous solidarity. It is not morally acceptable if the donor or his proxy has not given explicit consent. Moreover, it is not morally admissible to bring about the disabling mutilation or death of a human being, even in order to delay the death of other persons.

Respect for Bodily Integrity

2297. *Kidnapping* and *hostage taking* bring on a reign of terror; by means of threats they subject their victims to intolerable pressures. They are morally wrong. *Terrorism* threatens, wounds, and kills indiscriminately; it is gravely against justice and charity. *Torture* which uses physical or moral violence to extract confessions, punish the guilty, frighten opponents, or satisfy hatred is contrary to respect for the person and for human dignity. Except when performed for strictly therapeutic medical reasons, directly intended *amputations*, *mutilations*, and *sterilizations* performed on innocent persons are against the moral law.[91]

2298. In times past, cruel practices were commonly used by legitimate governments to maintain law and order, often without protest from the Pastors of the Church, who themselves adopted in their own tribunals the prescriptions of Roman law concerning torture. Regrettable as these facts are, the Church always taught the duty of clemency and mercy. She forbade clerics to shed blood. In recent times it has become evident that these cruel practices were neither necessary for public order, nor in conformity with the legitimate rights of the human person. On the contrary, these practices led to ones even more degrading. It is necessary to work for their abolition. We must pray for the victims and their tormentors.

Respect for the Dead

2299. The dying should be given attention and care to help them live their last moments in dignity and peace. They will be helped by the prayer of their relatives, who must see to it that the sick receive at the proper time the sacraments that prepare them to meet the living God.

2300. The bodies of the dead must be treated with respect and charity, in faith and hope of the Resurrection. The burial of the dead is a corporal work of mercy;[92] it honors the children of God, who are temples of the Holy Spirit.

2301. Autopsies can be morally permitted for legal inquests or scientific research. The free gift of organs after death is legitimate and can be meritorious.

The Church permits cremation, provided that it does not demonstrate a denial of faith in the resurrection of the body.[93]

III. Safeguarding Peace

Peace

2302. By recalling the commandment, "You shall not kill,"[94] our Lord asked for peace of heart and denounced murderous anger and hatred as immoral.

Anger is a desire for revenge. "To desire vengeance in order to do evil to someone who should be punished is illicit," but it is praiseworthy to impose restitution "to correct vices and maintain justice."[95] If anger reaches the point of a deliberate desire to kill or seriously wound a neighbor, it is gravely against charity; it is a mortal sin. The Lord says, "Everyone who is angry with his brother shall be liable to judgment."[96]

2303. Deliberate *hatred* is contrary to charity. Hatred of the neighbor is a sin when one deliberately wishes him evil. Hatred of the neighbor is a grave sin when one deliberately desires him grave harm. "But I say to you, Love your enemies and pray for those who persecute you, so that you may be sons of your Father who is in heaven."[97]

2304. Respect for and development of human life require peace. Peace is not merely the absence of war, and it is not limited to maintaining a balance of powers between adversaries. Peace cannot be attained on earth without safeguarding the goods of persons, free communication among men, respect for the dignity of persons and peoples, and the assiduous practice of fraternity. Peace is "the tranquility of order."[98] Peace is the work of justice and the effect of charity.[99]

2305. Earthly peace is the image and fruit of the *peace of Christ*, the messianic "Prince of Peace."[100] By the blood of his Cross, "in his own person he killed the hostility,"[101] he reconciled men with God and made his Church the sacrament of the unity of the human race and of its union with God. "He is our peace."[102] He has declared: "Blessed are the peacemakers."[103]

2306. Those who renounce violence and bloodshed and, in order to safeguard human rights, make use of those means of defense available to the weakest, bear witness to evangelical charity, provided they do so without harming the rights and obligations of other men and societies. They bear legitimate witness to the gravity of the physical and moral risks of recourse to violence, with all its destruction and death.[104]

Avoiding War

2307. The fifth commandment forbids the intentional destruction of human life. Because of the evils and injustices that accompany all war, the Church insistently urges everyone to prayer and to action so that the divine Goodness may free us from the ancient bondage of war.[105]

2308. All citizens and all governments are obliged to work for the avoidance of war.

However, "as long as the danger of war persists and there is no international authority with the necessary competence and power, governments cannot be denied the right of lawful self-defense, once all peace efforts have failed."[106]

2309. The strict conditions for *legitimate defense by military force* require rigorous consideration. The gravity of such a decision makes it subject to rigorous conditions of moral legitimacy. At one and the same time:

- The damage inflicted by the aggressor on the nation or community of nations must be lasting, grave, and certain;

- All other means of putting an end to it must have been shown to be impractical or ineffective;

- There must be serious prospects of success;

- The use of arms must not produce evils and disorders graver than the evil to be eliminated. The power of modern means of destruction weighs very heavily in evaluating this condition.

These are the traditional elements enumerated in what is called the "just war" doctrine.

The evaluation of these conditions for moral legitimacy belongs to the prudential judgment of those who have responsibility for the common good.

2310. Public authorities, in this case, have the right and duty to impose on citizens the *obligations necessary for national defense.*

Those who are sworn to serve their country in the armed forces are servants of the security and freedom of nations. If they carry out their duty honorably, they truly contribute to the common good of the nation and the maintenance of peace.[107]

2311. Public authorities should make equitable provision for those who for reasons of conscience refuse to bear arms; these are nonetheless obliged to serve the human community in some other way.[108]

2312. The Church and human reason both assert the permanent validity of the *moral law during armed conflict.* "The mere fact that war has regrettably broken out does not mean that everything becomes licit between the warring parties."[109]

2313. Non-combatants, wounded soldiers, and prisoners must be respected and treated humanely.

Actions deliberately contrary to the law of nations and to its universal principles are crimes, as are the orders that command such actions. Blind obedience does not suffice to excuse those who carry them out. Thus the extermination of a people, nation, or ethnic minority must be condemned as a mortal sin. One is morally bound to resist orders that command genocide.

2314. "Every act of war directed to the indiscriminate destruction of whole cities or vast areas with their inhabitants is a crime against God and man, which merits firm and unequivocal condemnation."[110] A danger of modern warfare is that it provides the opportunity to those who possess modern scientific weapons, especially atomic, biological, or chemical weapons to commit such crimes.

2315. The *accumulation of arms* strikes many as a paradoxically suitable way of deterring potential adversaries from war. They see it as the most effective means of ensuring peace among nations. This method of deterrence gives rise to strong moral reservations. The *arms race* does not ensure peace. Far from eliminating the causes of war, it risks aggravating them. Spending enormous sums to produce ever new types of weapons impedes efforts to aid needy populations;[111] it thwarts the development of peoples. *Over-armament* multiplies reasons for conflict and increases the danger of escalation.

2316. The *production and the sale of arms* affect the common good of nations and of the international community. Hence public authorities have the right and duty to regulate them. The short-term pursuit of private or collective interests cannot legitimate undertakings that promote violence and conflict among nations and compromise the international juridical order.

2317. Injustice, excessive economic or social inequalities, envy, distrust, and pride raging among men and nations constantly threaten peace and cause wars. Everything done to overcome these disorders contributes to building up peace and avoiding war:

Insofar as men are sinners, the threat of war hangs over them and will so continue until Christ comes again; but insofar as they can vanquish sin by coming together in charity, violence itself will be vanquished and these words will be fulfilled: "they shall beat their swords into plowshares, and their spears into pruning hooks; nation shall not lift up sword against nation, neither shall they learn war any more."[112]

NOTES
54   Ex 20:13; cf. Deut 5:17.
55   Mt 5:21-22.
56   CDF, instruction, *Donum Vitae*, intro. 5.
57   Cf. Gen 4:8-12.
58   Gen 4:10-11.
59   Gen 9:5-6.
60   Cf. Lev 17:14.
61   Ex 23:7.
62   Mt 5:21.
63   Cf. Mt 5:22-39; 5:44.
64   Cf. Mt 26:52.
65   St. Thomas Aquinas, *STh* II-II, 64, 7, corp. art.
66   St. Thomas Aquinas, *STh* II-II, 64, 7, corp. art.
67   Cf. Lk 23:4-43.
68   John Paul II, *Evangelium Vitae*, 56.
69   Cf. Gen 4:10.
70   Cf. GS 51 §3.
71   Cf. Am 8:4-10.
72   Cf. CDF, *Donum Vitae* I, 1.
73   Jer 1:5; cf. Job 10:8-12; Ps 22:10-11.
74   Ps 139:15.
75   *Didache* 2, 2: SCh 248, 148; cf. Ep. *Barnabae* 19, 5: PG 2, 777; *Ad Diognetum* 5, 6: PG 2, 1173; Tertullian, *Apol.* 9: PL 1, 319-320.
76   GS 51 §3.
77   CIC, can. 1398.
78   CIC, can. 1314.
79   Cf. CIC, cann. 1323-1324.
80   CDF, *Donum Vitae* III.
81   CDF, *Donum Vitae* III.
82   CDF, *Donum Vitae* I, 2.
83   CDF, *Donum Vitae* I, 3.
84   CDF, *Donum Vitae* I, 5.
85   CDF, *Donum Vitae* I, 6.
86   Mt 18:6; cf. 1 Cor 8:10-13.
87   Cf. Mt 7:15.
88   Pius XII, *Discourse*, June 1, 1941.
89   Cf. Eph 6:4; Col 3:21.
90   Lk 17:1.
91   Cf. DS 3722.
92   Cf. Tob 1:16-18.
93   Cf. CIC, can. 1176 § 3.
94   Mt 5:21.
95   St. Thomas Aquinas, *STh* II-II, 158, 1 ad 3.
96   Mt 5:22.

97   Mt 5:44-45.
98   St. Augustine, *De civ. Dei*, 19, 13, 1: PL 41, 640.
99   Isa 32:17; cf. GS 78 §§1-2.
100 Isa 9:5.
101 Eph 2:16 J.B.; cf. Col 1:20-22.
102 Eph 2:14.
103 Mt 5:9.
104 Cf. GS 78 §5.
105 Cf. GS 81 §4.
106 GS 79 §4.
107 Cf. GS 79 §5.
108 Cf. GS 79 §3.
109 GS 79 §4.
110 GS 80 §3.
111 Cf. Paul VI, PP 53.
112 GS 78 §6; cf. Is 2:4.

Article 7: The Seventh Commandment
(nos. 2401-2449)

You shall not steal.[186]

2401. The seventh commandment forbids unjustly taking or keeping the goods of one's neighbor and wronging him in any way with respect to his goods. It commands justice and charity in the care of earthly goods and the fruits of men's labor. For the sake of the common good, it requires respect for the universal destination of goods and respect for the right to private property. Christian life strives to order this world's goods to God and to fraternal charity.

I. The Universal Destination and the Private Ownership of Goods

2402. In the beginning God entrusted the earth and its resources to the common stewardship of mankind to take care of them, master them by labor, and enjoy their fruits.[187] The goods of creation are destined for the whole human race. However, the earth is divided up among men to assure the security of their lives, endangered by poverty and threatened by violence. The appropriation of property is legitimate for guaranteeing the freedom and dignity of persons and for helping each of them to meet his basic needs and the needs of those in his charge. It should allow for a natural solidarity to develop between men.

2403. The *right to private property*, acquired or received in a just way, does not do away with the original gift of the earth to the whole of mankind. The *universal destination of goods* remains primordial, even if the promotion of the common good requires respect for the right to private property and its exercise.

2404. "In his use of things man should regard the external goods he legitimately owns not merely as exclusive to himself but common to others also, in the sense that they can benefit others as well as himself."[188] The ownership of any property makes its holder a steward of Providence, with the task of making it fruitful and communicating its benefits to others, first of all his family.

2405. Goods of production—material or immaterial—such as land, factories, practical or artistic skills, oblige their possessors to employ them in ways that will benefit the greatest number. Those who hold goods for use and consumption should use them with moderation, reserving the better part for guests, for the sick and the poor.

2406. *Political authority* has the right and duty to regulate the legitimate exercise of the right to ownership for the sake of the common good.[189]

II. Respect for Persons and Their Goods

2407. In economic matters, respect for human dignity requires the practice of the virtue of *temperance*, so as to moderate attachment to this world's goods; the practice of the virtue of *justice*, to preserve our neighbor's rights and render him what is his due; and the practice of *solidarity*, in accordance with the golden rule and in keeping with the generosity of the Lord, who "though he was rich, yet for your sake . . . became poor so that by his poverty, you might become rich."[190]

Respect for the Goods of Others

2408. The seventh commandment forbids *theft*, that is, usurping another's property against the reasonable will of the owner. There is no theft if consent can be presumed or if refusal is contrary to reason and the universal destination of goods. This is the case in obvious and urgent necessity when the only way to provide for immediate, essential needs (food, shelter, clothing . . .) is to put at one's disposal and use the property of others.[191]

2409. Even if it does not contradict the provisions of civil law, any form of unjustly taking and keeping the property of others is against the seventh commandment: thus, deliberate retention of goods lent or of objects lost; business fraud; paying unjust wages; forcing up prices by taking advantage of the ignorance or hardship of another.[192]

The following are also morally illicit: speculation in which one contrives to manipulate the price of goods artificially in order to gain an advantage to the detriment of others; corruption in which one influences the judgment of those who must make decisions according to law; appropriation and use for private purposes of the common goods of an enterprise; work poorly done; tax evasion; forgery of checks and invoices; excessive expenses and waste. Willfully damaging private or public property is contrary to the moral law and requires reparation.

2410. Promises must be kept and contracts strictly observed to the extent that the commitments made in them are morally just. A significant part of economic and social life depends on the honoring of contracts between physical or moral persons—commercial contracts of purchase or sale, rental or labor contracts. All contracts must be agreed to and executed in good faith.

2411. Contracts are subject to *commutative justice* which regulates exchanges between persons and between institutions in accordance with a strict respect for their rights. Commutative justice obliges strictly; it requires safeguarding property rights, paying debts, and fulfilling obligations freely contracted. Without commutative justice, no other form of justice is possible.

One distinguishes *commutative* justice from *legal* justice, which concerns what the citizen owes in fairness to the community, and from distributive justice, which regulates what the community owes its citizens in proportion to their contributions and needs.

2412. In virtue of commutative justice, *reparation for injustice* committed requires the restitution of stolen goods to their owner:

Jesus blesses Zacchaeus for his pledge: "If I have defrauded anyone of anything, I restore it fourfold."[193] Those who, directly or indirectly, have taken possession of the goods of another are obliged to make restitution of them, or to return the equivalent in kind or in money if the goods have disappeared, as well as the profit or advantages their owner would have legitimately obtained from them. Likewise, all who in some manner have taken part in a theft or who have knowingly benefited from it—for example, those who ordered it, assisted in it, or received the stolen goods—are obliged to make restitution in proportion to their responsibility and to their share of what was stolen.

2413. *Games of chance* (card games, etc.) or wagers are not in themselves contrary to justice. They become morally unacceptable when they deprive someone of what is necessary to provide for his needs and those of others. The passion for gambling risks becoming an enslavement. Unfair wagers and cheating at games constitute grave matter, unless the damage inflicted is so slight that the one who suffers it cannot reasonably consider it significant.

2414. The seventh commandment forbids acts or enterprises that for any reason—selfish or ideological, commercial, or totalitarian—lead to the *enslavement of human beings*, to their being bought, sold, and exchanged like merchandise, in disregard for their personal dignity. It is a sin against the dignity of persons and their fundamental rights to reduce them by violence to their productive value or to a source of profit. St. Paul directed a Christian master to treat his Christian slave "no longer as a slave but more than a slave, as a beloved brother, . . . both in the flesh and in the Lord."[194]

Respect for the Integrity of Creation

2415. The seventh commandment enjoins respect for the integrity of creation. Animals, like plants and inanimate beings, are by nature destined for the common good of past, present, and future humanity.[195]

Use of the mineral, vegetable, and animal resources of the universe cannot be divorced from respect for moral imperatives. Man's dominion over inanimate and other living beings granted by the Creator is not absolute; it is limited by concern for the quality of life of his neighbor, including generations to come; it requires a religious respect for the integrity of creation.[196]

2416. *Animals* are God's creatures. He surrounds them with his providential care. By their mere existence they bless him and give him glory.[197] Thus men owe them kindness. We should recall the gentleness with which saints like St. Francis of Assisi or St. Philip Neri treated animals.

2417. God entrusted animals to the stewardship of those whom he created in his own image.[198] Hence it is legitimate to use animals for food and clothing. They may be domesticated to help man in his work and leisure. Medical and scientific experimentation on animals is a morally acceptable practice if it remains within reasonable limits and contributes to caring for or saving human lives.

2418. It is contrary to human dignity to cause animals to suffer or die needlessly. It is likewise unworthy to spend money on them that should as a priority go to the relief of human misery. One can love animals; one should not direct to them the affection due only to persons.

III. The Social Doctrine of the Church

2419. "Christian revelation . . . promotes deeper understanding of the laws of social living."[199] The Church receives from the Gospel the full revelation of the truth about man. When she fulfills her mission of proclaiming the Gospel, she bears witness to man, in the name of Christ, to his dignity and his vocation to the communion of persons. She teaches him the demands of justice and peace in conformity with divine wisdom.

2420. The Church makes a moral judgment about economic and social matters, "when the fundamental rights of the person or the salvation of souls requires it."[200] In the moral order she bears a mission distinct from that of political authorities: the Church is concerned with the temporal aspects of the common good because they are ordered to the sovereign Good, our ultimate end. She strives to inspire right attitudes with respect to earthly goods and in socio-economic relationships.

2421. The social doctrine of the Church developed in the nineteenth century when the Gospel encountered modern industrial society with its new structures for the production of consumer goods, its new concept of society, the state and authority, and its new forms of labor and ownership. The development of the doctrine of the Church on economic and social matters attests the permanent value of the Church's teaching at the same time as it attests the true meaning of her Tradition, always living and active.[201]

2422. The Church's social teaching comprises a body of doctrine, which is articulated as the Church interprets events in the course of history, with the assistance of the Holy Spirit, in the light of the whole of what has been revealed by Jesus Christ.[202] This teaching can be more easily accepted by men of good will, the more the faithful let themselves be guided by it.

2423. The Church's social teaching proposes principles for reflection; it provides criteria for judgment; it gives guidelines for action:

Any system in which social relationships are determined entirely by economic factors is contrary to the nature of the human person and his acts.[203]

2424. A theory that makes profit the exclusive norm and ultimate end of economic activity is morally unacceptable. The disordered desire for money cannot but produce perverse effects. It is one of the causes of the many conflicts which disturb the social order.[204]

A system that "subordinates the basic rights of individuals and of groups to the collective organization of production" is contrary to human dignity.[205] Every practice that reduces persons to nothing more than a means of profit enslaves man, leads to idolizing money, and contributes to the spread of atheism. "You cannot serve God and mammon."[206]

2425. The Church has rejected the totalitarian and atheistic ideologies associated in modern times with "communism" or "socialism." She has likewise refused to accept, in the practice of "capitalism," individualism and the absolute primacy of the law of the marketplace over human labor.[207] Regulating the economy solely by centralized planning perverts the basis of social bonds; regulating it solely by the law of the marketplace fails social justice, for "there are many human needs which cannot be satisfied by the market."[208] Reasonable regulation of the marketplace and economic initiatives, in keeping with a just hierarchy of values and a view to the common good, is to be commended.

IV. Economic Activity and Social Justice

2426. The development of economic activity and growth in production are meant to provide for the needs of human beings. Economic life is not meant solely to multiply goods produced and increase profit or power; it is ordered first of all to the service of persons, of the whole man, and of the entire human community. Economic activity, conducted according to its own proper methods, is to be exercised within the limits of the moral order, in keeping with social justice so as to correspond to God's plan for man.[209]

2427. *Human work* proceeds directly from persons created in the image of God and called to prolong the work of creation by subduing the earth, both with and for one another.[210] Hence work is a duty: "If any one will not work, let him not eat."[211] Work honors the Creator's gifts and the talents received from him. It can also be redemptive. By enduring the hardship of work[212] in union with Jesus, the carpenter of Nazareth and the one crucified on Calvary, man collaborates in a certain fashion with the Son of God in his redemptive work. He shows himself to be a disciple of Christ by carrying the cross, daily, in the work he is called to accomplish.[213] Work can be a means of sanctification and a way of animating earthly realities with the Spirit of Christ.

2428. In work, the person exercises and fulfills in part the potential inscribed in his nature. The primordial value of labor stems from man himself, its author and its beneficiary. Work is for man, not man for work.[214]

Everyone should be able to draw from work the means of providing for his life and that of his family, and of serving the human community.

2429. Everyone has the *right of economic initiative*; everyone should make legitimate use of his talents to contribute to the abundance that will benefit all and to harvest the just fruits of his labor. He should seek to observe regulations issued by legitimate authority for the sake of the common good.[215]

2430. *Economic life* brings into play different interests, often opposed to one another. This explains why the conflicts that characterize it arise.[216] Efforts should be made to reduce these conflicts by negotiation that respects the rights and duties of each social partner: those responsible for business enterprises, representatives of wage-earners (for example, trade unions), and public authorities when appropriate.

2431. The *responsibility of the state.* "Economic activity, especially the activity of a market economy, cannot be conducted in an institutional, juridical, or political vacuum. On the contrary, it presupposes sure guarantees of individual freedom and private property, as well as a stable currency and efficient public services. Hence the principal task of the state is to guarantee this security, so that those who work and produce can enjoy the fruits of their labors and thus feel encouraged to work efficiently and honestly. . . . Another task of the state is that of overseeing and directing the exercise of human rights in the economic sector. However, primary responsibility in this area belongs not to the state but to individuals and to the various groups and associations which make up society."[217]

2432. Those *responsible for business enterprises* are responsible to society for the economic and ecological effects of their operations.[218] They have an obligation to consider the good of persons and not only the increase of profits. Profits are necessary, however. They make possible the investments that ensure the future of a business and they guarantee employment.

2433. *Access to employment* and to professions must be open to all without unjust discrimination: men and women, healthy and disabled, natives and immigrants.[219] For its part society should, according to circumstances, help citizens find work and employment.[220]

2434. A *just wage* is the legitimate fruit of work. To refuse or withhold it can be a grave injustice.[221] In determining fair pay both the needs and the contributions of each person must be taken into account. "Remuneration for work should guarantee man the opportunity to provide a dignified livelihood for himself and his family on the material, social, cultural and spiritual level, taking into account the role and the productivity of each, the state of the business, and the common good."[222] Agreement between the parties is not sufficient to justify morally the amount to be received in wages.

2435. Recourse to a *strike* is morally legitimate when it cannot be avoided, or at least when it is necessary to obtain a proportionate benefit. It becomes morally unacceptable when accompanied by violence, or when objectives are included that are not directly linked to working conditions or are contrary to the common good.

2436. It is unjust not to pay the social security contributions required by legitimate authority.

Unemployment almost always wounds its victim's dignity and threatens the equilibrium of his life. Besides the harm done to him personally, it entails many risks for his family.[223]

V. Justice and Solidarity
Among Nations

2437. On the international level, inequality of resources and economic capability is such that it creates a real "gap" between nations.[224] On the one side there are those nations possessing and developing the means of growth and, on the other, those accumulating debts.

2438. Various causes of a religious, political, economic, and financial nature today give "the social question a worldwide dimension."[225] There must be solidarity among nations which are already politically interdependent. It is even more essential when it is a question of dismantling the "perverse mechanisms" that impede the development of the less advanced countries.[226] In place of abusive if not usurious financial systems, iniquitous commercial relations among nations, and the arms race, there must be substituted a common effort to mobilize resources toward objectives of moral, cultural, and economic development, "redefining the priorities and hierarchies of values."[227]

2439. *Rich nations* have a grave moral responsibility toward those which are unable to ensure the means of their development by themselves or have been prevented from doing so by tragic historical events. It is a duty in solidarity and charity; it is also an obligation in justice if the prosperity of the rich nations has come from resources that have not been paid for fairly.

2440. *Direct aid* is an appropriate response to immediate, extraordinary needs caused by natural catastrophes, epidemics, and the like. But it does not suffice to repair the grave damage resulting from destitution or to provide a lasting solution to a country's needs. It is also necessary to *reform* international economic and financial *institutions* so that they will better promote equitable relationships with less advanced countries.[288] The efforts of poor countries working for growth and liberation must be supported.[229] This doctrine must be applied especially in the area of agricultural labor. Peasants, especially in the Third World, form the overwhelming majority of the poor.

2441. An increased sense of God and increased self-awareness are fundamental to any *full development of human society*. This development multiplies material goods and puts them at the service of the person and his freedom. It reduces dire poverty and economic exploitation. It makes for growth in respect for cultural identities and openness to the transcendent.[230]

2442. It is not the role of the Pastors of the Church to intervene directly in the political structuring and organization of social life. This task is part of the vocation of the *lay faithful*, acting on their own initiative with their fellow citizens. Social action can assume various concrete forms. It should always have the common good in view and be in conformity with the message of the Gospel and the teaching of the Church. It is the role of the laity "to animate temporal realities with Christian commitment, by which they show that they are witnesses and agents of peace and justice."[231]

VI. Love for the Poor

2443. God blesses those who come to the aid of the poor and rebukes those who turn away from them: "Give to him who begs from you, do not refuse him who would borrow from you;" "you received without pay, give without pay."[232] It is by what they have done for the poor that Jesus Christ will recognize his chosen ones.[233] When "the poor have the good news preached to them," it is the sign of Christ's presence.[234]

2444. "The Church's love for the poor . . . is a part of her constant tradition." This love is inspired by the Gospel of the Beatitudes, of the poverty of Jesus, and of his concern for the poor.[235] Love for the poor is even one of the motives for the duty of working so as to "be able to give to those in need."[236] It extends not only to material poverty but also to the many forms of cultural and religious poverty.[237]

2445. Love for the poor is incompatible with immoderate love of riches or their selfish use:

> Come now, you rich, weep and howl for the miseries that are coming upon you. Your riches have rotted and your garments are moth-eaten. Your gold and silver have rusted, and their rust will be evidence against you and will eat your flesh like fire. You have laid up treasure for the last days. Behold, the wages of the laborers who mowed your fields, which you kept back by fraud, cry out; and the cries of the harvesters have reached the ears of the Lord of hosts. You have lived on the earth in luxury and in pleasure; you have fattened your hearts in a day of slaughter. You have condemned, you have killed the righteous man; he does not resist you.[238]

2446. St. John Chrysostom vigorously recalls this: "Not to enable the poor to share in our goods is to steal from them and deprive them of life. The goods we possess are not ours, but theirs."[239] "The demands of justice must be satisfied first of all; that which is already due in justice is not to be offered as a gift of charity":[240]

When we attend to the needs of those in want, we give them what is theirs, not ours. More than performing works of mercy, we are paying a debt of justice.[241]

2447. The *works of mercy* are charitable actions by which we come to the aid of our neighbor in his spiritual and bodily necessities.[242] Instructing, advising, consoling, comforting are spiritual works of mercy, as are forgiving and bearing wrongs patiently. The corporal works of mercy consist especially in feeding the hungry, sheltering the homeless, clothing the naked, visiting the sick and imprisoned, and burying the dead.[243] Among all these, giving alms to the poor is one of the chief witnesses to fraternal charity: it is also a work of justice pleasing to God:[244]

> He who has two coats, let him share with him who has none and he who has food must do likewise.[245] But give for alms those things which are within; and behold, everything is clean for you.[246] If a brother or sister is ill-clad and in lack of daily food, and one of you says to them, "Go in peace, be warmed and filled," without giving them the things needed for the body, what does it profit?[247]

2448. "In its various forms—material deprivation, unjust oppression, physical and psychological illness and death—*human misery* is the obvious sign of the inherited condition of frailty and need for salvation in which man finds himself as a consequence of original sin. This misery elicited the compassion of Christ the Savior, who willingly took it upon himself and identified himself with the least of his brethren. Hence, those who are oppressed by poverty are the object of *a preferential love* on the part of the Church which, since her origin and in spite of the failings of many of her members, has not ceased to work for their relief, defense, and liberation through numerous works of charity which remain indispensable always and everywhere."[248]

2449. Beginning with the Old Testament, all kinds of juridical measures (the jubilee year of forgiveness of debts, prohibition of loans at interest and the keeping of collateral, the obligation to tithe, the daily payment of the day-laborer, the right to glean vines and fields) answer the exhortation of *Deuteronomy*: "For the poor will never cease out of the land; therefore I command you, 'You shall open wide your hand to your brother, to the needy and to the poor in the land.'"[249] Jesus makes these words his own: "The poor you always have with you, but you do not always have me."[250] In so doing he does not soften the vehemence of former oracles against "buying the poor for silver and the needy for a pair of sandals . . . ," but invites us to recognize his own presence in the poor who are his brethren:[251]

> When her mother reproached her for caring for the poor and the sick at home, St. Rose of Lima said to her: "When we serve the poor and the sick, we serve Jesus. We must not fail to help our neighbors, because in them we serve Jesus.[252]

NOTES

186 Ex 20:15; Deut 5:19; Mt 19:18.
187 Cf. Gen 1:26-29.
188 GS 69 §1.
189 Cf. GS 71 §4; SRS 42; CA 40; 48.
190 2 Cor 8:9.
191 Cf. GS 69 §1.
192 Cf. Deut 25:13-16; 24:14-15; Jas 5:4; Am 8:4-6.
193 Lk 19:8.
194 Philem 16.
195 Cf. Gen 1:28-31.
196 Cf. CA 37-38.
197 Cf. Mt 6:26; Dan 3:79-81.
198 Cf. Gen 2:19-20; 9:1-4.
199 GS 23 §1.
200 GS 76 §5.
201 Cf. CA 3.
202 Cf. SRS 1; 41.
203 Cf. CA 24.
204 Cf. GS 63 §3; LE 7:20; CA 35.
205 GS 65 §2.
206 Mt 6:24; Lk 16:13.
207 Cf. CA 10; 13; 44.
208 CA 34.
209 Cf. GS 64.
210 Cf. Gen 1:28; GS 34; CA 31.
211 2 Thes 3:10; cf. 1 Thes 4:11.
212 Cf. Gen 3:14-19.
213 Cf. LE 27.
214 Cf. LE 6.
215 Cf. CA 32; 34.
216 Cf. LE 11.
217 CA 48.
218 Cf CA 37.
219 Cf. LE 19; 22-23.
220 Cf. CA 48.
221 Cf. Lev 19:13; Deut 24:14-15; Jas 5:4.
222 GS 67 §2.
223 Cf. LE 18.

224 Cf. SRS 14.
225 SRS 9.
226 Cf. SRS 17; 45.
227 CA 28; cf. 35.
228 Cf. SRS 16.
229 Cf. CA 26.
230 Cf. SRS 32; CA 51.
231 SRS 47 §6; cf. 42.
232 Mt 5:42; 10:8.
233 Cf. Mt 25:31-36.
234 Mt 11:5; cf. Lk 4:18.
235 CA 57; cf. Lk 6:20-22, Mt 8:20; Mk 12:41-44.
236 Eph 4:28.
237 Cf. CA 57.
238 Jas 5:1-6.
239 St. John Chrysostom, *Hom. in Lazaro* 2, 5: PG 48, 992.
240 AA 8 §5.
241 St. Gregory the Great, *Regula Pastoralis*. 3, 21: PL 77, 87.
242 Cf. Isa 58:6-7; Heb 13:3.
243 Cf. Mt 25:31-46.
244 Cf. Tob 4:5-11; Sir 17:22; Mt 6:2-4.
245 Lk 3:11.
246 Lk 11:41.
247 Jas 2:15-16; cf. 1 Jn 3:17.
248 CDF, instruction, *Libertatis Conscientia*, 68.
249 Deut 15:11.
250 Jn 12:8.
251 Am 8:6; cf. Mt 25:40.
252 P. Hansen, *Vita mirabilis* (Louvain, 1668).

Doctrinal Note on Some Questions Regarding the Participation of Catholics in Political Life

Congregation for the Doctrine of the Faith, 2002

The Congregation for the Doctrine of the Faith, having received the opinion of the Pontifical Council for the Laity, has decided that it would be appropriate to publish the present Doctrinal Note on Some Questions Regarding the Participation of Catholics in Political Life. *This Note is directed to the Bishops of the Catholic Church and, in a particular way, to Catholic politicians and all lay members of the faithful called to participate in the political life of democratic societies.*

I. A Constant Teaching

1. The commitment of Christians in the world has found a variety of expressions in the course of the past 2,000 years. One such expression has been Christian involvement in political life: Christians, as one Early Church writer stated, "play their full role as citizens."[1] Among the saints, the Church venerates many men and women who served God through their generous commitment to politics and government. Among these, St. Thomas More, who was proclaimed Patron of Statesmen and Politicians, gave witness by his martyrdom to "the inalienable dignity of the human conscience."[2] Though subjected to various forms of psychological pressure, St. Thomas More refused to compromise, never forsaking the "constant fidelity to legitimate authority and institutions" which distinguished him; he taught by his life and his death that "man cannot be separated from God, nor politics from morality."[3]

It is commendable that in today's democratic societies, in a climate

Congregation for the Doctrine of the Faith, *Doctrinal Note on Some Questions Regarding the Participation of Catholics in Political Life* (November 24, 2002). See http://www.vatican.va/roman_curia/congregations/cfaith/documents/rc_con_cfaith_doc_20021124_politica_en.html (accessed May 10, 2005).

of true freedom, everyone is made a participant in directing the body politic.[4] Such societies call for new and fuller forms of participation in public life by Christian and non-Christian citizens alike. Indeed, all can contribute, by voting in elections for lawmakers and government officials, and in other ways as well, to the development of political solutions and legislative choices which, in their opinion, will benefit the common good.[5] The life of a democracy could not be productive without the active, responsible, and generous involvement of everyone, "albeit in a diversity and complementarity of forms, levels, tasks, and responsibilities."[6]

By fulfilling their civic duties, "guided by a Christian conscience,"[7] in conformity with its values, the lay faithful exercise their proper task of infusing the temporal order with Christian values, all the while respecting the nature and rightful autonomy of that order,[8] and cooperating with other citizens according to their particular competence and responsibility.[9] The consequence of this fundamental teaching of the Second Vatican Council is that "the lay faithful are never to relinquish their participation in 'public life,' that is, in the many different economic, social, legislative, administrative and cultural areas, which are intended to promote organically and institutionally the common good."[10] This would include the promotion and defense of goods such as public order and peace, freedom and equality, respect for human life and for the environment, justice, and solidarity.

The present *Note* does not seek to set out the entire teaching of the Church on this matter, which is summarized in its essentials in the *Catechism of the Catholic Church*, but intends only to recall some principles proper to the Christian conscience, which inspire the social and political involvement of Catholics in democratic societies.[11] The emergence of ambiguities or questionable positions in recent times, often because of the pressure of world events, has made it necessary to clarify some important elements of Church teaching in this area.

II. Central Points in the Current Cultural and Political Debate

2. Civil society today is undergoing a complex cultural process as the end of an era brings with it a time of uncertainty in the face of something new. The great strides made in our time give evidence of humanity's progress in attaining conditions of life which are more in keeping with human dignity. The growth in the sense of responsibility towards countries still on the path of development is without doubt an impor-

tant sign, illustrative of a greater sensitivity to the common good. At the same time, however, one cannot close one's eyes to the real dangers which certain tendencies in society are promoting through legislation, nor can one ignore the effects this will have on future generations.

A kind of cultural relativism exists today, evident in the conceptualization and defense of an ethical pluralism, which sanctions the decadence and disintegration of reason and the principles of the natural moral law. Furthermore, it is not unusual to hear the opinion expressed in the public sphere that such ethical pluralism is the very condition for democracy.[12] As a result, citizens claim complete autonomy with regard to their moral choices, and lawmakers maintain that they are respecting this freedom of choice by enacting laws which ignore the principles of natural ethics and yield to ephemeral cultural and moral trends,[13] as if every possible outlook on life were of equal value. At the same time, the value of tolerance is disingenuously invoked when a large number of citizens, Catholics among them, are asked not to base their contribution to society and political life—through the legitimate means available to everyone in a democracy—on their particular understanding of the human person and the common good. The history of the twentieth century demonstrates that those citizens were right who recognized the falsehood of relativism, and with it, the notion that there is no moral law rooted in the nature of the human person, which must govern our understanding of man, the common good, and the state.

3. Such relativism, of course, has nothing to do with the legitimate freedom of Catholic citizens to choose among the various political opinions that are compatible with faith and the natural moral law, and to select, according to their own criteria, what best corresponds to the needs of the common good. Political freedom is not—and cannot be—based upon the relativistic idea that all conceptions of the human person's good have the same value and truth, but rather, on the fact that politics are concerned with very concrete realizations of the true human and social good in given historical, geographic, economic, technological, and cultural contexts. From the specificity of the task at hand and the variety of circumstances, a plurality of morally acceptable policies and solutions arises. It is not the Church's task to set forth specific political solutions—and even less to propose a single solution as the acceptable one—to temporal questions that God has left to the free and responsible judgment of each person. It is, however, the Church's right

and duty to provide a moral judgment on temporal matters when this is required by faith or the moral law.[14] If Christians must "recognize the legitimacy of differing points of view about the organization of worldly affairs,"[15] they are also called to reject, as injurious to democratic life, a conception of pluralism that reflects moral relativism. Democracy must be based on the true and solid foundation of non-negotiable ethical principles, which are the underpinning of life in society.

On the level of concrete political action, there can generally be a plurality of political parties in which Catholics may exercise—especially through legislative assemblies—their right and duty to contribute to the public life of their country.[16] This arises because of the contingent nature of certain choices regarding the ordering of society, the variety of strategies available for accomplishing or guaranteeing the same fundamental value, the possibility of different interpretations of the basic principles of political theory, and the technical complexity of many political problems. It should not be confused, however, with an ambiguous pluralism in the choice of moral principles or essential values. The legitimate plurality of temporal options is at the origin of the commitment of Catholics to politics and relates directly to Christian moral and social teaching. It is in the light of this teaching that lay Catholics must assess their participation in political life so as to be sure that it is marked by a coherent responsibility for temporal reality.

The Church recognizes that while democracy is the best expression of the direct participation of citizens in political choices, it succeeds only to the extent that it is based on a correct understanding of the human *person*.[17] Catholic involvement in political life cannot compromise on this principle, for otherwise the witness of the Christian faith in the world, as well as the unity and interior coherence of the faithful, would be non-existent. The democratic structures on which the modern state is based would be quite fragile were its foundation not the centrality of the human person. It is respect for the person that makes democratic participation possible. As the Second Vatican Council teaches, the protection of "the rights of the person is, indeed, a necessary condition for citizens, individually and collectively, to play an active part in public life and administration."[18]

4.   The complex array of today's problems branches out from here, including some never faced by past generations. Scientific progress has resulted in advances that are unsettling for the consciences of men and

women and call for solutions that respect ethical principles in a coherent and fundamental way. At the same time, legislative proposals are put forward which, heedless of the consequences for the existence and future of human beings with regard to the formation of culture and social behavior, attack the very inviolability of human life. Catholics, in this difficult situation, have the right and the duty to recall society to a deeper understanding of human life and to the responsibility of everyone in this regard. John Paul II, continuing the constant teaching of the Church, has reiterated many times that those who are directly involved in lawmaking bodies have a *"grave and clear obligation to oppose"* any law that attacks human life. For them, as for every Catholic, it is impossible to promote such laws or to vote for them.[19] As John Paul II has taught in his Encyclical Letter *Evangelium vitae* regarding the situation in which it is not possible to overturn or completely repeal a law allowing abortion which is already in force or coming up for a vote, "an elected official, whose absolute personal opposition to procured abortion was well known, could licitly support proposals aimed at *limiting the harm* done by such a law and at lessening its negative consequences at the level of general opinion and public morality."[20]

In this context, it must be noted also that a well-formed Christian conscience does not permit one to vote for a political program or an individual law which contradicts the fundamental contents of faith and morals. The Christian faith is an integral unity, and thus it is incoherent to isolate some particular element to the detriment of the whole of Catholic doctrine. A political commitment to a single isolated aspect of the Church's social doctrine does not exhaust one's responsibility towards the common good. Nor can a Catholic think of delegating his Christian responsibility to others; rather, the Gospel of Jesus Christ gives him this task, so that the truth about man and the world might be proclaimed and put into action.

When political activity comes up against moral principles that do not admit of exception, compromise, or derogation, the Catholic commitment becomes more evident and laden with responsibility. In the face of *fundamental and inalienable ethical demands*, Christians must recognize that what is at stake is the essence of the moral law, which concerns the integral good of the human person. This is the case with laws concerning *abortion* and *euthanasia* (not to be confused with the decision to forgo *extraordinary treatments*, which is morally legitimate). Such laws must defend the basic right to life from conception to natural death. In the same way, it is necessary to recall the duty to respect and protect the rights of the *human embryo*. Analogously, the *family* needs to be safeguarded and promoted, based on monogamous marriage between a man and a woman, and protected in its unity and stability in the face of modern laws on divorce: in no way can other forms of cohabitation be placed on the same level as marriage, nor can they receive legal recognition as such. The same is true for the freedom of parents regarding the *education* of their children; it is an inalienable right recognized also by the Universal Declaration on Human Rights. In the same way, one must consider *society's protection of minors* and freedom from *modern forms of slavery* (drug abuse and prostitution, for example). In addition, there is the right to *religious freedom* and the development of an economy that is at the service of the human person and of the common good, with respect for social justice, the principles of human solidarity and subsidiarity, according to which "the rights of all individuals, families, and organizations and their practical implementation must be acknowledged."[21] Finally, the question of *peace* must be mentioned. Certain pacifistic and ideological visions tend at times to secularize the value of peace, while, in other cases, there is the problem of summary ethical judgments which forget the complexity of the issues involved. Peace is always "the work of justice and the effect of charity."[22] It demands the absolute and radical rejection of violence and terrorism and requires a constant and vigilant commitment on the part of all political leaders.

III. Principles of Catholic Doctrine on the Autonomy of the Temporal Order and on Pluralism

5.   While a plurality of methodologies reflective of different sensibilities and cultures can be legitimate in approaching such questions, no Catholic can appeal to the principle of pluralism or to the autonomy of lay involvement in political life to support policies affecting the common good which compromise or undermine fundamental ethical requirements. This is not a question of "confessional values" per se, because such ethical precepts are rooted in human nature itself and belong to the natural moral law. They do not require from those who defend them the profession of the Christian faith, although the Church's teaching confirms and defends them always and everywhere

as part of her service to the truth about man and about the common good of civil society. Moreover, it cannot be denied that politics must refer to principles of absolute value precisely because these are at the service of the dignity of the human person and of true human progress.

6.   The appeal often made to *"the rightful autonomy of the participation of lay Catholics"* in politics needs to be clarified. Promoting the common good of society, according to one's conscience, has nothing to do with "confessionalism" or religious intolerance. For Catholic moral doctrine, the rightful autonomy of the political or civil sphere from that of religion and the Church—*but not from that of morality*—is a value that has been attained and recognized by the Catholic Church and belongs to inheritance of contemporary civilization.[23] John Paul II has warned many times of the dangers which follow from confusion between the religious and political spheres. "Extremely sensitive situations arise when a specifically religious norm becomes or tends to become the law of a state without due consideration for the distinction between the domains proper to religion and to political society. In practice, the identification of religious law with civil law can stifle religious freedom, even going so far as to restrict or deny other inalienable human rights."[24] All the faithful are well aware that specifically religious activities (such as the profession of faith, worship, administration of sacraments, theological doctrines, interchange between religious authorities and the members of religions) are outside the state's responsibility. The state must not interfere, nor in any way require or prohibit these activities, except when it is a question of public order. The recognition of civil and political rights, as well as the allocation of public services may not be made dependent upon citizens' religious convictions or activities.

The right and duty of Catholics and all citizens to seek the truth with sincerity and to promote and defend, by legitimate means, moral truths concerning society, justice, freedom, respect for human life, and the other rights of the person, is something quite different. The fact that some of these truths may also be taught by the Church does not lessen the political legitimacy or the rightful "autonomy" of the contribution of those citizens who are committed to them, irrespective of the role that reasoned inquiry or confirmation by the Christian faith may have played in recognizing such truths. Such "autonomy" refers first of all to the attitude of the person who respects the truths that derive from natural knowledge regarding man's life in society, even if such truths may also be taught by a specific religion, because truth is one. It would be a mistake to confuse the proper *autonomy* exercised by Catholics in political life with the claim of a principle that prescinds from the moral and social teaching of the Church.

By its interventions in this area, the Church's Magisterium does not wish to exercise political power or eliminate the freedom of opinion of Catholics regarding contingent questions. Instead, it intends—as is its proper function—to instruct and illuminate the consciences of the faithful, particularly those involved in political life, so that their actions may always serve the integral promotion of the human person and the common good. The social doctrine of the Church is not an intrusion into the government of individual countries. It is a question of the lay Catholic's duty to be morally coherent, found within one's conscience, which is one and indivisible. "There cannot be two parallel lives in their existence: on the one hand, the so-called 'spiritual life', with its values and demands; and on the other, the so-called 'secular' life, that is, life in a family, at work, in social responsibilities, in the responsibilities of public life and in culture. The branch, engrafted to the vine which is Christ, bears its fruit in every sphere of existence and activity. In fact, every area of the lay faithful's lives, as different as they are, enters into the plan of God, who desires that these very areas be the 'places in time' where the love of Christ is revealed and realized for both the glory of the Father and service of others. Every activity, every situation, every precise responsibility— as, for example, skill and solidarity in work, love and dedication in the family and the education of children, service to society and public life and the promotion of truth in the area of culture—are the occasions ordained by providence for a 'continuous exercise of faith, hope and charity (*Apostolicam Actuositatem*, 4)."[25] Living and acting in conformity with one's own conscience on questions of politics is not slavish acceptance of positions alien to politics or some kind of confessionalism, but rather the way in which Christians offer their concrete contribution so that, through political life, society will become more just and more consistent with the dignity of the human person.

In democratic societies, all proposals are freely discussed and examined. Those who, on the basis of respect for individual conscience, would view the moral duty of Christians to act according to their conscience as something that disqualifies them from political life, denying the legitimacy of their political involvement following from their convictions about the common good, would be guilty of a form of intolerant *secularism*. Such a position would seek to deny not only any engagement of Christianity in public or political life, but even the possibility of natural ethics itself. Were this the case, the road would be open to moral anarchy, which would be anything but legitimate pluralism. The oppression of the weak by the strong would be the obvious consequence. The marginalization of Christianity, moreover, would not bode well for the future of society or for consensus among peoples; indeed, it would threaten the very spiritual and cultural foundations of civilization.[26]

IV. Considerations Regarding Particular Aspects

7. In recent years, there have been cases within some organizations founded on Catholic principles, in which support has been given to political forces or movements with positions contrary to the moral and social teaching of the Church on fundamental ethical questions. Such activities, in contradiction to basic principles of Christian conscience, are not compatible with membership in organizations or associations which define themselves as Catholic. Similarly, some Catholic periodicals in certain countries have expressed perspectives on political choices that have been ambiguous or incorrect, by misinterpreting the idea of the political autonomy enjoyed by Catholics and by not taking into consideration the principles mentioned above.

Faith in Jesus Christ, who is "the way, the truth, and the life" (Jn 14:6), calls Christians to exert a greater effort in building a culture which, inspired by the Gospel, will reclaim the values and contents of the Catholic Tradition. The presentation of the fruits of the spiritual, intellectual, and moral heritage of Catholicism in terms understandable to modern culture is a task of great urgency today, in order to avoid also a kind of Catholic cultural diaspora. Furthermore, the cultural achievements and mature experience of Catholics in political life in various countries, especially since the Second World War, do not permit any kind of "inferiority complex" in comparison with political programs which recent history has revealed to be weak or totally ruinous. It is insufficient and reductive to think that the commitment of Catholics in society can be limited to a simple transformation of structures, because if at the basic level there is no culture capable of receiving, justifying, and putting into practice positions deriving from faith and morals, the changes will always rest on a weak foundation.

Christian faith has never presumed to impose a rigid framework on social and political questions, conscious that the historical dimension requires men and women to live in imperfect situations, which are also susceptible to rapid change. For this reason, Christians must reject political positions and activities inspired by a utopian perspective which, turning the tradition of Biblical faith into a kind of prophetic vision without God, makes ill use of religion by directing consciences towards a hope which is merely earthly and which empties or reinterprets the Christian striving towards eternal life.

At the same time, the Church teaches that authentic freedom does not exist without the truth. "Truth and freedom either go together hand in hand or together they perish in misery."[27] In a society in which truth is neither mentioned nor sought, every form of authentic exercise of freedom will be weakened, opening the way to libertine and individualistic distortions and undermining the protection of the good of the human person and of the entire society.

8.   In this regard, it is helpful to recall a truth which today is often not perceived or formulated correctly in public opinion: the right to freedom of conscience and, in a special way, to religious freedom, taught in the Declaration *Dignitatis Humanae* of the Second Vatican Council, is based on the ontological dignity of the human person and not on a non-existent equality among religions or cultural systems of human creation.[28] Reflecting on this question, Paul VI taught that "in no way does the Council base this right to religious freedom on the fact that all religions and all teachings, including those that are erroneous, would have more or less equal value; it is based rather on the dignity of the human person, which demands that he not be subjected to external limitations which tend to constrain the conscience in its search for the true religion or in adhering to it."[29] The teaching on freedom of conscience and on religious freedom does not therefore contradict the condemnation of indifferentism and religious relativism by Catholic doctrine;[30] on the contrary, it is fully in accord with it.

V. Conclusion

9.   The principles contained in the present *Note* are intended to shed light on one of the most important aspects of the unity of Christian life: coherence between faith and life, Gospel and culture, as recalled by the

Second Vatican Council. The Council exhorted Christians "to fulfill their duties faithfully in the spirit of the Gospel. It is a mistake to think that, because we have here no lasting city, but seek the city which is to come, we are entitled to shirk our earthly responsibilities; this is to forget that by our faith we are bound all the more to fulfill these responsibilities according to the vocation of each. . . . May Christians . . . be proud of the opportunity to carry out their earthly activity in such a way as to integrate human, domestic, professional, scientific and technical enterprises with religious values, under whose supreme direction all things are ordered to the glory of God."[31]

NOTES

1   *Letter to Diognetus*, 5, 5; cf. *Catechism of the Catholic Church*, no. 2240.

2   John Paul II, Apostolic Letter Motu Proprio *Proclaiming St. Thomas More Patron of Statesmen and Politicians*, 1: AAS 93 (2001), 76.

3   Ibid., 4.

4   Cf. Second Vatican Council, Pastoral Constitution *Gaudium et Spes*, 31; *Catechism of the Catholic Church*, no. 1915.

5   Cf. Second Vatican Council, Pastoral Constitution *Gaudium et Spes*, 75.

6   John Paul II, Apostolic Exhortation, *Christifideles Laici*, 42: AAS 81 (1989), 472. The present doctrinal Note refers to the involvement in political life of lay members of the faithful. The Bishops of the Church have the right and the duty to set out the moral principles relating to the social order; "nevertheless active participation in political parties is reserved to the lay faithful" (ibid., 60). Cf. Congregation for the Clergy, *Directory for the Ministry and Life of Priests* (March 31, 1994), 33.

7   Second Vatican Council, Pastoral Constitution *Gaudium et Spes*, 76.

8   Cf. Second Vatican Council, Pastoral Constitution *Gaudium et Spes*, 36.

9   Cf. Second Vatican Council, Decree *Apostolicam actuositatem*, 7; Dogmatic Constitution *Lumen Gentium*, 36; Pastoral Constitution *Gaudium et Spes*, 31 and 43.

10 John Paul II, Apostolic Exhortation *Christifideles Laici*, 42.

11 In the last two centuries, the Papal Magisterium has spoken on the principal questions regarding the social and political order. Cf. Leo XIII, Encyclical Letter *Diuturnum illud*: ASS 14 (1881-1882), 4ff.; Encyclical Letter *Immortale Dei*: ASS 18 (1885-1886), 162ff.; Encyclical Letter *Libertas præstantissimum*: ASS 20 (1887-1888), 593ff.; Encyclical Letter *Rerum Novarum*: ASS 23 (1890-1891), 643ff.; Benedict XV, Encyclical Letter *Pacem Dei munus pulcherrimum*: AAS 12 (1920), 209ff.; Pius XI, Encyclical Letter *Quadragesimo Anno*: AAS 23 (1931), 190ff.; Encyclical Letter *Mit brennender Sorge*: AAS 29 (1937), 145-167; Encyclical Letter *Divini Redemptoris*: AAS 29 (1937), 78ff.; Pius XII, Encyclical Letter *Summi Pontificatus*: AAS 31 (1939), 423ff.; *Radiomessaggi natalizi* 1941-1944; John XXIII, Encyclical Letter *Mater et Magistra*: AAS 53 (1961), 401-464; Encyclical Letter *Pacem in Terris*: AAS 55 (1963), 257-304; Paul VI, Encyclical Letter *Populorum Progressio*: AAS 59 (1967), 257-299; Apostolic Letter *Octogesima Adveniens*: AAS 63 (1971), 401-441.

12 Cf. John Paul II, Encyclical Letter *Centesimus Annus*, 46: AAS 83 (1991); Encyclical Letter *Veritatis Splendor*, 101: AAS 85 (1993), 1212-1213; *Discourse to the Italian Parliament*, 5: *L'Osservatore Romano* (November 15, 2002).

13 Cf. John Paul II, Encyclical Letter *Evangelium Vitae*, 22: AAS 87 (1995), 425-426.

14 Cf. Second Vatican Council, Pastoral Constitution *Gaudium et Spes*, 76.

15 Second Vatican Council, Pastoral Constitution *Gaudium et Spes*, 75.

16   Cf. Second Vatican Council, Pastoral Constitution *Gaudium et Spes*, 43 and 75.

17   Cf. Second Vatican Council, Pastoral Constitution *Gaudium et Spes*, 25.

18   Second Vatican Council, Pastoral Constitution *Gaudium et Spes*, 73.

19   Cf. John Paul II, Encyclical Letter *Evangelium Vitae*, 73.

20   Ibid.

21   Second Vatican Council, Pastoral Constitution *Gaudium et Spes*, 75.

22   *Catechism of the Catholic Church*, no. 2304.

23   Cf. Second Vatican Council, Pastoral Constitution *Gaudium et Spes*, 76.

24   John Paul II, *Message for the 1991 World Day of Peace: "If you want peace, respect the conscience of every person,"* 4: AAS 83 (1991), 414-415.

25   John Paul II, Apostolic Exhortation *Christifideles Laici*, 59.

26   Cf. John Paul II, *Address to the Diplomatic Corps accredited to the Holy See: L'Osservatore Romano* (January 11, 2002).

27   John Paul II, Encyclical Letter *Fides et ratio*, 90: AAS 91 (1999), 75.

28   Cf. Second Vatican Council, Declaration *Dignitatis Humanae*, 1: "This Sacred Council begins by professing that God himself has made known to the human race how men by serving him can be saved and reach the state of the blessed. We believe that this one true religion subsists in the Catholic and Apostolic Church." This does not lessen the sincere respect that the Church has for the various religious traditions, recognizing in them "elements of truth and goodness." *See also* Second Vatican Council, Dogmatic Constitution *Lumen Gentium*, 16; Decree *Ad gentes*, 11; Declaration Nostra aetate, 2; John Paul II, Encyclical Letter *Redemptoris Missio*, 55: AAS 83 (1991), 302-304; Congregation for the Doctrine of the Faith, Declaration *Dominus Iesus*, 2, 8, 21: AAS 92 (2000), 742-765.

29   Paul VI, *Address to the Sacred College and to the Roman Prelature: in Insegnamenti di Paolo VI*, 14 (1976), 1088-1089.

30   Cf. Pius IX, Encyclical Letter *Quanta cura*: ASS 3 (1867), 162; Leo XIII, Encyclical Letter *Immortale Dei*: ASS 18 (1885), 170-171; Pius XI, Encyclical Letter *Quas primas*: AAS 17 (1925), 604-605; *Catechism of the Catholic Church*, no. 2108; Congregation for the Doctrine of the Faith, Declaration *Dominus Iesus*, 22.

31   Second Vatican Council, Pastoral Constitution *Gaudium et Spes*, 43; see also John Paul II, Apostolic Exhortation *Christifideles Laici*, 59.

Compendium of the
Social Doctrine of the Church

Pontifical Council for Justice and Peace, 2005

CHAPTER FOUR:
PRINCIPLES OF THE CHURCH'S SOCIAL DOCTRINE

IV. THE PRINCIPLE OF SUBSIDIARITY

a. Origin and Meaning

185. Subsidiarity is among the most constant and characteristic directives of the Church's social doctrine and has been present since the first
great social encyclical.[395] It is impossible to promote the dignity of the
person without showing concern for the family, groups, associations,
local territorial realities; in short, for that aggregate of economic, social,
cultural, sports-oriented, recreational, professional, and political
expressions to which people spontaneously give life and which make it
possible for them to achieve effective social growth.[396] This is the realm
of civil society, understood as the sum of the relationships between
individuals and intermediate social groupings, which are the first relationships to arise and which come about thanks to "the creative subjectivity of the citizen."[397] This network of relationships strengthens the
social fabric and constitutes the basis of a true community of persons,
making possible the recognition of higher forms of social activity.[398]

186. The necessity of defending and promoting the original expressions of social life is emphasized by the Church in the Encyclical
Quadragesimo Anno, in which the principle of subsidiarity is indicated as
a most important principle of "social philosophy." "Just as it is gravely
wrong to take from individuals what they can accomplish by their own

Pontifical Council for Justice and Peace, *Compendium of the Social Doctrine of the Church* (Washington,
DC: United States Conference of Catholic Bishops–Libreria Editrice Vaticana, 2005).

initiative and industry and give it to the community, so also it is an injustice and at the same time a grave evil and disturbance of right order to assign to a greater and higher association what lesser and subordinate organizations can do. For every social activity ought of its very nature to furnish help to the members of the body social, and never destroy and absorb them."[399]

On the basis of this principle, all societies of a superior order must adopt attitudes of help ("subsidium")—therefore of support, promotion, development—with respect to lower-order societies. In this way, intermediate social entities can properly perform the functions that fall to them without being required to hand them over unjustly to other social entities of a higher level, by which they would end up being absorbed and substituted, in the end seeing themselves denied their dignity and essential place.

Subsidiarity, understood in the positive sense as economic, institutional, or juridical assistance offered to lesser social entities, entails a corresponding series of negative implications that require the State to refrain from anything that would de facto restrict the existential space of the smaller essential cells of society. Their initiative, freedom, and responsibility must not be supplanted.

b. Concrete Indications

187. The principle of subsidiarity protects people from abuses by higher-level social authority and calls on these same authorities to help individuals and intermediate groups to fulfill their duties. This principle is imperative because every person, family and intermediate group has something original to offer to the community. Experience shows that the denial of subsidiarity, or its limitation in the name of an alleged democratization or equality of all members of society, limits and sometimes even destroys the spirit of freedom and initiative.

The principle of subsidiarity is opposed to certain forms of centralization, bureaucratization, and welfare assistance and to the unjustified and excessive presence of the State in public mechanisms. "By intervening directly and depriving society of its responsibility, the Social Assistance State leads to a loss of human energies and an inordinate increase of public agencies, which are dominated more by bureaucratic ways of thinking than by concern for serving their clients, and which are accompanied by an enormous increase in spending."[400] An absent or insufficient recognition of private initiative—in economic matters also—and the failure to recognize its public function contribute to the undermining of the principle of subsidiarity, as monopolies do as well.

In order for the principle of subsidiarity to be put into practice there is a corresponding need for respect and effective promotion of the human person and the family; ever greater appreciation of associations and intermediate organizations in their fundamental choices and in those that cannot be delegated to or exercised by others; the encouragement of private initiative so that every social entity remains at the service of the common good, each with its own distinctive characteristics; the presence of pluralism in society and due representation of its vital components; safeguarding human rights and the rights of minorities; bringing about bureaucratic and administrative decentralization; striking a balance between the public and private spheres, with the resulting recognition of the social function of the private sphere; appropriate methods for making citizens more responsible in actively "being a part" of the political and social reality of their country.

188. *Various circumstances may make it advisable that the State step in to supply certain functions.*[401] One may think, for example, of situations in which it is necessary for the State itself to stimulate the economy because it is impossible for civil society to support initiatives on its own. One may also envision the reality of serious social imbalance or injustice where only the intervention of the public authority can create conditions of greater equality, justice, and peace. In light of the principle of subsidiarity, however, this institutional substitution must not continue any longer than is absolutely necessary, since justification for such intervention is found only in the *exceptional nature* of the situation. In any case, the common good correctly understood, the demands of which will never in any way be contrary to the defense and promotion of the primacy of the person and the way this is expressed in society, must remain the criteria for making decisions concerning the application of the principle of subsidiarity.

NOTES

395 Cf. Leo XIII, Encyclical Letter *Rerum Novarum*: Acta Leonis XIII, 11 (1892), 101-102, 123.

396 Cf. *Catechism of the Catholic Church*, 1882.

397   John Paul II, Encyclical Letter *Sollicitudo Rei Socialis*, 15: AAS 80 (1988), 529; cf. Pius XI, Encyclical Letter *Quadragesimo Anno*: AAS 23 (1931), 203; John XXIII, Encyclical Letter *Mater et Magistra*: AAS 53 (1961), 439; Second Vatican Ecumenical Council, Pastoral Constitution *Gaudium et Spes*, 65: AAS 58 (1966), 1086-1087; Congregation for the Doctrine of the Faith, Instruction *Libertatis Conscientia*, 73, 85-86: AAS 79 (1987), 586, 592-593; John Paul II, Encyclical Letter *Centesimus Annus*, 48: AAS 83 (1991), 852-854; *Catechism of the Catholic Church*, 1883-1885.

398   Cf. John Paul II, Encyclical Letter *Centesimus Annus*, 49: AAS 83 (1991), 854-856; John Paul II, Encyclical Letter *Sollicitudo Rei Socialis*, 15: AAS 80 (1988), 528-530.

399   Pius XI, Encyclical Letter *Quadragesimo Anno*: AAS 23 (1931), 203; cf. John Paul II, Encyclical Letter *Centesimus Annus*, 48: AAS 83 (1991), 852-854; *Catechism of the Catholic Church*, 1883.

400   John Paul II, Encyclical Letter *Centesimus Annus*, 48: AAS 83 (1991), 854.

401   Cf. John Paul II, Encyclical Letter *Centesimus Annus*, 48: AAS 83 (1991), 852-854.

CHAPTER EIGHT:
THE POLITICAL COMMUNITY

III. POLITICAL AUTHORITY

a. The Foundation of Political Authority

393. *The Church has always considered different ways of understanding authority, taking care to defend and propose a model of authority that is founded on the social nature of the person.* "Since God made men social by nature, and since no society can hold together unless some one be over all, directing all to strive earnestly for the common good, every civilized community must have a ruling authority, and this authority, no less than society itself, has its source in nature, and has, consequently, God for its author."[799] *Political authority is therefore necessary*[800] *because of the responsibilities assigned to it. Political authority is and must be a positive and irreplaceable component of civil life.*[801]

394. *Political authority must guarantee an ordered and upright community life without usurping the free activity of individuals and groups but disciplining and orienting this freedom, by respecting and defending the independence of the individual and social subjects, for the attainment of the common good.* Political authority is an instrument of coordination and direction by means of which the many individuals and intermediate bodies must move towards an order in which relationships, institutions, and procedures are put at the service of integral human growth. Political authority, in fact, "whether in the community as such or in institutions representing the State, must always be exercised within the limits of morality and on behalf of the dynamically conceived common good, according to a juridical order enjoying legal status. When such is the case citizens are conscience-bound to obey."[802]

395. *The subject of political authority is the people considered in its entirety as those who have sovereignty.* In various forms, this people transfers the exercise of sovereignty to those whom it freely elects as its representatives, but it preserves the prerogative to assert this sovereignty in evaluating the work of those charged with governing and also in replacing them when they do not fulfill their functions satisfactorily. Although this right is operative in every State and in every kind of political regime, a democratic form of government, due to its procedures for verification, allows and guarantees its fullest application.[803] The mere consent of the people is not, however, sufficient for considering "just" the ways in which political authority is exercised.

b. Authority as Moral Force

396. *Authority must be guided by the moral law.* All of its dignity derives from its being exercised within the context of the moral order,[804] "which in turn has God for its first source and final end."[805] Because of its necessary reference to the moral order, which precedes it and is its basis, and because of its purpose and the people to whom it is directed, authority cannot be understood as a power determined by criteria of a solely sociological or historical character. "There are some indeed who go so far as to deny the existence of a moral order which is transcendent, absolute, universal and equally binding upon all. And where the same law of justice is not adhered to by all, men cannot hope to come to open and full agreement on vital issues."[806] This order "has no existence except in God; cut off from God it must necessarily disintegrate."[807] It is from the moral order that authority derives its power to impose obligations [808] and its moral legitimacy,[809] not from some arbitrary will or from the thirst for power,[810] and it is to translate this order into concrete actions to achieve the common good.[811]

397. *Authority must recognize, respect and promote essential human and moral values.* These are innate and "flow from the very truth of the human being and express and safeguard the dignity of the person; values which no individual, no majority and no State can ever create, modify or destroy."[812] These values do not have their foundation in provisional and changeable "majority" opinions, but must simply be recognized, respected and promoted as elements of an objective moral law, the natural law written in the human heart (cf. *Rom* 2:15), and as the normative point of reference for civil law itself.[813] If, as a result of the tragic clouding of the collective conscience, skepticism were to succeed in casting doubt on the basic principles of the moral law,[814] the legal structure of the State itself would be shaken to its very foundations, being reduced to nothing more than a mechanism for the pragmatic regulation of different and opposing interests.[815]

398. *Authority must enact just laws, that is, laws that correspond to the dignity of the human person and to what is required by right reason.* "Human law is law insofar as it corresponds to right reason and therefore is derived from the eternal law. When, however, a law is contrary to reason, it is called an unjust law; in such a case it ceases to be law and becomes instead an act of violence."[816] Authority that governs according to reason places citizens in a relationship not so much of subjection to another person as of obedience to the moral order and, therefore, to God himself who is its ultimate source.[817] Whoever refuses to obey an authority that is acting in accordance with the moral order "resists what God has appointed" (Rom 13:2).[818] Analogously, whenever public authority—which has its foundation in human nature and belongs to the order preordained by God[819]—fails to seek the common good, it abandons its proper purpose and so delegitimizes itself.

c. The Right to Conscientious Objection

399. *Citizens are not obligated in conscience to follow the prescriptions of civil authorities if their precepts are contrary to the demands of the moral order, to the fundamental rights of persons, or to the teachings of the Gospel.*[820] Unjust laws pose dramatic problems of conscience for morally upright people: *when they are called to cooperate in morally evil acts they must refuse.*[821] Besides being a moral duty, such a refusal is also a basic human

right which, precisely as such, civil law itself is obliged to recognize and protect. "Those who have recourse to conscientious objection must be protected not only from legal penalties but also from any negative effects on the legal, disciplinary, financial and professional plane."[822]

It is a grave duty of conscience not to cooperate, not even formally, in practices which, although permitted by civil legislation, are contrary to the Law of God. Such cooperation in fact can never be justified, not by invoking respect for the freedom of others nor by appealing to the fact that it is foreseen and required by civil law. No one can escape the moral responsibility for actions taken, and all will be judged by God himself based on this responsibility (cf. Rom 2:6; 14:12).

d. The Right to Resist

400. *Recognizing that natural law is the basis for and places limits on positive law means admitting that it is legitimate to resist authority should it violate in a serious or repeated manner the essential principles of natural law.* St. Thomas Aquinas writes that "one is obliged to obey . . . insofar as it is required by the order of justice."[823] Natural law is therefore the basis of the right to resistance.

There can be many different concrete ways this right may be exercised; there are also many different *ends* that may be pursued. Resistance to authority is meant to attest to the validity of a different way of looking at things, whether the intent is to achieve partial change, for example, modifying certain laws, or to fight for a radical change in the situation.

401. *The Church's social doctrine indicates the criteria for exercising the right to resistance*: "Armed resistance to oppression by political authority is not legitimate, unless all the following conditions are met: (1) there is certain, grave and prolonged violation of fundamental rights, (2) all other means of redress have been exhausted, (3) such resistance will not provoke worse disorders, (4) there is well-founded hope of success; and (5) it is impossible reasonably to foresee any better solution."[824] Recourse to arms is seen as an extreme remedy for putting an end to a "manifest, long-standing tyranny which would do great damage to fundamental personal rights and dangerous harm to the common good of the country."[825] The gravity of the danger that recourse to violence entails today makes it preferable in any case that *passive resistance* be

practiced, which is "a way more conformable to moral principles and having no less prospects for success."[826]

e. Inflicting Punishment

402. *In order to protect the common good, the lawful public authority must exercise the right and the duty to inflict punishments according to the seriousness of the crimes committed.*[827] The State has the twofold responsibility to *discourage* behavior that is harmful to human rights and the fundamental norms of civil life, and to repair, through the penal system, the disorder created by criminal activity. In a State ruled by law the power to inflict punishment is correctly entrusted to the Courts: "In defining the proper relationships between the legislative, executive and judicial powers, the Constitutions of modern States guarantee the judicial power the necessary independence in the realm of law."[828]

403. *Punishment does not serve merely the purpose of defending the public order and guaranteeing the safety of persons; it becomes as well an instrument for the correction of the offender, a correction that also takes on the moral value of expiation when the guilty party voluntarily accepts his punishment.*[829] There is a twofold purpose here. On the one hand, encouraging the re-insertion of the condemned person into society; on the other, fostering a justice that reconciles, a justice capable of restoring harmony in social relationships disrupted by the criminal act committed.

In this regard, the activity that prison chaplains are called to undertake is important, not only in the specifically religious dimension of this activity but also in defense of the dignity of those detained. Unfortunately, the conditions under which prisoners serve their time do not always foster respect for their dignity; and often, prisons become places where new crimes are committed. Nonetheless, the environment of penal institutions offers a privileged forum for bearing witness once more to Christian concern for social issues: "I was . . . in prison and you came to me" (Mt 25:35-36).

404. *The activity of offices charged with establishing criminal responsibility, which is always personal in character, must strive to be a meticulous search for truth and must be conducted in full respect for the dignity and rights of the human person;* this means guaranteeing the rights of the guilty as well as those of the innocent. The juridical principle by which punish-

ment cannot be inflicted if a crime has not first been proven must be borne in mind.

In carrying out investigations, the regulation against the use of torture, even in the case of serious crimes, must be strictly observed: "Christ's disciple refuses every recourse to such methods, which nothing could justify and in which the dignity of man is as much debased in his torturer as in the torturer's victim."[830] International juridical instruments concerning human rights correctly indicate a prohibition against torture as a principle which cannot be contravened under any circumstances.

Likewise ruled out is "the use of detention for the sole purpose of trying to obtain significant information for the trial."[831] Moreover, it must be ensured that "trials are conducted swiftly: their excessive length is becoming intolerable for citizens and results in a real injustice."[832]

Officials of the court are especially called to exercise due discretion in their investigations so as not to violate the rights of the accused to confidentiality and in order not to undermine the principle of the presumption of innocence. Since even judges can make mistakes, it is proper that the law provide for suitable compensation for victims of judicial errors.

405. The Church sees as a sign of hope "a growing public opposition to the death penalty, even when such a penalty is seen as a kind of 'legitimate defense' on the part of society. Modern society in fact has the means of effectively suppressing crime by rendering criminals harmless without definitively denying them the chance to reform."[833] Whereas, presuming the full ascertainment of the identity and responsibility of the guilty party, the traditional teaching of the Church does not exclude the death penalty "when this is the only practicable way to defend the lives of human beings effectively against the aggressor."[834] Bloodless methods of deterrence and punishment are preferred as "they better correspond to the concrete conditions of the common good and are more in conformity to the dignity of the human person."[835] The growing number of countries adopting provisions to abolish the death penalty or suspend its application is also proof of the fact that cases in which it is absolutely necessary to execute the offender "are very rare, if not practically non-existent."[836] The growing aversion of public opinion towards the death penalty and the various provisions aimed at abolishing it or suspending its application constitute visible manifestations of a heightened moral awareness.

IV. THE DEMOCRATIC SYSTEM

406. *The Encyclical* Centesimus Annus *contains an explicit and articulate judgment with regard to democracy*: "The Church values the democratic system inasmuch as it ensures the participation of citizens in making political choices, guarantees to the governed the possibility both of electing and holding accountable those who govern them, and of replacing them through peaceful means when appropriate. Thus she cannot encourage the formation of narrow ruling groups which usurp the power of the State for individual interests or for ideological ends. Authentic democracy is possible only in a State ruled by law, and on the basis of a correct conception of the human person. It requires that the necessary conditions be present for the advancement both of the individual through education and formation in true ideals, and of the 'subjectivity' of society through the creation of structures of participation and shared responsibility."[837]

a. Values and Democracy

407. *An authentic democracy is not merely the result of a formal observation of a set of rules but is the fruit of a convinced acceptance of the values that inspire democratic procedures: the dignity of every human person, the respect of human rights, commitment to the common good as the purpose and guiding criterion for political life.* If there is no general consensus on these values, the deepest meaning of democracy is lost and its stability is compromised.

The Church's social doctrine sees ethical relativism, which maintains that there are no objective or universal criteria for establishing the foundations of a correct hierarchy of values, as one of the greatest threats to modern-day democracies. "Nowadays there is a tendency to claim that agnosticism and skeptical relativism are the philosophy and the basic attitude which correspond to democratic forms of political life. Those who are convinced that they know the truth and firmly adhere to it are considered unreliable from a democratic point of view, since they do not accept that truth is determined by the majority, or that it is subject to variation according to different political trends. It must be observed in this regard that if there is no ultimate truth to guide and direct political action, then ideas and convictions can easily be manipulated for reasons of power. As history demonstrates, a democracy without values easily turns into open or thinly disguised totalitarianism."[838] Democracy is fundamentally "a 'system' and as such is a means and not an end. Its 'moral' value is not automatic, but depends on conformity to the moral law to which it, like every other form of human behavior, must be subject: in other words, its morality depends on the morality of the ends which it pursues and of the means which it employs."[839]

b. Institutions and Democracy

408. *The Magisterium recognizes the validity of the principle concerning the division of powers in a State*: "it is preferable that each power be balanced by other powers and by other spheres of responsibility which keep it within proper bounds. This is the principle of the 'rule of law,' in which the law is sovereign, and not the arbitrary will of individuals."[840]

In the democratic system, political authority is accountable to the people. Representative bodies must be subjected to effective social control. This control can be carried out above all in free elections which allow the selection and change of representatives. The obligation on the part of those elected to *give an accounting* of their work—which is guaranteed by respecting electoral terms—is a constitutive element of democratic representation.

409. *In their specific areas (drafting laws, governing, setting up systems of checks and balances), elected officials must strive to seek and attain that which will contribute to making civil life proceed well in its overall course.*[841] Those who govern have the obligation to answer to those governed, but this does not in the least imply that representatives are merely passive agents of the electors. The control exercised by the citizens does not in fact exclude the freedom that elected officials must enjoy in order to fulfill their mandate with respect to the objectives to be pursued. These do not depend exclusively on special interests, but in a much greater part on the function of synthesis and mediation that serve the common good, one of the essential and indispensable goals of political authority.

c. Moral Components of Political Representation

410. *Those with political responsibilities must not forget or underestimate the moral dimension of political representation*, which consists in the commitment to share fully in the destiny of the people and to seek solutions to social problems. In this perspective, responsible authority also means authority exercised with those virtues that make it possible to *put power into practice as service*[842] (patience, modesty, moderation, charity, efforts to share), an authority exercised by persons who are able to accept the common good, and not prestige or the gaining of personal advantages, as the true goal of their work.

411. Among the deformities of the democratic system, political corruption is one of the most serious[843] because it betrays at one and the same time both moral principles and the norms of social justice. It compromises the correct functioning of the State, having a negative influence on the relationship between those who govern and the governed. It causes a growing distrust with respect to public institutions, bringing about a progressive disaffection in the citizens with regard to politics and its representatives, with a resulting weakening of institutions. Corruption radically distorts the role of representative institutions, because they become an arena for political bartering between clients' requests and governmental services. In this way political choices favor the narrow objectives of those who possess the means to influence these choices and are an obstacle to bringing about the common good of all citizens.

412. *As an instrument of the State, public administration at any level— national, regional, community—is oriented towards the service of citizens*: "Being at the service of its citizens, the State is the steward of the people's resources, which it must administer with a view to the common good."[844] *Excessive bureaucratization* is contrary to this vision and arises when "institutions become complex in their organization and pretend to manage every area at hand. In the end they lose their effectiveness as a result of an impersonal functionalism, an overgrown bureaucracy, unjust private interests and an all-too-easy and generalized disengagement from a sense of duty."[845] The role of those working in public administration is not to be conceived as impersonal or bureaucratic, but rather as an act of generous assistance for citizens, undertaken with a spirit of service.

d. Instruments for Political Participation

413. *Political parties have the task of fostering widespread participation and making public responsibilities accessible to all.* Political parties are called to

interpret the aspirations of civil society, orienting them towards the common good,[846] offering citizens the effective possibility of contributing to the formulation of political choices. They must be democratic in their internal structure, and capable of political synthesis and planning.

Another instrument of political participation is the referendum, whereby a form of direct access to political decisions is practiced. The institution of representation in fact does not exclude the possibility of asking citizens directly about the decisions of great importance for social life.

e. Information and Democracy

414. *Information is among the principal instruments of democratic participation.* Participation without an understanding of the situation of the political community, the facts and the proposed solutions to problems is unthinkable. It is necessary to guarantee a real pluralism in this delicate area of social life, ensuring that there are many forms and instruments of information and communications. It is likewise necessary to facilitate conditions of equality in the possession and use of these instruments by means of appropriate laws. Among the obstacles that hinder the full exercise of the right to objectivity in information,[847] special attention must be given to the phenomenon of the news media being controlled by just a few people or groups. This has dangerous effects for the entire democratic system when this phenomenon is accompanied by ever closer ties between governmental activity and the financial and information establishments.

415. *The media must be used to build up and sustain the human community in its different sectors: economic, political, cultural, educational, and religious.*[848] "The information provided by the media is at the service of the common good. Society has a right to information based on truth, freedom, justice and solidarity."[849]

The essential question is whether the current information system is contributing to the betterment of the human person; that is, does it make people more spiritually mature, more aware of the dignity of their humanity, more responsible or more open to others, in particular to the neediest and the weakest. A further aspect of great importance is the requisite that new technologies respect legitimate cultural differences.

416. *In the world of the media the intrinsic difficulties of communications are often exacerbated by ideology, the desire for profit and political control, rivalry and conflicts between groups, and other social evils.* Moral values and principles apply also to the media. "The ethical dimension relates not just to the content of communication (the message) and the process of communication (how the communicating is done) but to fundamental structural and systemic issues, often involving large questions of policy bearing upon the distribution of sophisticated technology and product (who shall be information rich and who shall be information poor?)."[850]

In all three areas—the message, the process, and structural issues—one fundamental moral principle always applies: the human person and the human community are the end and measure of the use of the media. A second principle is complementary to the first: the good of human beings cannot be attained independently of the common good of the community to which they belong.[851] It is necessary that citizens participate in the decision-making process concerning media policies. This participation, which is to be public, has to be genuinely representative and not skewed in favor of special interest groups when the media are a money-making venture.[852]

V. THE POLITICAL COMMUNITY AT THE SERVICE OF CIVIL SOCIETY

a. Value of Civil Society

417. *The political community is established to be of service to civil society, from which it originates.* The Church has contributed to the distinction between the political community and civil society above all by her vision of man, understood as an autonomous, relational being who is open to the Transcendent. This vision is challenged by political ideologies of an individualistic nature and those of a totalitarian character, which tend to absorb civil society into the sphere of the State. The Church's commitment on behalf of social pluralism aims at bringing about a more fitting attainment of the common good and democracy itself, according to the principles of solidarity, subsidiarity, and justice.

Civil society is the sum of relationships and resources, cultural and associative, that are relatively independent from the political sphere and the economic sector. "The purpose of civil society is universal, since it concerns the common good, to which each and every citizen has a right in due proportion."[853] This is marked by a planning capacity that aims at fostering a freer and more just social life, in which the various groups of citizens can form associations, working to develop and express their preferences, in order to meet their fundamental needs and defend their legitimate interests.

b. Priority of Civil Society

418. *The political community and civil society, although mutually connected and interdependent, are not equal in the hierarchy of ends.* The political community is essentially at the service of civil society and, in the final analysis, the persons and groups of which civil society is composed.[854] Civil society, therefore, cannot be considered an extension or a changing component of the political community; rather, it has priority because it is in civil society itself that the political community finds its justification.

The State must provide an adequate legal framework for social subjects to engage freely in their different activities and it must be ready to intervene, when necessary and with respect for the principle of subsidiarity, so that the interplay between free associations and democratic life may be directed to the common good. Civil society is in fact multifaceted and irregular; it does not lack its ambiguities and contradictions. It is also the arena where different interests clash with one another, with the risk that the stronger will prevail over the weaker.

c. Application of the Principle of Subsidiarity

419. *The political community is responsible for regulating its relations with civil society according to the principle of subsidiarity.*[855] It is essential that the growth of democratic life begin within the fabric of society. The activities of civil society—above all *volunteer organizations* and *cooperative endeavors* in the *private-social* sector, all of which are succinctly known as the *"third sector,"* to distinguish from the State and the market—represent the most appropriate ways to develop the social dimension of the person, who finds in these activities the necessary space to express himself fully. The progressive expansion of social initiatives beyond the State-controlled sphere creates new areas for the active presence and direct action of citizens, integrating the functions of the State. This important phenomenon has often come about largely through informal means and has given rise to new and positive ways of exercising personal rights, which have brought about a qualitative enrichment of democratic life.

420. *Cooperation, even in its less structured forms, shows itself to be one of the most effective responses to a mentality of conflict and unlimited competition that seems so prevalent today.* The relationships that are established in a climate of cooperation and solidarity overcome ideological divisions, prompting people to seek out what unites them rather than what divides them.

Many experiences of volunteer work are examples of great value that call people to look upon civil society as a place where it is possible to rebuild a public ethic based on solidarity, concrete cooperation, and fraternal dialogue. All are called to look with confidence to the potentialities that thus present themselves and to lend their own personal efforts for the good of the community in general and, in particular, for the good of the weakest and the neediest. In this way, the principle of the "subjectivity of society" is also affirmed.[856]

VI. THE STATE AND RELIGIOUS COMMUNITIES

A. RELIGIOUS FREEDOM, A FUNDAMENTAL HUMAN RIGHT

421. *The Second Vatican Council committed the Catholic Church to the promotion of religious freedom.* The Declaration *Dignitatis Humanae* explains in its subtitle that it intends to proclaim "the right of the person and of communities to social and civil freedom in religious matters." In order that this freedom, willed by God and inscribed in human nature, may be exercised, no obstacle should be placed in its way, since "the truth cannot be imposed except by virtue of its own truth."[857] The dignity of the person and the very nature of the quest for God require that all men and women should be free from every constraint in the area of religion.[858] Society and the State must not force a person to act against his conscience or prevent him from acting in conformity with it.[859] Religious freedom is not a moral license to adhere to error, nor as an implicit right to error.[860]

422. *Freedom of conscience and religion "concerns man both individually and socially."*[861] The right to religious freedom must be recognized in the juridical order and sanctioned as a civil right; [862] nonetheless, it is not of itself an unlimited right. The *just limits* of the exercise of religious freedom must be determined in each social situation with political prudence, according to the requirements of the common good, and ratified by the civil authority through legal norms consistent with the objective moral order. Such norms are required by "the need for the effective safeguarding of the rights of all citizens and for the peaceful settlement of conflicts of rights, also by the need for an adequate care of genuine public peace, which comes about when men live together in good order and in true justice, and finally by the need for a proper guardianship of public morality."[863]

423. *Because of its historical and cultural ties to a nation, a religious community might be given special recognition on the part of the State. Such recognition must in no way create discrimination within the civil or social order for other religious groups.*[864] The vision of the relations between States and religious organizations promoted by the Second Vatican Council corresponds to the requirements of a State ruled by law and to the norms of international law.[865] The Church is well aware that this vision is not shared by all; the right to religious freedom, unfortunately, "is being violated by many States, even to the point that imparting catechesis, having it imparted, and receiving it become punishable offences."[866]

B. THE CATHOLIC CHURCH AND THE POLITICAL COMMUNITY

a. Autonomy and Independence

424. *Although the Church and the political community both manifest themselves in visible organizational structures, they are by nature different because of their configuration and because of the ends they pursue.* The Second Vatican Council solemnly reaffirmed that, "in their proper spheres, the political community and the Church are mutually independent and self-governing."[867] The Church is organized in ways that are suitable to meet the spiritual needs of the faithful, while the different political communities give rise to relationships and institutions that are at the service of everything that is part of the temporal common good. The autonomy and independence of these two realities is particularly evident with regards to their ends.

The duty to respect religious freedom requires that the political community guarantee the Church the space needed to carry out her mission. For her part, the Church has no particular area of competence concerning the structures of the political community: "The Church respects the legitimate autonomy of the democratic order and is not entitled to express preferences for this or that institutional or constitutional solution,"[868] nor does it belong to her to enter into questions of the merit of political programs, except as concerns their religious or moral implications.

b. Cooperation

425. *The mutual autonomy of the Church and the political community does not entail a separation that excludes cooperation.* Both of them, although by different titles, serve the personal and social vocation of the same human beings. The Church and the political community, in fact, express themselves in organized structures that are not ends in themselves but are intended for the service of man, to help him to exercise his rights fully, those inherent in his reality as a citizen and a Christian, and to fulfill correctly his corresponding duties. The Church and the political community can more effectively render this service "for the good of all if each works better for wholesome mutual cooperation in a way suitable to the circumstances of time and place."[869]

426. *The Church has the right to the legal recognition of her proper identity.* Precisely because her mission embraces all of human reality, the Church, sensing that she is "truly and intimately linked with mankind and its history,"[870] claims the freedom to express her moral judgment on this reality, whenever it may be required to defend the fundamental rights of the person or for the salvation of souls.[871]

The Church therefore seeks: freedom of expression, teaching and evangelization; freedom of public worship; freedom of organization and of her own internal government; freedom of selecting, educating, naming, and transferring her ministers; freedom for constructing religious buildings; freedom to acquire and possess sufficient goods for her activity; and freedom to form associations not only for religious purposes but also for educational, cultural, health care, and charitable purposes.[872]

427. In order to prevent or attenuate possible conflicts between the Church and the political community, the juridical experience of the Church and the State have variously defined stable forms of contact and suitable instruments for guaranteeing harmonious relations. This experience is an essential reference point for all cases in which the State has the presumption to invade the Church's area of action, impairing the freedom of her activity to the point of openly persecuting her or, vice versa, for cases in which church organizations do not act properly with respect to the State.

NOTES

799 John XXIII, Encyclical Letter *Pacem in Terris*: AAS 55 (1963), 269; Leo XIII, Encyclical Letter *Immortale Dei*, in *Acta Leonis XIII*, V, 1885, 120.

800 Cf. *Catechism of the Catholic Church*, 1898; St. Thomas Aquinas, *De Regno. Ad Regem Cypri*, I, 1: Ed. Leon. 42, 450: "Si igitur naturale est homini quod in societate multorum uiuat, necesse est in omnibus esse aliquid per quod multitudo regatur. Multis enim existentibus hominibus et unoquoque id quod est sibi congruum prouidente, multitudo in diuersa dispergetur nisi etiam esset aliquid de eo quod ad bonum multitudinis pertinet curam habens, sicut et corpus hominis et cuiuslibet animalis deflueret nisi esset aliqua uis regitiua communis in corpore, quae ad bonum commune omnium membrorum intenderet. Quod considerans Salomon dixit: 'Ubi non est gubernator, dissipabitur populus.'"

801 Cf. *Catechism of the Catholic Church*, 1897; John XXIII, Encyclical Letter *Pacem in Terris*: AAS 55 (1963), 279.

802 Second Vatican Ecumenical Council, Pastoral Constitution *Gaudium et Spes*, 74: AAS 58 (1966), 1096.

803 Cf. John Paul II, Encyclical Letter *Centesimus Annus*, 46: AAS 83 (1991), 850- 851; John XXIII, Encyclical Letter *Pacem in Terris*: AAS 55 (1963), 271.

804 Cf. Second Vatican Ecumenical Council, Pastoral Constitution *Gaudium et Spes*, 74: AAS 58 (1966), 1095-1097.

805 John XXIII, Encyclical Letter *Pacem in Terris*: AAS 55 (1963), 270; cf. Pius XII, Christmas Radio Message of 24 December 1944: AAS 37 (1945), 15; *Catechism of the Catholic Church*, 2235.

806 John XXIII, Encyclical Letter *Mater et Magistra*: AAS 53 (1961), 449-450.

807 John XXIII, Encyclical Letter *Mater et Magistra*: AAS 53 (1961), 450.

808 Cf. John XXIII, Encyclical Letter *Pacem in Terris*: AAS 55 (1963), 269-270.

809 Cf. *Catechism of the Catholic Church*, 1902.

810 Cf. John XXIII, Encyclical Letter *Pacem in Terris*: AAS 55 (1963), 258-259.

811 Cf. Pius XII, Encyclical Letter *Summi Pontificatus*: AAS 31 (1939), 432-433.

812 John Paul II, Encyclical Letter *Evangelium Vitae*, 71: AAS 87 (1995), 483.

813 Cf. John Paul II, Encyclical Letter *Evangelium Vitae*, 70: AAS 87 (1995), 481-483; John XXIII, Encyclical Letter *Pacem in Terris*: AAS 55 (1963), 258-259, 279-280.

814 Cf. Pius XII, Encyclical Letter *Summi Pontificatus*: AAS 31 (1939), 423.

815 Cf. John Paul II, Encyclical Letter *Evangelium Vitae*, 70: AAS 87 (1995), 481-483; John Paul II, Encyclical Letter *Veritatis Splendor*, 97, 99: AAS 85 (1993), 1209-1211; Congregation for the Doctrine of the Faith, *Doctrinal Note on Some Questions Regarding the Participation of Catholics in Political Life Questions Regarding the Participation of Catholics in Political Life* (24 November 2002), 5-6, Libreria Editrice Vaticana, Vatican City 2002, pp. 11-14.

816   St. Thomas Aquinas, *Summa Theologiae*, I-II, q. 93, a. 3, ad 2um: Ed. Leon. 7, 164: "Lex humana intantum habet rationem legis, inquantum est secundum rationem rectam: et secundum hoc manifestum est quod a lege aeterna derivatur. Inquantum vero a ratione recedit, sic dicitur lex iniqua: et sic non habet rationem legis, sed magis violentiae cuiusdam."

817   Cf. John XXIII, Encyclical Letter *Pacem in Terris*: AAS 55 (1963), 270.

818   Cf. *Catechism of the Catholic Church*, 1899-1900.

819   Cf. Second Vatican Ecumenical Council, Pastoral Constitution *Gaudium et Spes*, 74: AAS 58 (1966), 1095-1097; *Catechism of the Catholic Church*, 1901.

820   Cf. *Catechism of the Catholic Church*, 2242.

821   Cf. John Paul II, Encyclical Letter *Evangelium Vitae*, 73: AAS 87 (1995), 486-487.

822   John Paul II, Encyclical Letter *Evangelium Vitae*, 74: AAS 87 (1995), 488.

823   Saint Thomas Aquinas, *Summa Theologiae*, II-II, q. 104, a. 6, ad 3um: Ed. Leon. 9, 392: "principibus saecularibus intantum homo oboedire tenetur, inquantum ordo iustitiae requirit."

824   *Catechism of the Catholic Church*, 2243.

825   Paul VI, Encyclical Letter *Populorum Progressio*, 31: AAS 59 (1967), 272.

826   Congregation for the Doctrine of the Faith, Instruction *Libertatis Conscientia*, 79: AAS 79 (1987), 590.

827   Cf. *Catechism of the Catholic Church*, 2266.

828   John Paul II, Address to the Italian Association of Judges (31 March 2000), 4: AAS 92 (2000), 633.

829   Cf. *Catechism of the Catholic Church*, 2266.

830   John Paul II, Address to the International Committee of the Red Cross, Geneva (15 June 1982), 5: *L'Osservatore Romano*, English edition, 26 July 1982, p. 3.

831   John Paul II, Address to the Italian Association of Judges (31 March 2000), 4: AAS 92 (2000), 633.

832   John Paul II, Address to the Italian Association of Judges (31 March 2000), 4: AAS 92 (2000), 633.

833   John Paul II, Encyclical Letter *Evangelium Vitae*, 27: AAS 87 (1995), 432.

834   *Catechism of the Catholic Church*, 2267.

835   *Catechism of the Catholic Church*, 2267.

836   John Paul II, Encyclical Letter *Evangelium Vitae*, 56: AAS 87 (1995), 464; cf. also John Paul II, Message for the 2001 World Day of Peace, 19: AAS 93 (2001), 244, where recourse to the death penalty is described as "unnecessary."

837   John Paul II, Encyclical Letter *Centesimus Annus*, 46: AAS 83 (1991), 850.

838   John Paul II, Encyclical Letter *Centesimus Annus*, 46: AAS 83 (1991), 850.

839   John Paul II, Encyclical Letter *Evangelium Vitae*, 70: AAS 87 (1995), 482.

840   John Paul II, Encyclical Letter *Centesimus Annus*, 44: AAS 83 (1991), 848.

841   Cf. *Catechism of the Catholic Church*, 2236.

842   Cf. John Paul II, Post-Synodal Apostolic Exhortation *Christifideles Laici*, 42: AAS 81 (1989), 472-476.

843   Cf. John Paul II, Encyclical Letter *Sollicitudo Rei Socialis*, 44: AAS 80 (1988), 575-577; John Paul II, Encyclical Letter *Centesimus Annus*, 48: AAS 83 (1991), 852-854; John Paul II, Message for the 1999 World Day of Peace, 6: AAS 91 (1991), 381-382.

844   John Paul II, Message for the 1998 World Day of Peace, 5: AAS 90 (1998), 152.

845   John Paul II, Post-Synodal Apostolic Exhortation *Christifideles Laici*, 41: AAS 81 (1989), 471-472.

846   Cf. Second Vatican Ecumenical Council, Pastoral Constitution *Gaudium et Spes*, 75: AAS 58 (1966), 1097-1099.

847   Cf. John XXIII, Encyclical Letter *Pacem in Terris*: AAS 55 (1963), 260.

848 Cf. Second Vatican Ecumenical Council, Decree *Inter Mirifica*, 3: AAS 56 (1964), 146; Paul VI, Apostolic Exhortation *Evangelii Nuntiandi*, 45: AAS 68 (1976), 35-36; John Paul II, Encyclical Letter *Redemptoris Missio*, 37: AAS 83 (1991), 282-286; Pontifical Council for Social Communications, *Communio et Progressio*. 126-134: AAS 63 (1971), 638-640; Pontifical Council for Social Communications, *Aetatis Novae*, 11: AAS 84 (1992), 455-456; Pontifical Council for Social Communications, *Ethics in Advertising* (22 February 1997), 4-8: *L'Osservatore Romano*,English edition, 16 April 1997, pp. I-II.

849 *Catechism of the Catholic Church*, 2494; cf. Second Vatican Ecumenical Council, Decree *Inter Mirifica*, 11: AAS 56 (1964), 148-149.

850 Pontifical Council for Social Communications, *Ethics in Communications* (4 June 2000), 20, Libreria Editrice Vaticana, Vatican City 2000, p. 22.

851 Cf. Pontifical Council for Social Communications, *Ethics in Communications* (4 June 2000), 22, Libreria Editrice Vaticana, Vatican City 2000, pp. 23-25.

852 Cf. Pontifical Council for Social Communications, *Ethics in Communications* (4 June 2000), 24, Libreria Editrice Vaticana, Vatican City 2000, pp. 26-28.

853 Leo XIII, Encyclical Letter *Rerum Novarum*: *Acta Leonis XIII*, 11 (1892), 134.

854 Cf. *Catechism of the Catholic Church*, 1910.

855 Cf. Pius XI, Encyclical Letter *Quadragesimo Anno*: AAS 23 (1931), 203; *Catechism of the Catholic Church*, 1883-1885.

856 Cf. John Paul II, Encyclical Letter *Centesimus Annus*, 49: AAS 83 (1991), 855.

857 Second Vatican Ecumenical Council, Declaration *Dignitatis Humanae*, 1: AAS 58 (1966), 929.

858 Cf. Second Vatican Ecumenical Council, Declaration *Dignitatis Humanae*, 2: AAS 58 (1966), 930-931; *Catechism of the Catholic Church*, 2106.

859 Cf. Second Vatican Ecumenical Council, Declaration *Dignitatis Humanae*, 3: AAS 58 (1966), 931-932.

860 Cf. *Catechism of the Catholic Church*, 2108.

861 *Catechism of the Catholic Church*, 2105.

862 Cf. Second Vatican Ecumenical Council, Declaration *Dignitatis Humanae*, 2: AAS 58 (1966), 930-931; *Catechism of the Catholic Church*, 2108.

863 Second Vatican Ecumenical Council, Declaration *Dignitatis Humanae*, 7: AAS 58 (1966), 935; *Catechism of the Catholic Church*, 2109.

864 Cf. Second Vatican Ecumenical Council, Declaration *Dignitatis Humanae*, 6: AAS 58 (1966), 933-934; *Catechism of the Catholic Church*, 2107.

865 Cf. John Paul II, Message for the 1999 World Day of Peace, 5: AAS 91 (1999), 380-381.

866 John Paul II, Apostolic Exhortation *Catechesi Tradendae*, 14: AAS 71 (1979), 1289.

867 Second Vatican Ecumenical Council, Pastoral Constitution *Gaudium et Spes*, 76: AAS 58 (1966), 1099; cf. *Catechism of the Catholic Church*, 2245.

868 John Paul II, Encyclical Letter *Centesimus Annus*, 47: AAS 83 (1991), 852.

869 Second Vatican Ecumenical Council, Pastoral Constitution *Gaudium et Spes*, 76: AAS 58 (1966), 1099.

870 Second Vatican Ecumenical Council, Pastoral Constitution *Gaudium et Spes*, 1: AAS 58 (1966), 1026.

871 Cf. *Code of Canon Law*, canon 747 §2; *Catechism of the Catholic Church*, 2246.

872 Cf. John Paul II, Letter to the Heads of State Signing the Final Helsinki Act (1 September 1980), 4: AAS 72 (1980), 1256-1258.

⬚

CHAPTER TWELVE:
SOCIAL DOCTRINE AND ECCLESIAL ACTION

II. SOCIAL DOCTRINE AND THE
COMMITMENT OF THE LAY FAITHFUL

a. The Lay Faithful

541. *The essential characteristic of the lay faithful who work in the Lord's vineyard (cf. Mt 20:1-16) is the secular nature of their Christian discipleship, which is carried out precisely in the world.* "It belongs to the laity to seek the kingdom of God by engaging in temporal affairs and directing them according to God's will."[1139] By Baptism, the laity are incorporated into Christ and are made participants in his life and mission according to their specific identity. "The term 'laity' is here understood to mean all the faithful except those in Holy Orders and those who belong to a religious state approved by the Church. That is, the faithful who, by Baptism are incorporated into Christ, are placed in the People of God and in their own way share the priestly, prophetic and kingly office of Christ, and to the best of their ability carry on the mission of the whole Christian people in the Church and in the world."[1140]

542. *The identity of the lay faithful is born in and nourished by the sacraments of Baptism, Confirmation, and the Eucharist.* Baptism conforms the person to Christ, Son of the Father, first-born of every creature, sent to all as Teacher and Redeemer. Confirmation configures the individual to Christ, sent to give new life to creation and to every being through the outpouring of his Spirit. The Eucharist makes the believer a participant in the unique and perfect sacrifice that Christ offered to the Father, in his own flesh, for the salvation of the world.

Lay Catholics are disciples of Christ starting with the sacraments, that is, by virtue of what God has wrought in them, marking them with the very image of his Son Jesus Christ. It is from this divine gift of grace, and not from human concession, that is born the threefold *"munus"* (*gift and duty*) that characterizes the lay person as *prophet, priest, and king,* according to his secular nature.

543. It is the proper duty of the lay faithful to proclaim the Gospel with an exemplary witness of life rooted in Christ and lived in temporal realities: the family; professional commitment in the world of work, culture, science, and research; the exercise of social, economic, and political responsibilities. All secular human realities—both personal and social, including various environments and historical situations, as well as structures and institutions—are the context in which the lay Christian lives and works. These realities are places where God's love is received; the commitment of the lay faithful must correspond to this vision and is to be considered an expression of evangelical charity; "for the lay faithful to be present and active in the world is not only an anthropological and sociological reality, but in a specific way, a theological and ecclesiological reality as well."[1141]

NOTES

1139 Second Vatican Ecumenical Council, Dogmatic Constitution *Lumen Gentium,* 31: AAS 57 (1965), 37.

1140 Second Vatican Ecumenical Council, Dogmatic Constitution *Lumen Gentium,* 31: AAS 57 (1965), 37.

1141 John Paul II, Post-Synodal Apostolic Exhortation *Christifideles Laici,* 15: AAS 81 (1989), 415.

c. Acting with Prudence

547. *The lay faithful should act according to the dictates of prudence, the virtue that makes it possible to discern the true good in every circumstance and to choose the right means for achieving it. Thanks to this virtue, moral principles are applied correctly to particular cases.* We can identify three distinct moments as prudence is exercised to clarify and evaluate situations, to inspire decisions, and to prompt action. The first moment is seen in the *reflection and consultation* by which the question is studied and the necessary opinions sought. The second moment is that of *evaluation,* as the reality is *analyzed and judged* in the light of God's plan. The third moment, that of *decision,* is based on the preceding steps and makes it possible to choose between the different actions that may be taken.

548. Prudence makes it possible to make decisions that are consistent, and to make them with realism and a sense of responsibility for the consequences of one's action. The rather widespread opinion that equates prudence with shrewdness, with utilitarian calculations, with diffidence or with timidity or indecision, is far from the correct understanding of this virtue. It is a characteristic of practical reason and offers assistance in deciding with wisdom and courage the course of action that should be followed, becoming the measure of the other virtues. Prudence affirms the good as a duty and shows in what manner the person should accomplish it.[1146] In the final analysis, it is a virtue that requires the mature exercise of thought and responsibility in an objective understanding of a specific situation and in making decisions according to a correct will.[1147]

NOTES

1146   Cf. *Catechism of the Catholic Church*, 1806.

1147   The exercise of prudence calls for a progressive formation in order to acquire the necessary qualities: "*memory*" as the capacity to remember one's own past experience with objectivity, without falsification (cf. St. Thomas Aquinas, *Summa Theologiae*, II-II, q. 49, a. 1: Ed. Leon. 8, 367); "*docilitas*" (docility) that allows one to learn from others and to profit from their experience on the basis of an authentic love for truth (cf. St. Thomas Aquinas, *Summa Theologiae*, II-II, q. 49, a. 3: Ed. Leon. 8, 368- 369); "*solertia*" (diligence), that is, the ability to face the unexpected with objectivity in order to turn every situation to the service of good, overcoming the temptation of intemperance, injustice, and cowardice (cf. St. Thomas Aquinas, *Summa Theologiae*, II-II, q. 49, a. 4: Ed. Leon. 8, 369-370). These cognitive dispositions permit the development of the necessary conditions for the moment of decision: "*providencia*" (foresight), which is the capacity of weighing the efficacy of a given conduct for the attainment of a moral end (cf. St. Thomas Aquinas, *Summa Theologiae*, II-II, q. 49, a. 6: Ed. Leon. 8, 371) and "*circumspectio*" (circumspection), or the capacity of weighing the circumstances that contribute to the creation of the situation in which a given action will be carried out (cf. St. Thomas Aquinas, *Summa Theologiae*, II-II, q. 49, a. 7: Ed. Leon. 8, 372). In the social context, prudence can be specified under two particular forms: "*regnative*" prudence, that is, the capacity to order all things for the greatest good of society (cf. St. Thomas Aquinas, *Summa Theologiae*, II-II, q. 50, a. 1: Ed. Leon. 8, 374), and "*political*" prudence, which leads citizens to obey, carrying out the indications of authority (cf. St. Thomas Aquinas, *Summa Theologiae*, II-II, q. 50, a. 2: Ed. Leon. 8, 375), without compromising their dignity as a human person (cf. St. Thomas Aquinas, *Summa Theologiae*, II-II, qq. 47-56: Ed. Leon. 8, 348-406).

e. Service in the Various Sectors of Social Life

551. The presence of the laity in social life is characterized by service, the sign and expression of love, which is seen in the areas of the family, culture, work, economics, and politics according to specific aspects. Complying with the different demands of their particular area of work, lay men and women express the truth of their faith and, at the same time, the truth of the Church's social doctrine, which fully becomes a reality when it is lived concretely in order to resolve social problems. In fact, the credibility of this social doctrine comes more immediately from the witness of action than from its internal consistency or logic.[1153]

Having entered into the Third Millennium of the Christian era, the lay faithful will open themselves, through their witness, to all people with whom they will take on the burden of the most pressing calls of our time. "Drawn from the treasures of the teaching of the Church, the proposals of this Council are intended for all men, whether they believe in God or whether they do not explicitly acknowledge him; they are intended to help them to a keener awareness of their own destiny, to make the work conform better to the surpassing dignity of man, to strive for a more deeply rooted sense of universal brotherhood and to meet the pressing appeals of our times with a generous and common effort of love."[1154]

1. Service to the Human Person

552. Among the areas of the social commitment of the laity, service to the human person emerges as a priority. Promoting the dignity of every person, the most precious possession of men and women, is the "essential task, in a certain sense, the central and unifying task of the service which the Church, and the lay faithful in her, are called to render to the human family."[1155]

The first form in which this task is undertaken consists in the commitment and efforts to renew oneself interiorly, because human history is not governed by an impersonal determinism but by a plurality of subjects whose free acts shape the social order. Social institutions do not of themselves guarantee, as if automatically, the common good; the internal "renewal of the Christian spirit"[1156] must precede the commitment to improve society "according to the mind of the Church on the firmly established basis of social justice and social charity."[1157]

It is from the conversion of hearts that there arises concern for others, loved as brothers or sisters. This concern helps us to understand the obligation and commitment to heal institutions, structures, and conditions of life that are contrary to human dignity. The laity must therefore work at the same time for the conversion of hearts and the improvement of structures, taking historical situations into account and using legitimate means so that the dignity of every man and woman will be truly respected and promoted within institutions.

553. Promoting human dignity implies above all affirming the inviolability of the right to life, from conception to natural death, the first among all rights and the condition for all other rights of the person.[1158] Respect for personal dignity requires, moreover, that the religious dimension of the person be recognized. "This is not simply a requirement 'concerning matters of faith,' but a requirement that finds itself inextricably bound up with the very reality of the individual."[1159] The effective recognition of the right to freedom of conscience and religious freedom is one of the highest goods and one of the most serious duties of every people that truly wishes to ensure the good of the individual and of society.[1160] In the present cultural context, there is a particularly urgent need to defend marriage and the family, which can be adequately met only if one is convinced of the unique and singular value of these two realities for an authentic development of human society.[1161]

2. Service in Culture

554. Culture must represent a privileged area for the presence and commitment of the Church and individual Christians. The Second Vatican Council sees the separation of Christian faith and daily life as one of the most serious errors of our day.[1162] Without a metaphysical perspective, the loss of a longing for God in self-serving narcissism and the varied means found in a consumeristic lifestyle; the primacy given to technology and scientific research as ends in themselves; the emphasis placed on appearance, the quest for an image, communication techniques: all of these phenomena must be understood in their cultural aspects and placed in relation to the central issue of the human person, of integral human growth, of the human capacity to communicate and relate with other people, and of the constant human search for an

answer to the great questions that run throughout life. It must be kept in mind that "culture is that through which man, as man, becomes more man, 'is' more, has more access to 'being.'"[1163]

555. Fostering a social and political culture inspired by the Gospel must be an area of particular importance for the lay faithful. Recent history has shown the weakness and radical failure of commonly held cultural perspectives that prevailed for a long time, especially on the social and political levels. In this area, particularly in the decades following the Second World War, Catholics in different countries have been involved at high levels, which shows with ever greater clarity today the consistency of their inspiration and of their heritage of values. The social and political involvement of Catholics, in fact, has never been limited to the mere transformation of structures, because this involvement takes place at the foundations of a culture that receives and listens to the reasoning made by faith and morality, including them as the basis and goal of concrete planning. When this awareness is lacking, Catholics themselves are condemned to cultural dispersion and their proposals are rendered insufficient and limited. An urgent priority today is also found in the need to present the patrimony of Catholic tradition, its values and content, and the entire spiritual, intellectual, and moral heritage of Catholicism in culturally up-to-date terms. Faith in Jesus Christ, who described himself as "the way and the truth and the life" (Jn 14:6), prompts Christians to commit themselves with firm and ever new resolve to building a social and political culture inspired by the Gospel.[1164]

556. The integral perfection of the person and the good of the whole of society are the essential ends of culture;[1165] the ethical dimension of culture is therefore a priority in the social action of the laity. Failure to pay attention to this dimension easily transforms culture into an instrument that impoverishes humanity. A culture can become sterile and headed for decadence when it "becomes inward looking, and tries to perpetuate obsolete ways of living by rejecting any exchange or debate with regard to the truth about man."[1166] The formation of a culture capable of enriching men and women requires on the contrary the involvement of the whole person, who, in the cultural sphere, expresses his creativity, his intelligence, his knowledge of the world and of human persons; someone moreover who puts to good use his capacity

for self-control, personal sacrifice, solidarity, and readiness to promote the common good.[1167]

557. The social and political involvement of the lay faithful in the area of culture moves today in specific directions. The first is that of seeking to guarantee the right of each person to a human and civil culture "in harmony with the dignity of the human person, without distinction of race, sex, nation, religion, or social circumstances."[1168] This right implies the right of families and persons to free and open schools; freedom of access to the means of social communication together with the avoidance of all forms of monopolies and ideological control of this field; freedom of research, sharing one's thoughts, debate, and discussion. At the root of the poverty of so many peoples are also various forms of cultural deprivation and the failure to recognize cultural rights. The commitment to the education and formation of the person has always represented the first concern of Christian social action.

558. The second challenge for Christian commitment concerns the content of culture, that is, truth. The question of truth is essential for culture because "it remains each man's duty to retain an understanding of the whole human person in which the values of intellect, will, conscience and fraternity are pre-eminent."[1169] A correct anthropology is the criterion for shedding light on and verifying every historical form of culture. The Christian commitment in the field of culture is opposed to all reductionistic and ideological perspectives of man and life. The dynamism of openness to the truth is guaranteed above all by the fact that "different cultures are basically different ways of facing the question of the meaning of personal existence."[1170]

559. *Christians must work so that the full value of the religious dimension of culture is seen. This is a very important and urgent task for the quality of human life, at both the individual and social levels.* The question arising from the mystery of life and referring to the greater mystery of God is in fact at the center of every culture; when it is eliminated, culture and the moral life of nations are corrupted.[1171] The authentic religious dimension is an essential part of man and allows him to open his diverse activities to the horizon in which they find meaning and direction. Human religiosity or spirituality is manifested in the forms taken on by a culture, to which it gives vitality and inspiration. The countless works of art of every

period bear witness to this. When the religious dimension of the person or of a people is denied, culture itself starts to die off, sometimes disappearing completely.

NOTES

1153   Cf. John XXIII, Encyclical Letter *Mater et Magistra*: AAS 53 (1961) 454; John Paul II, Encyclical Letter *Centesimus Annus*, 57: AAS 83 (1991), 862-863.

1154   Second Vatican Ecumenical Council, Pastoral Constitution *Gaudium et Spes*, 91: AAS 58 (1966), 1113.

1155   John Paul II, Post-Synodal Apostolic Exhortation *Christifideles Laici*, 37: AAS 81 (1989), 460.

1156   Pius XI, Encyclical Letter *Quadragesimo Anno*: AAS 23 (1931), 218.

1157   Pius XI, Encyclical Letter *Quadragesimo Anno*: AAS 23 (1931), 218.

1158   Cf. Congregation for the Doctrine of the Faith, Instruction *Donum Vitae* (22 February 1987): AAS 80 (1988) 70-102.

1159   John Paul II, Post-Synodal Apostolic Exhortation *Christifideles Laici*, 39: AAS 81 (1989), 466.

1160   Cf. John Paul II, Post-Synodal Apostolic Exhortation *Christifideles Laici*, 39: AAS 81 (1989), 466.

1161   Cf. John Paul II, Post-Synodal Apostolic Exhortation *Familiaris Consortio*, 42-48: AAS 74 (1982), 134-140.

1162   Cf. Second Vatican Ecumenical Council, Pastoral Constitution *Gaudium et Spes*, 43: AAS 58 (1966), 1062.

1163   John Paul II, Address to UNESCO (2 June 1980), 7: *L'Osservatore Romano*, English edition, 23 June 1980, p. 9.

1164   Cf. Congregation for the Doctrine of the Faith, *Doctrinal Note on Some Questions Regarding the Participation of Catholics in Political Life* (24 November 2002), 7: Libreria Editrice Vaticana, Vatican City 2002, p. 15.

1165   Cf. Second Vatican Ecumenical Council, Pastoral Constitution *Gaudium et Spes*, 59: AAS 58 (1966), 1079-1080.

1166   John Paul II, Encyclical Letter *Centesimus Annus*, 50: AAS 83 (1991), 856.

1167   Cf. John Paul II, Address to UNESCO (2 June 1980), 11: *L'Osservatore Romano*, English edition, 23 June 1980, p. 10.

1168   Second Vatican Ecumenical Council, Pastoral Constitution *Gaudium et Spes*, 60: AAS 58 (1966), 1081.

1169   Second Vatican Ecumenical Council, Pastoral Constitution *Gaudium et Spes*, 61: AAS 58 (1966), 1082.

1170   John Paul II, Encyclical Letter *Centesimus Annus*, 24: AAS 83 (1991), 822.

1171   Cf. John Paul II, Encyclical Letter *Centesimus Annus*, 24: AAS 83 (1991), 821-822.

4. Service in Politics

565. *For the lay faithful, political involvement is a worthy and demanding expression of the Christian commitment of service to others.*[1183] The pursuit of the common good in a spirit of service, the development of justice with particular attention to situations of poverty and suffering, respect for the autonomy of earthly realities, the principle of subsidiarity, the promotion of dialogue and peace in the context of solidarity: these are the criteria that must inspire the Christian laity in their political activity. All believers, insofar as they possess rights and duties as citizens, are obligated to respect these guiding principles. Special attention must be paid to their observance by those who occupy institutional positions dealing with the complex problems of the public domain, whether in local administrations or national and international institutions.

566. The tasks accompanying responsibilities in social and political institutions demand a strict and articulated commitment that is able to demonstrate clearly the absolute necessity of the moral dimension in social and political life through thoughtful contributions to the political debate, planning and the chosen actions. Inadequate attention to the moral dimension leads to the dehumanization of life in society and of social and political institutions, thereby consolidating "structures of sin":[1184] "Living and acting in conformity with one's own conscience on questions of politics is not slavish acceptance of positions alien to politics or some kind of confessionalism, but rather the way in which Christians offer their concrete contribution so that, through political life, society will become more just and more consistent with the dignity of the human person."[1185]

567. In the context of the laity's political commitment, particular attention must be given to preparing believers to exercise the power that will be theirs, especially when they are entrusted with such duties by their fellow citizens in accordance with democratic rules. They must show appreciation for the democratic system "inasmuch as it ensures the participation of citizens in making political choices, guarantees to the governed the possibility both of electing and holding accountable those who govern them, and of replacing them through peaceful means when appropriate."[1186] They must also reject all secret organizations that seek to influence or subvert the functioning of legitimate institutions. The exercise of authority must take on the character of service to be carried out always in the context of moral law for the attainment of the common good.[1187] Those who exercise political authority must see to it that the energies of all citizens are directed towards the common good; and they are to do so not in an authoritarian style but by making use of moral power sustained in freedom.

568. The lay faithful are called to identify steps that can be taken in concrete political situations in order to put into practice the principles and values proper to life in society. This calls for a method of discernment,[1188] at both the personal and community levels, structured around certain key elements: knowledge of the situations, analyzed with the help of the social sciences and other appropriate tools; systematic reflection on these realities in the light of the unchanging message of the Gospel and the Church's social teaching; identification of choices aimed at assuring that the situation will evolve positively. When reality is the subject of careful attention and proper interpretation, concrete and effective choices can be made. However, an absolute value must never be attributed to these choices because no problem can be solved once and for all. "Christian faith has never presumed to impose a rigid framework on social and political questions, conscious that the historical dimension requires men and women to live in imperfect situations, which are also susceptible to rapid change."[1189]

569. *A characteristic context for the exercise of discernment can be found in the functioning of the democratic system, understood by many today in agnostic and relativistic terms that lead to the belief that truth is something determined by the majority and conditioned by political considerations.*[1190] In such circumstances, discernment is particularly demanding when it is exercised with regard to the objectivity and accuracy of information, scientific research, and economic decisions that affect the life of the poorest people. It is likewise demanding when dealing with realities that involve fundamental and unavoidable moral duties, such as the sacredness of life, the indissolubility of marriage, the promotion of the family founded on marriage between a man and a woman.

In such situations certain fundamental criteria are useful: the distinction and, simultaneously, the connection between the legal order and the moral order; fidelity to one's own identity and, at the same time, the willingness to engage in dialogue with all people; the need, in the social judgment and activity of Christians, to refer to the observance of three inseparable values—*natural values*, with respect for the legitimate autonomy of temporal realities; *moral values*, promoting an awareness of the intrinsic ethical dimension of every social and political issue; *supernatural values*, in order to fulfill one's duty in the spirit of the Gospel of Jesus Christ.

570. *When—concerning areas or realities that involve fundamental ethical duties—legislative or political choices contrary to Christian principles and values are proposed or made, the Magisterium teaches that "a well-formed Christian conscience does not permit one to vote for a political program or an individual law which contradicts the fundamental contents of faith and morals."*[1191] In cases where it is not possible to avoid the implementation of such political programs or to block or abrogate such laws, the Magisterium teaches that a parliamentary representative, whose personal absolute opposition to these programs or laws is clear and known to all, may legitimately support proposals aimed at limiting the damage caused by such programs or laws and at diminishing their negative effects on the level of culture and public morality. In this regard, a typical example of such a case would be a law permitting abortion.[1192] The representative's vote, in any case, cannot be interpreted as support of an unjust law but only as a contribution to reducing the negative consequences of a legislative provision, the responsibility for which lies entirely with those who have brought it into being.

Faced with the many situations involving fundamental and indispensable moral duties, it must be remembered that Christian witness is to be considered a fundamental obligation that can even lead to the sacrificing of one's life, to martyrdom in the name of love and human dignity.[1193] The history of the past twenty centuries, as well as that of the last century, is filled with martyrs for Christian truth, witnesses to the faith, hope, and love founded on the Gospel. Martyrdom is the witness of one who has been personally conformed to Jesus crucified, expressed in the supreme form of shedding one's blood according to the teaching of the Gospel: if "a grain of wheat falls into the earth and dies . . . it bears much fruit" (Jn 12:24).

571. *The political commitment of Catholics is often placed in the context of the "autonomy" of the State, that is, the distinction between the political and religious spheres.*[1194] This distinction "is a value that has been attained and recognized by the Catholic Church and belongs to the inheritance of contemporary civilization."[1195] Catholic moral doctrine, however, clearly rejects the prospects of an autonomy that is understood as independence from the moral law: "Such 'autonomy' refers first of all to the attitude of the person who respects the truths that derive from natural knowledge regarding man's life in society, even if such truths may also be taught by a specific religion, because truth is one."[1196] A sincere quest for the truth, using legitimate means to promote and defend the moral

truths concerning social life—justice, freedom, respect for life and for other human rights—is a right and duty of all members of a social and political community.

When the Church's Magisterium intervenes in issues concerning social and political life, it does not fail to observe the requirements of a correctly understood autonomy, for "the Church's Magisterium does not wish to exercise political power or eliminate the freedom of opinion of Catholics regarding contingent questions. Instead, it intends—as is its proper function—to instruct and illuminate the consciences of the faithful, particularly those involved in political life, so that their actions may always serve the integral promotion of the human person and the common good. The social doctrine of the Church is not an intrusion into the government of individual countries. It is a question of the lay Catholic's duty to be morally coherent, found within one's conscience, which is one and indivisible."[1197]

572. *The principle of autonomy involves respect for every religious confession on the part of the State, which "assures the free exercise of ritual, spiritual, cultural and charitable activities by communities of believers. In a pluralistic society, secularity is a place for communication between the different spiritual traditions and the nation."*[1198]

Unfortunately, even in democratic societies, there still remain expressions of secular intolerance that are hostile to granting any kind of political or cultural relevance to religious faiths. Such intolerance seeks to exclude the activity of Christians from the social and political spheres because Christians strive to uphold the truths taught by the Church and are obedient to the moral duty to act in accordance with their conscience. These attitudes even go so far, and radically so, as to deny the basis of a natural morality. This denial, which is the harbinger of a moral anarchy with the obvious consequence of the stronger prevailing over the weaker, cannot be accepted in any form by legitimate pluralism, since it undermines the very foundations of human society. In the light of this state of affairs, "the marginalization of Christianity . . . would not bode well for the future of society or for consensus among peoples; indeed, it would threaten the very spiritual and cultural foundations of civilization."[1199]

573. *A particular area for discernment on the part of the lay faithful concerns the choice of political instruments, that is, membership in a party or in other*

types of political participation. A choice must be made that is consistent with values, taking into account actual circumstances. In every case, whatever choice is made must be rooted in charity and tend towards the attainment of the common good.[1200] It is difficult for the concerns of the Christian faith to be adequately met in one sole political entity; to claim that one party or political coalition responds completely to the demands of faith or of Christian life would give rise to dangerous errors. Christians cannot find one party that fully corresponds to the ethical demands arising from faith and from membership in the Church. Their adherence to a political alliance will never be ideological but always critical; in this way the party and its political platform will be prompted to be ever more conscientious in attaining the true common good, including the spiritual end of the human person.[1201]

574. *The distinction that must be made on the one hand between the demands of faith and socio-political options, and on the other hand between the choices made by individual Christians and the Christian community as such, means that membership in a party or in a political alliance should be considered a personal decision, legitimate at least within the limits of those parties and positions that are not incompatible with Christian faith and values.*[1202] However, the choice of a party, a political alliance, the persons to whom public life is to be entrusted, while involving the conscience of each person, can never be an *exclusively* individual choice. "It is up to the Christian community to analyze with objectivity the situation which is proper to their own country, to shed on it the light of the Gospel's inalterable words and to draw principles of reflection, norms of judgment and directives for action from the social teaching of the Church."[1203] In any case, "no one is permitted to identify the authority of the Church exclusively with his own opinion";[1204] believers should rather "try to guide each other by sincere dialogue in a spirit of mutual charity and with anxious interest above all in the common good."[1205]

NOTES

1183   Cf. Paul VI, Apostolic Letter *Octogesima Adveniens*, 46: AAS 63 (1971), 433-436.

1184   Cf. John Paul II, Encyclical Letter *Sollicitudo Rei Socialis*, 36: AAS 80 (1988), 561-563.

1185   Congregation for the Doctrine of the Faith, *Doctrinal Note on Some Questions Regarding the Participation of Catholics in Political Life Questions Regarding the Participation of Catholics in Political Life* (24 November 2002), 6: Libreria Editrice Vaticana, Vatican City 2002, p. 13.

1186   John Paul II, Encyclical Letter *Centesimus Annus*, 46: AAS 83 (1991), 850.

1187 Cf. Second Vatican Ecumenical Council, Pastoral Constitution *Gaudium et Spes*, 74: AAS 58 (1966), 1095-1097.

1188 Cf. Congregation for Catholic Education, Guidelines for the Study and Teaching of the Church's Social Doctrine in the Formation of Priests, 8, Vatican Polyglot Press, Rome 1988, pp. 13-14.

1189 Congregation for the Doctrine of the Faith, *Doctrinal Note on Some Questions Regarding the Participation of Catholics in Political Life Questions Regarding the Participation of Catholics in Political Life* (24 November 2002), 7: Libreria Editrice Vaticana, Vatican City 2002, pp. 15-16.

1190 Cf. John Paul II, *Centesimus Annus*, 46: AAS 83 (1991), 850-851.

1191 Congregation for the Doctrine of the Faith, *Doctrinal Note on Doctrinal Note on Some Questions Regarding the Participation of Catholics in Political Life Questions Regarding the Participation of Catholics in Political Life* (24 November 2002), 4: Libreria Editrice Vaticana, Vatican City 2002, p. 9.

1192 Cf. John Paul II, Encyclical Letter *Evangelium Vitae*, 73: AAS 87 (1995),486-487.

1193 Cf. John Paul II, Post-Synodal Exhortation, *Christifideles Laici*, 39: AAS 81 (1989), 466-468.

1194 Cf. Second Vatican Ecumenical Council, Pastoral Constitution *Gaudium et Spes*, 76: AAS 58 (1966), 1099-1100.

1195 Congregation for the Doctrine of the Faith, *Doctrinal Note on Some Questions Regarding the Participation of Catholics in Political Life Questions Regarding the Participation of Catholics in Political Life* (24 November 2002), 6: Libreria Editrice Vaticana, Vatican City 2002, p. 11.

1196 Congregation for the Doctrine of the Faith, *Doctrinal Note on Some Questions Regarding the Participation of Catholics in Political Life Questions Regarding the Participation of Catholics in Political Life* (24 November 2002), 6: Libreria Editrice Vaticana, Vatican City 2002, p. 12.

1197 Congregation for the Doctrine of the Faith, *Doctrinal Note on Some Questions Regarding the Participation of Catholics in Political Life Questions Regarding the Participation of Catholics in Political Life* (24 November 2002), 6: Libreria Editrice Vaticana, Vatican City 2002, pp. 12-13.

1198 John Paul II, Address to the Diplomatic Corps (12 January 2004), 3: *L'Osservatore Romano*, English edition, 21 January 2004, p. 3.

1199 Congregation for the Doctrine of the Faith, *Doctrinal Note on Some Questions Regarding the Participation of Catholics in Political Life Questions Regarding the Participation of Catholics in Political Life* (24 November 2002), 6: Libreria Editrice Vaticana, Vatican City 2002, p. 14.

1200 Cf. Paul VI, Apostolic Letter *Octogesima Adveniens*, 46: AAS 63 (1971), 433-435.

1201 Cf. Paul VI, Apostolic Letter *Octogesima Adveniens*, 46: AAS 63 (1971), 433-435.

1202 Cf. Paul VI, Apostolic Letter *Octogesima Adveniens*, 50: AAS 63 (1971), 439-440.

1203 Paul VI, Apostolic Letter *Octogesima Adveniens*, 4: AAS 63 (1971), 403-404.

1204 Second Vatican Ecumenical Council, Pastoral Constitution *Gaudium et Spes*, 43: AAS 58 (1966), 1063.

1205 Second Vatican Ecumenical Council, Pastoral Constitution *Gaudium et Spes*, 43: AAS 58 (1966), 1063.

Documents
of the
Bishops of the
United States

✝ ✝ ✝

Resolution on Abortion

United States Conference of Catholic Bishops, 1989

As leaders of the Catholic community in the United States, we acknowledge our right and responsibility to help establish laws and social policies protecting the right to life of unborn children, providing care and services for women and children, and safeguarding human life at every stage and in every circumstance. At this particular time, abortion has become the fundamental human rights issue for all men and women of good will. The duty to respect life in all its stages and especially in the womb is evident when one appreciates the unborn child's membership in our human family, and the grave consequences of denying moral or legal status to any class of human beings because of their age or condition of dependency.

We therefore call upon Catholics to commit themselves vigorously to the implementation of all three elements of the Pastoral Plan—an education and public information effort, pastoral care for pregnant women and their children, and a public policy program in defense of human life in all its stages, especially the unborn. Our long and short range public policy goals include (1) constitutional protection for the right to life of unborn children to the maximum degree possible; (2) federal and state laws and administrative policies that restrict support for and the practice of abortion; (3) continual refinement and ultimate reversal of Supreme Court and other court decisions that deny the inalienable right to life; (4) supportive legislation to provide morally acceptable alternatives to abortion, and social policy initiatives which provide support to pregnant women for prenatal care and extended support for low-income women and their children. We urge public officials, especially Catholics, to advance these goals in recognition of their moral responsibility to protect the weak and defenseless among us.

Resolution adopted unanimously by the Catholic bishops of the United States at their annual meeting in November 1989.

National Conference of Catholic Bishops, *Resolution on Abortion* (November 7, 1989). See http://www.usccb.org/prolife/tdocs/resabort89.htm (accessed May 10, 2005).

Living the Gospel of Life:
A Challenge to American Catholics

United States Conference of Catholic Bishops, 1998

Now the word of the Lord came to me saying,
Before I formed you in the womb I knew you, before
you were born, I consecrated you;
I appointed you a prophet to the nations.

Jeremiah 1:5

Brothers and sisters in the Lord:

At the conclusion of the 1998 *Ad Limina* visits of the bishops of the United States, our Holy Father Pope John Paul II spoke these words:

> Today I believe the Lord is saying to us all: do not hesitate, do not be afraid to engage the good fight of the faith (cf. 1 Tim 6:12). When we preach the liberating message of Jesus Christ we are offering the words of life to the world. Our prophetic witness is an urgent and essential service not just to the Catholic community but to the whole human family.

In this statement we attempt to fulfill our role as teachers and pastors in proclaiming the Gospel of Life. We are confident that the proclamation of the truth in love is an indispensable way for us to exercise our pastoral responsibility.

United States Conference of Catholic Bishops, *Living the Gospel of Life: A Challenge to American Catholics* (Washington, DC: USCCB, 1998). See http://www.usccb.org/prolife/gospel.htm (accessed May 10, 2005).

I. The American Century

"Your country stands upon the world scene as a model of a democratic society at an advanced stage of development. Your power of example carries with it heavy responsibilities. Use it well, America!"

Pope John Paul II, Newark, 1995

1.   When Henry Luce published his appeal for an "American century" in 1941, he could not have known how the coming reality would dwarf his dream. Luce hoped that the "engineers, scientists, doctors . . . builders of roads [and] teachers" of the United States would spread across the globe to promote economic success and American ideals: "a love of freedom, a feeling for the quality of opportunity, a tradition of self-reliance and independence and also cooperation."[1] Exactly this, and much more, has happened in the decades since. U.S. economic success has reshaped the world. But the nobility of the American experiment flows from its founding principles, not from its commercial power. In this century alone, hundreds of thousands of Americans have died defending those principles. Hundreds of thousands more have lived lives of service to those principles—both at home and on other continents—teaching, advising, and providing humanitarian assistance to people in need. As Pope John Paul has observed, "At the center of the moral vision of [the American] founding documents is the recognition of the rights of the human person. . . ." The greatness of the United States lies "especially [in its] respect for the dignity and sanctity of human life in all conditions and at all stages of development."[2]

2.   This nobility of the American spirit endures today in those who struggle for social justice and equal opportunity for the disadvantaged. The United States has thrived because, at its best, it embodies a commitment to human freedom, human rights and human dignity. This is why the Holy Father tells us: " . . . [As] Americans, you are rightly proud of your country's great achievements."[3]

3.   But success often bears the seeds of failure. U.S. economic and military power has sometimes led to grave injustices abroad. At home, it has

fueled self-absorption, indifference, and consumerist excess. Overconfidence in our power, made even more pronounced by advances in science and technology, has created the illusion of a life without natural boundaries and actions without consequences. The standards of the marketplace, instead of being guided by sound morality, threaten to displace it. We are now witnessing the gradual restructuring of American culture according to ideals of utility, productivity, and cost-effectiveness. It is a culture where moral questions are submerged by a river of goods and services and where the misuse of marketing and public relations subverts public life.

4.   The losers in this ethical sea change will be those who are elderly, poor, disabled and politically marginalized. None of these pass the utility test; and yet, they at least have a presence. They at least have the possibility of organizing to be heard. *Those who are unborn, infirm, and terminally ill have no such advantage.* They have no "utility," and worse, they have no voice. As we tinker with the beginning, the end, and even the intimate cell structure of life, we tinker with our own identity as a free nation dedicated to the dignity of the human person. When American political life becomes an experiment on people rather than for and by them, it will no longer be worth conducting. We are arguably moving closer to that day. Today, when the inviolable rights of the human person are proclaimed and the value of life publicly affirmed, the most basic human right, "the right to life, is being denied or trampled upon, especially at the more significant moments of existence: the moment of birth and the moment of death" (Pope John Paul II, *The Gospel of Life* [*Evangelium Vitae*], no. 18).

5.   The nature and urgency of this threat should not be misunderstood. Respect for the dignity of the human person demands a commitment to human rights across a broad spectrum: "Both as Americans and as followers of Christ, American Catholics must be committed to the defense of life in all its stages and in every condition."[4] The culture of death extends beyond our shores: famine and starvation, denial of health care and development around the world, the deadly violence of armed conflict, and the scandalous arms trade that spawns such conflict. Our nation is witness to domestic violence, the spread of drugs, sexual activity which poses a threat to lives, and a reckless tampering with the world's ecological balance. Respect for human life calls us to defend life

from these and other threats. It calls us as well to enhance the conditions for human living by helping to provide food, shelter, and meaningful employment, beginning with those who are most in need. We live the Gospel of Life when we live in solidarity with the poor of the world, standing up for their lives and dignity. Yet abortion and euthanasia have become preeminent threats to human dignity because they directly attack life itself, the most fundamental human good and the condition for all others. They are committed against those who are weakest and most defenseless, those who are genuinely "the poorest of the poor." They are endorsed increasingly without the veil of euphemism, as supporters of abortion and euthanasia freely concede these are killing even as they promote them. Sadly, they are practiced in those communities which ordinarily provide a safe haven for the weak—the family and the healing professions. Such direct attacks on human life, once crimes, are today legitimized by governments sworn to protect the weak and marginalized.

6.   It needn't be so. God, the Father of all nations, has blessed the American people with a tremendous reservoir of goodness. He has also graced our founders with the wisdom to establish political structures enabling all citizens to participate in promoting the inalienable rights of all. As Americans, as Catholics and as pastors of our people, we write therefore today *to call our fellow citizens back to our country's founding principles, and most especially to renew our national respect for the rights of those who are unborn, weak, disabled and terminally ill.* Real freedom rests on the inviolability of every person as a child of God. The inherent value of human life, at every stage and in every circumstance, is not a sectarian issue any more than the Declaration of Independence is a sectarian creed.

7.   In a special way, we call on U.S. Catholics, especially those in positions of leadership—whether cultural, economic, or political—to recover their identity as followers of Jesus Christ and to be leaders in the renewal of American respect for the sanctity of life. "Citizenship" in the work of the Gospel is also a sure guarantee of responsible citizenship in American civic affairs. Every Catholic, without exception, should remember that he or she is called by our Lord to proclaim his message. Some proclaim it by word, some by action, and all by example. But every believer shares responsibility for the Gospel. Every Catholic is a missionary of the Good News of human dignity redeemed through the cross.

While our personal vocation may determine the form and style of our witness, Jesus calls each of us to be a leaven in society, and we will be judged by our actions. No one, least of all someone who exercises leadership in society, can rightfully claim to share fully and practically the Catholic faith and yet act publicly in a way contrary to that faith.

8.   Our attitude toward the sanctity of life in these closing years of the "American century" will say volumes about our true character as a nation. It will also shape the discourse about the sanctity of human life in the next century, because what happens here, in our nation, will have global consequences. It is primarily U.S. technology, U.S. microchips, U.S. fiberoptics, U.S. satellites, U.S. habits of thought and entertainment which are building the neural network of the new global mentality. What America has indelibly imprinted on the emerging global culture is its spirit. And the ambiguity of that spirit is why the pope appealed so passionately to the American people in 1995. "It is vital for the human family," he said, "that in continuing to seek advancement in many different fields—science, business, education and art, and wherever else your creativity leads you—America keeps compassion, generosity and concern for others at the very heart of its efforts."[5] That will be no easy task.

II. The Abolition of Man

"In our time, political speech and writing are largely the defense of the indefensible."

George Orwell, Politics and the English Language

9. Nations are not machines or equations. They are like ecosystems. A people's habits, beliefs, values, and institutions intertwine like a root system. Poisoning one part will eventually poison it all. As a result, bad laws and bad court decisions produce degraded political thought and behavior, and vice versa. So it is with the legacy of *Roe vs. Wade. Roe* effectively legalized abortion throughout pregnancy for virtually any reason, or none at all. It is responsible for the grief of millions of women and men, and the killing of millions of unborn children in the past quarter century. Yet the weaknesses of the Supreme Court's 1973 reasoning are well known. They were acknowledged by the Supreme Court itself in the

subsequent 1992 *Casey* decision, which could find no better reason to uphold *Roe* than the habits *Roe* itself created by surviving for twenty years.[6] The feebleness and confusion of the *Casey* decision flow directly out of *Roe's* own confusion. They are part of the same root system. Taking a distorted "right to privacy" to new heights, and developing a new moral calculus to justify it, *Roe* has spread through the American political ecology with toxic results.

10.   *Roe* effectively *rendered the definition of human personhood flexible and negotiable.* It also implicitly excluded unborn children from human status. In doing so, *Roe* helped create an environment in which infanticide—a predictable next step along the continuum of killing—is now open to serious examination. Thanks ultimately to *Roe*, some today speculate publicly and sympathetically why a number of young American women kill their newborn babies or leave them to die. Even the word "infanticide" is being replaced by new and less emotionally charged words like "neonaticide" (killing a newborn on the day of his or her birth) and "filicide" (killing the baby at some later point). Revising the name given to the killing *reduces its perceived gravity.* This is the ecology of law, moral reasoning, and language in action. Bad law and defective moral reasoning produce the evasive language to justify evil. Nothing else can explain the verbal and ethical gymnastics required by elected officials to justify their support for partial-birth abortion, a procedure in which infants are brutally killed during the process of delivery. The same sanitized marketing is now deployed on behalf of physician-assisted suicide, fetal experimentation, and human cloning. Each reduces the human person to a problem or an object. Each can trace its lineage in no small part to *Roe*.

11.   Obviously *Roe* is only one of several social watersheds which have shaped the America of the late 1990s. But it is a uniquely destructive one. In the twenty-five years since *Roe*, our society's confusion about the relationship of law, moral reasoning, and language has created more and more cynicism in the electorate. As words become unmoored from their meaning (as in "choice" or "terminating a pregnancy"), and as the ideas and ideals which bind us together erode, democratic participation inevitably declines. So too does a healthy and appropriate patriotism.

12.   At Baltimore's Camden Yards, Pope John Paul spoke prophetically when he said: "Today the challenge facing America is to find freedom's fulfillment in truth; the truth that is intrinsic to human life created in God's image and likeness, the truth that is written on the human heart, the truth that can be known by reason and can therefore form the basis of a profound and universal dialogue among people about the direction they must give to their lives and their activities."[7]

III. We Hold These Truths to Be Self-Evident

"For the power of Man to make himself what he pleases means, as we have seen, the power of some men to make other men what they please."

C.S. Lewis, The Abolition of Man

13.   We believe that universal understandings of freedom and truth are "written on the human heart." America's founders also believed this to be true. In 1776 John Dickinson, one of the framers of our Constitution, affirmed: "Our liberties do not come from charters; for these are only the declaration of pre-existing rights. They do not depend on parchments or seals, but come from the king of kings and the Lord of all the earth."[8] The words of the Declaration of Independence speak of the "Laws of Nature and of Nature's God," and proceed to make the historic assertion: "We hold these truths to be self-evident, that all men are created equal, that they are endowed by their Creator with certain unalienable Rights, that among these are Life, Liberty and the pursuit of Happiness. . . ." Today, more than two centuries of the American experiment have passed. We tend to take these words for granted. But for the founders, writing on the brink of armed revolution, these phrases were invested not just with their philosophy but with their lives. This is why they closed with a "firm reliance on the protection of divine Providence." The words of the Declaration of Independence illuminate the founding principles of the American Republic, principles explicitly grounded in unchanging truths about the human person.

14.   The principles of the Declaration were not fully reflected in the social or political structures of its own day. Then human slavery and other

social injustices stood in tension to the high ideals the Founders articulated. Only after much time and effort have these contradictions been reduced. In a striking way, we see today a heightening of the tension between our nation's founding principles and political reality. We see this in diminishing respect for the inalienable right to life and in the elimination of legal protections for those who are most vulnerable. There can be no genuine justice in our society until the truths on which our nation was founded are more perfectly realized in our culture and law.

15. One of those truths is our own essential creatureliness. Virtual reality and genetic science may give us the illusion of power, but we are not gods. We are not our own, or anyone else's, creator. Nor, for our own safety, should we ever seek to be. Even parents, entrusted with a special guardianship over new life, do not "own" their children any more than one adult can own another. And therein lies our only security. *No one but the Creator is the sovereign of basic human rights—beginning with the right to life.* We are daughters and sons of the one God who, outside and above us all, grants us the freedom, dignity, and rights of personhood which no one else can take away. Only in this context, the context of a Creator who authors our human dignity, do words like "truths" and "self-evident" find their ultimate meaning. Without the assumption that a Creator exists who has ordained certain irrevocable truths about the human person, no rights are "unalienable," and nothing about human dignity is axiomatic.

16. This does not make America sectarian. It does, however, underline the crucial role God's sovereignty has played in the architecture of American politics. While the founders were a blend of Enlightenment rationalists and traditional Christians, generations of Jews, Muslims, other religious groups, and non-believers have all found a home in the United States. This is so because the tolerance of our system is rooted in the Jewish-Christian principle that even those who differ from one another in culture, appearance, and faith *still share the same rights*. We believe that this principle still possesses the power to enlighten our national will.

17. The Second Vatican Council, in its *Pastoral Constitution on the Church in the Modern World* (*Gaudium et Spes*), praises those women and men who have a vocation to public office. It encourages active citizenship. It also reminds us that "the political community . . . exists for the

common good: This is its full justification and meaning, and the source of its specific and basic right to exist. The common good embraces all those conditions of social life which enable individuals, families and organizations to achieve complete and efficacious fulfillment" (no. 74). In pursuing the common good, citizens should "cultivate a generous and loyal spirit of patriotism, but without narrow-mindedness . . . [they must also] be conscious of their specific and proper role in the political community: They should be a shining example by their sense of responsibility and their dedication to the common good . . ." (no. 75).

18.   As to the role of the Church in this process: ". . . The political community and the Church are autonomous and independent of each other in their own fields. Nevertheless, both are devoted to the personal vocation of man, though under different titles . . . [yet] at all times and in all places, the Church should have the true freedom to teach the faith, to proclaim its teaching about society, to carry out its task among men without hindrance, *and to pass moral judgment even in matters relating to politics, whenever the fundamental rights of man or the salvation of souls requires it*" (no. 76; emphasis added).

19.   Pope John Paul II elaborates on this responsibility in his 1988 apostolic exhortation *The Vocation and the Mission of the Lay Faithful in the Church and in the World* (*Christifideles Laici*): "The inviolability of the person, which is a reflection of the absolute inviolability of God, finds its primary and fundamental expression in the inviolability of human life. Above all, the common outcry, which is justly made on behalf of human rights—for example, the right to health, to home, to work, to family, to culture—is false and illusory if *the right to life*, the most basic and fundamental right and the condition of all other personal rights, is not defended with maximum determination. . . . The human being is entitled to such rights in every phase of development, from conception until natural death, whether healthy or sick, whole or handicapped, rich or poor. . . . [Moreover, if,] indeed, everyone has the mission and responsibility of acknowledging the personal dignity of every human being and of defending the right to life, some lay faithful are given particular title to this task: such as *parents, teachers, health workers and the many who hold economic and political power*" (no. 38).

20.   We believe that the Gospel of Jesus Christ is a "Gospel of life." It invites all persons and societies to a new life lived abundantly in respect for human dignity. We believe that this Gospel is not only a complement to American political principles, but also the cure for the spiritual sickness now infecting our society. As Scripture says, no house can stand divided against itself (Lk 11:17). We cannot simultaneously commit ourselves to human rights and progress while eliminating or marginalizing the weakest among us. Nor can we practice the Gospel of life only as a private piety. American Catholics must live it *vigorously* and publicly, as a matter of national leadership and witness, or we will not live it at all.

IV. Living the Gospel of Life: The Virtues We Need

"It is impossible to further the common good without acknowledging and defending the right to life, upon which all the other inalienable rights of individuals are founded and from which they develop."

Pope John Paul II, Evangelium Vitae (no. 101)

21.   Bringing a respect for human dignity to practical politics can be a daunting task. There is such a wide spectrum of issues involving the protection of human life and the promotion of human dignity. Good people frequently disagree on which problems to address, which policies to adopt, and how best to apply them. But for citizens and elected officials alike, the basic principle is simple: *We must begin with a commitment never to intentionally kill, or collude in the killing, of any innocent human life, no matter how broken, unformed, disabled, or desperate that life may seem.* In other words, the choice of certain ways of acting is *always and radically incompatible* with the love of God and the dignity of the human person created in his image. Direct abortion is *never* a morally tolerable option. It is always a grave act of violence against a woman and her unborn child. This is so even when a woman does not see the truth because of the pressures she may be subjected to, often by the child's father, her parents, or friends. Similarly, euthanasia and assisted suicide are never acceptable acts of mercy. They *always* gravely exploit the suffer-

ing and desperate, extinguishing life in the name of the "quality of life" itself. This same teaching against direct killing of the innocent condemns all direct attacks on innocent civilians in time of war.

22.   Pope John Paul II has reminded us that we must respect every life, even that of criminals and unjust aggressors. It is increasingly clear in modern society that capital punishment is unnecessary to protect people's safety and the public order, so that cases where it may be justified are "very rare, if not practically non-existent." No matter how serious the crime, punishment that does not take life is "more in conformity with the dignity of the human person" (*Evangelium Vitae*, nos. 56-57). Our witness to respect for life shines most brightly when we demand respect for each and every human life, including the lives of those who fail to show that respect for others. The antidote to violence is love, not more violence.

23.   As we stressed in our 1995 statement *Political Responsibility*, "the application of Gospel values to real situations is an essential work of the Christian community." Adopting a consistent ethic of life, the Catholic Church promotes a broad spectrum of issues "seeking to protect human life and promote human dignity from the inception of life to its final moment."[9] Opposition to abortion and euthanasia does not excuse indifference to those who suffer from poverty, violence, and injustice. Any politics of human life must work to resist the violence of war and the scandal of capital punishment. Any politics of human dignity must seriously address issues of racism, poverty, hunger, employment, education, housing, and health care. Therefore, Catholics should eagerly involve themselves as advocates for the weak and marginalized in all these areas. Catholic public officials are obliged to address each of these issues as they seek to build consistent policies which promote respect for the human person at all stages of life. *But being "right" in such matters can never excuse a wrong choice regarding direct attacks on innocent human life.* Indeed, the failure to protect and defend life in its most vulnerable stages renders suspect any claims to the "rightness" of positions in other matters affecting the poorest and least powerful of the human community. If we understand the human person as the "temple of the Holy Spirit"—the living house of God—then these latter issues fall logically into place as the crossbeams and walls of that house. *All direct attacks on innocent human life, such as abortion and euthanasia, strike at the house's*

foundation. These directly and immediately violate the human person's most fundamental right—the right to life. Neglect of these issues is the equivalent of building our house on sand. Such attacks cannot help but lull the social conscience in ways ultimately destructive of other human rights. As Pope John Paul II reminds us, the command never to kill establishes a minimum which we must respect and from which we must start out "in order to say 'yes' over and over again, a 'yes' which will gradually embrace the *entire horizon of the good*" (*Evangelium Vitae*, no. 75).

24. Since the entry of Catholics into the U.S. political mainstream, believers have struggled to balance their faith with the perceived demands of democratic pluralism. As a result, some Catholic elected officials have adopted the argument that, while they personally oppose evils like abortion, they cannot force their religious views onto the wider society. This is seriously mistaken on several key counts. First, regarding abortion, the point when human life begins is not a religious belief but a scientific fact—a fact on which there is clear agreement even among leading abortion advocates. Second, the sanctity of human life is not merely Catholic doctrine but part of humanity's global ethical heritage, and our nation's founding principle. Finally, democracy is not served by silence. Most Americans would recognize the contradiction in the statement, "While I am personally opposed to slavery or racism or sexism I cannot force my personal view on the rest of society." *Real pluralism depends on people of conviction struggling vigorously to advance their beliefs by every ethical and legal means at their disposal.*

25. Today, Catholics risk cooperating in a false pluralism. Secular society will allow believers to have whatever moral convictions they please—as long as they keep them on the private preserves of their consciences, in their homes and churches, and out of the public arena. Democracy is not a substitute for morality, nor a panacea for immorality. Its value stands—or falls—with the values which it embodies and promotes. *Only* tireless promotion of the truth about the human person can infuse democracy with the right values. This is what Jesus meant when he asked us to be leaven in society. American Catholics have long sought to assimilate into U.S. cultural life. But in assimilating, we have too often been digested. We have been changed by our culture too much, and we have *changed it not enough.* If we are leaven, we must bring to our culture the whole Gospel, which is a *Gospel of life and joy.* That is our vocation as believers. And there is no better place to start than promoting the beauty and sanctity of human life. Those who would claim to promote the cause of life through violence or the threat of violence contradict this Gospel at its core.

26.   Scripture calls us to "be doers of the word and not hearers only . . . [for] faith by itself, if it has no works, is dead" (Jas 1:22, 2:17). Jesus himself directs us to "Go therefore and make disciples of all nations . . . teaching them to observe all that I have commanded you . . ." (Mt 28:19-20). Life in Christ is a life of *active witness.* It demands *moral leadership.* Each and every person baptized in the truth of the Catholic faith is a member of the "people of life" sent by God to evangelize the world.

27.   God is always ready to answer our prayers for help with the virtues we need to do his will. First and foremost we need the *courage and the honesty* to speak the truth about human life, no matter how high the cost to ourselves. The great lie of our age is that we are powerless in the face of the compromises, structures, and temptations of mass culture. But we are not powerless. We can make a difference. We belong to the Lord, in him is our strength, and through his grace, we can change the world. We also need the humility to listen well to both friend and opponent on the abortion issue, learning from each and forgetting ourselves. We need *the perseverance* to continue the struggle for the protection of human life, no matter what the setbacks, trusting in God and in the ultimate fruitfulness of the task he has called us to. We need *the prudence* to know when and how to act in the public arena—and also to recognize and dismiss that fear of acting which postures as prudence itself. And finally we need the great foundation of every apostolic life: *faith, hope, and charity. Faith* not in moral or political abstractions, but in the personal presence of God; *hope* not in our own ingenuity, but in his goodness and mercy; and *love* for others, including those who oppose us, rooted in the love God showers down on us.

28.   These virtues, like the *Gospel of Life* which they help animate, have serious implications for every Christian involved in any way in the public life of the nation.

29.   As *bishops,* we have the responsibility to call Americans to conversion, including political leaders, and especially those publicly identified

as Catholic. As the Holy Father reminds us in *The Splendor of the Truth* (*Veritatis Splendor*): " . . . [It] is part of our pastoral ministry to see to it that [the Church's] moral teaching is faithfully handed down, and to have recourse to appropriate measures to ensure that the faithful are guarded from every doctrine and theory contrary to it" (no. 116). As chief teachers in the Church, we must therefore explain, persuade, correct, and admonish those in leadership positions who contradict the Gospel of life through their actions and policies. Catholic public officials who disregard Church teaching on the inviolability of the human person indirectly collude in the taking of innocent life. A private call to conversion should always be the first step in dealing with these leaders. Through prayer, through patiently speaking the truth in love, and by the witness of our lives, we must strive always to open their hearts to the God-given dignity of the unborn and of all vulnerable persons. So also we must remind these leaders of their duty to exercise genuine moral leadership in society. They do this not by unthinking adherence to public opinion polls or by repeating empty pro-choice slogans, but by educating and sensitizing themselves and their constituents to the humanity of the unborn child. At the same time we need to redouble our efforts to evangelize and catechize our people on the dignity of life and the wrongness of abortion. Nonetheless, some Catholic officials may exclude themselves from the truth by refusing to open their minds to the Church's witness. In all cases, bishops have the duty and pastoral responsibility to continue to challenge those officials on the issue in question and persistently call them to a change of heart. As bishops we reflect particularly on the words of the Office of Readings:

> Let us be neither dogs that do not bark nor silent onlookers nor paid servants who run away before the wolf. Instead, let us be careful shepherds watching over Christ's flock. Let us preach the whole of God's plan to the powerful and the humble, to rich and to poor, to men of every rank and age, as far as God gives us the strength, in season and out of season, as St. Gregory writes in his book of Pastoral Instruction.[10]

30. *Priests, religious, catechists, Catholic school teachers, family life ministers, and theologians* all share, each in their appropriate way, in the Church's task of forming the Catholic faithful in a reverence for the sanctity of life. We call them to a renewed commitment to that task. In their

words and example, they should witness loyally and joyfully to the truth that every human life, at every stage of development, is a gift from God. *Physicians, nurses, and healthcare workers* can touch the lives of women and girls who may be considering abortion with practical assistance, counseling, and adoption alternatives. Equally important, they should be conscious evangelizers of their own professions, witnessing by word and example that God is the Lord of life.

31. *Catholics who are privileged to serve in public leadership positions* have an obligation to place their faith at the heart of their public service, particularly on issues regarding the sanctity and dignity of human life. Thomas More, the former chancellor of England who preferred to give his life rather than betray his Catholic convictions, went to his execution with the words, "I die the king's good servant, but God's first." In the United States in the late 1990s, elected officials safely keep their heads. But some will face a political penalty for living their public office in accord with their pro-life convictions. To those who choose this path, we assure them that their course is just, they save lives through their witness, and God and history will not forget them. Moreover, the risk of witness should not be exaggerated, and the power of witness should not be underestimated. In an age of artifice, many voters are hungry for substance. They admire and support political figures who speak out sincerely for their moral convictions. For our part we commend Catholic and other public officials who, with courage and determination, use their positions of leadership to promote respect for all human life.

32. We urge those Catholic officials who choose to depart from Church teaching on the inviolability of human life in their public life to consider the consequences for their own spiritual well-being, as well as the scandal they risk by leading others into serious sin. We call on them to reflect on the grave contradiction of assuming public roles and presenting themselves as credible Catholics when their actions on fundamental issues of human life are not in agreement with Church teaching. No public official, especially one claiming to be a faithful and serious Catholic, can responsibly advocate for or actively support direct attacks on innocent human life. Certainly there are times when it may be impossible to overturn or prevent passage of a law which allows or promotes a moral evil—such as a law allowing the destruction of nascent human life. In such cases, an elected official, whose position in

favor of life is known, could seek legitimately to limit the harm done by the law. However, no appeal to policy, procedure, majority will, or pluralism ever excuses a public official from defending life to the greatest extent possible. As is true of leaders in all walks of life, no political leader can evade accountability for his or her exercise of power (*Evangelium Vitae*, nos. 73-74). Those who justify their inaction on the grounds that abortion is the law of the land need to recognize that there is a higher law, the law of God. No human law can validly contradict the Commandment: "Thou shalt not kill."

33.   The Gospel of life must be proclaimed, and human life defended, in all places and all times. The arena for moral responsibility includes not only the halls of government, but the voting booth as well. Laws that permit abortion, euthanasia, and assisted suicide are profoundly unjust, and we should work peacefully and tirelessly to oppose and change them. Because they are unjust they cannot bind citizens in conscience, be supported, acquiesced in, or recognized as valid. Our nation cannot countenance the continued existence in our society of such fundamental violations of human rights.

34.   We encourage *all citizens*, particularly Catholics, to embrace their citizenship not merely as a duty and privilege, but as an opportunity meaningfully to participate *in building the culture of life*. Every voice matters in the public forum. Every vote counts. Every act of responsible citizenship is an exercise of significant individual power. We must exercise that power in ways that defend human life, especially those of God's children who are unborn, disabled, or otherwise vulnerable. We get the public officials we deserve. Their virtue—or lack thereof—is a judgment not only on them, but on us. Because of this, we urge our fellow citizens to *see beyond party politics, to analyze campaign rhetoric critically, and to choose their political leaders according to principle, not party affiliation or mere self-interest.*

35.   We urge parents to recall the words of the Second Vatican Council and our Holy Father in *On the Family* (*Familiaris Consortio*), that the family is "the first and vital cell of society" (no. 42).[11] As the family goes, so goes our culture. Parents are the primary educators of their children, especially in the important areas of human sexuality and the transmission of human life. They shape society toward a respect for human life

by first *being open to new life themselves;* then by forming their children—through personal example—with a reverence for the poor, the elderly, and developing life in the womb. Families which live the Gospel of life are *important agents of evangelization through their witness.* But additionally, they should organize "to see that the laws and institutions of the state not only do not offend, but support and actively defend the rights and duties of the family," for the purpose of transforming society and advancing the sanctity of life (no. 44).

36.   *Women* have a unique role in the transmission and nurturing of human life. They can best understand the bitter trauma of abortion and the hollowness and sterility at the heart of the vocabulary of "choice." Therefore, we ask women to assume a special role in promoting the Gospel of life with a new pro-life feminism. Women are uniquely qualified to counsel and support other women facing unexpected pregnancies, and they have been in the vanguard of establishing and staffing the more than three thousand pregnancy aid centers in the United States. They, in a way more fruitful than any others, can help elected officials to understand that any political agenda which hopes to uphold equal rights for all must affirm the equal rights of every child, born and unborn. They can remind us that our nation's declaration of God-given rights, coupled with the command "Thou shalt not kill," are the starting points of true freedom. To choose any other path is to contradict our own identity as a nation dedicated to "life, liberty and the pursuit of happiness."

37.   We commend all who *proclaim and serve the Gospel of life.* By their peaceful activism, education, and prayer, they witness to God's truth and embody our Lord's command to love one another as he loved us. By their service to women who have experienced abortion, they bring his peace and consolation. We urge them to persevere in this difficult work, and not to be discouraged. Like the Cross of our Lord, faithful dedication to the Gospel of life is a "sign of contradiction" in our times.

38.   As Pope John Paul II has said: "It is a tribute to the Church and to the openness of American society that so many Catholics in the United States are involved in political life." He reminds us that "democracy is . . . a moral adventure, a continuing test of a people's capacity to govern themselves in ways that serve the common good and the good

of individual citizens. The survival of a particular democracy depends not only on its institutions, but to an even greater extent on the spirit which inspires and permeates its procedures for legislating, administering and judging. The future of *democracy in fact depends on a culture capable of forming men and women who are prepared to defend certain truths and values.*"[12]

39.   As we conclude the American century and approach a new era for our own nation and the world, we believe that the purpose of the United States remains hopeful and worthy. In the words of Robert Frost, our vocation is to take "the road less traveled," *the road of human freedom rooted in law; law which is rooted, in turn, in the truth about the sanctity of the human person.* But the future of a nation is decided by every new generation. Freedom always implies the ability to choose between two roads: one which leads to life; the other, death (Dt 30:19). *It is now our turn to choose.* We appeal to all people of the United States, especially those in authority, and among them most especially Catholics, to understand this critical choice before us. We urge all persons of good will to work earnestly to bring about the cultural transformation we need, a true renewal in our public life and institutions based on the sanctity of all human life. And finally, as God entrusted his Son to Mary nearly two thousand years ago for the redemption of the world, we close this letter today by entrusting to Mary all our people's efforts to witness the Gospel of life effectively in the public square.

> *Mary, patroness of America, renew in us a love for the beauty and sanctity of the human person from conception to natural death; and as your Son gave his life for us, help us to live our lives serving others. Mother of the Church, Mother of our Savior, open our hearts to the Gospel of life, protect our nation, and make us witnesses to the truth.*

NOTES

1   Henry Luce, "The American Century," *Life* (February 17, 1941).

2   Pope John Paul II, Departure from Baltimore/Washington International Airport, Departure Remarks, October 8, 1995; 25 *Origins*, p. 318 (October 19, 1995).

3   Pope John Paul II, Homily in Giants Stadium, October 5, 1995; 25 *Origins*, p. 305 (October 19, 1995).

4   Pope John Paul II, Homily in Giants Stadium, October 5, 1995; 25 *Origins*, p. 303 (October 19, 1995).

5   Pope John Paul II, Arrival in Newark, Airport Remarks, October 4, 1995; 25 *Origins*, p. 301 (October 19, 1995).

6   In *Planned Parenthood v. Casey*, 505 U.S. 833 (1992), the Supreme Court upheld most of the challenged provisions of a Pennsylvania law regulating abortion. The Court declined, however, to overturn what it called the "central holding" of *Roe v. Wade* and said: "For two decades of economic and social developments, people have organized intimate relationships and made choices that define their views of themselves and their places in society, in reliance on the availability of abortion in the event that contraception should fail" 505 U.S. at 856.

7   Pope John Paul II, Homily at Camden Yards, "What Freedom Is," October 8, 1995; 25 *Origins*, p. 314 (October 19, 1995).

8   Pope John Paul II, Remarks on Accepting the Credentials of the U.S. Ambassador to the Holy See, December 16, 1997; 27 *Origins*, p. 488 (January 8, 1998) [citing C. Herman Pritchett, *The American Constitution* (McGraw-Hill 1977), p. 2].

9   Administrative Board, Unites States Catholic Conference, *Political Responsibility: Proclaiming the Gospel of Life, Protecting the Least Among Us, and Pursuing the Common Good* (1995), p. 12.

10   Boniface, Ep. 78: MGH, Epistolae, 3, 352, 354; from *Liturgy of the Hours According to the Roman Rite* (New York: Catholic Book Publishing Co. 1975).

11   Cf. also *Decree on the Apostolate of Lay People* (*Apostolicam Actuositatem*), 11.

12   Pope John Paul II, *Ad Limina* Remarks to the Bishops of Texas, Oklahoma, and Arkansas (June 27, 1998); 28 *Origins*, p. 282 (October 1, 1998).

Everyday Christianity:
To Hunger and Thirst for Justice

A Pastoral Reflection on Lay Discipleship
for Justice in a New Millennium

United States Conference of Catholic Bishops, 1998

Introduction

One of the great challenges for Christians is as old as our faith, but it takes on special urgency today as we approach the Third Christian Millennium. How do we connect worship on Sunday to work on Monday? How is the Gospel proclaimed not only in the pulpits of our parishes, but also in the everyday lives of Catholic people? How does the Church gathered on the Sabbath act as the People of God scattered and active every day of the week? How can we best carry the values of our faith into family life, the market place, and the public square? How do we love our neighbor, pursue peace, and seek justice in everyday choices and commitments?

In these reflections, we highlight one essential dimension of the lay vocation which is sometimes overlooked or neglected: the social mission of Christians in the world.[1] Every believer is called to serve "the least of these," to "hunger and thirst for justice," to be a "peacemaker."[2] Catholics are called by God to protect human life, to promote human dignity, to defend the poor and to seek the common good. This social mission of the Church belongs to all of us. It is an essential part of what it is to be a believer.

This social mission is advanced in many ways—by the prophetic teaching of our Holy Father; by the efforts of our bishops' Conference; and by many structures of charity and justice within our community of faith. But the most common and, in many ways, the most important Christian witness is often neither very visible nor highly structured. It is

United States Conference of Catholic Bishops, *Everyday Christianity: To Hunger and Thirst for Justice—A Pastoral Reflection on Lay Discipleship for Justice in a New Millennium* (Washington, DC: USCCB, 1998). See http://www.usccb.org/sdwp/projects/everyday.htm (accessed May 10, 2005).

the sacrifice of parents trying to raise children with concern for others; the service and creativity of workers who do their best and reach out to those in need; the struggle of business owners trying to reconcile the bottom line and the needs of employees and customers; and the hard choices of public officials who seek to protect the weak and pursue the common good. The Church's social mission is advanced by teachers and scientists, by family farmers and bankers, by sales persons and entertainers.

The Catholic social mission is also carried forward by believers who join unions, neighborhood organizations, business groups, civic associations, the pro-life movement, groups working for justice, or environmental, civil rights or peace groups. It is advanced by Christians who stand up for the values of the Gospel. This mission is the task of countless Christians living their faith without much fanfare or recognition, who are quietly building a better society by their choices and actions day by day. They protect human life, defend those who are poor, seek the common good, work for peace, and promote human dignity.

Working for justice in everyday life is not easy. There are complex and sometimes difficult challenges encountered by women and men as they try to live their faith in the world. We applaud the efforts of all Catholics to live the Gospel by pursuing justice and peace in their everyday choices and commitments.

The Catholic Layperson: Discipleship and the Pursuit of Justice

Being a believer means that one lives a certain way—walking with the Lord, doing justice, loving kindness, living peaceably among all people. Christian discipleship means practicing what Jesus preached. Discipleship is found in a relationship with Christ and a commitment to his mission of bringing "glad tidings to the poor. / . . . liberty to captives / and recovery of sight to the blind, / to let the oppressed go free."[3]

For Catholics, this takes on special meaning today. According to the Second Vatican Council,

It is the special vocation of the laity to seek the kingdom of God by engaging in temporal affairs and directing them according to God's will. They live in the world, in each and every one of the world's occupations and callings and in the ordinary circumstances of social and family life which, as it were, form the context of their existence. There they are called by God to contribute to the sanctification of the world within, like leaven, in the spirit of the Gospel, by fulfilling their own particular duties.[4]

We welcome and affirm the growing participation of lay women and men in the internal life of the Church. Service within the Church should form and strengthen believers for their mission in the world. With this pastoral statement we are addressing in a special way the demands of discipleship in the pursuit of justice and peace in everyday activity.

Followers of the Lord Jesus live their discipleship as spouses and parents, single adults and youth, employers and employees, consumers and investors, citizens and neighbors. We renew the warning of the Second Vatican Council, "One of the gravest errors of our time is the dichotomy between the faith which many profess and their day-to-day conduct."[5] By our baptism and confirmation every member of our community is called to live his or her faith in the world.

Called to Justice in Everyday Life

Catholicism does not call us to abandon the world, but to help shape it. This does not mean leaving worldly tasks and responsibilities, but transforming them. Catholics are everywhere in this society. We are corporate executives and migrant farm workers, politicians and welfare recipients, educators and day care workers, tradesmen and farmers, office and factory workers, union leaders and small business owners. Our entire community of faith must help Catholics to be instruments of God's grace and creative power in business and politics, in factories and offices, in homes and schools, and in all the events of daily life. Social justice and the common good are built up or torn down day by day in the countless decisions and choices we make. This vocation to pursue justice is not simply an individual task; it is a call to work with others to humanize and shape the institutions that touch so many people. The lay vocation for justice cannot be carried forward alone, but only as members of a community called to be the "leaven" of the Gospel.

- Our **families** are the starting point and the center of a vocation for justice. How we treat our parents, spouses, and children is a reflection of our commitment to Christ's love and justice. We demonstrate our commitment to the Gospel by how we spend our time and money, and whether our family life includes an ethic of charity, service, and action for justice. The lessons we teach our children through what we do as well as what we say determine whether they care for the "least among us" and are committed to work for justice.[6]

- **Workers** are called to pursue justice. In the Catholic tradition, work is not a burden, not just how we make a living. Work is a way of supporting our family, realizing our dignity, promoting the common good, and participating in God's creation. This means often doing the ordinary well, making the most of our talents and opportunities, treating others fairly and with dignity, and working with integrity and creativity. Believers should be encouraged to choose their work based on how they can best use the gifts God has given them. Decisions made at work can make important contributions to an ethic of justice. Catholics have the often difficult responsibility of choosing between competing values in the workplace. This is a measure of holiness. Associations that enable workers, owners, or managers to pursue justice often make the witness of the individual more effective.[7]

- **Owners**, **managers**, and **investors** face important opportunities to seek justice and pursue peace. Ethical responsibility is not just avoiding evil, but doing right, especially for the weak and vulnerable. Decisions about the use of capital have moral implications: Are companies creating and preserving quality jobs at living wages? Are they building up community through the goods and services they provide? Do policies and decisions reflect respect for human life and dignity, promote peace, and preserve God's creation? While economic returns are important, they should not take precedence over the rights of workers or protection of the environment. Investors should examine ownership, management, and economic decisions in the light of the Catholic call to protect life, defend those who are poor, and seek the common good. These decisions promote human dignity or undermine it.[8]

- As **consumers**, believers can promote social justice or injustice. In an affluent culture that suggests that what we have defines who we are, we can live more simply. When we purchase goods and services, we can choose to support companies that defend human life, treat workers fairly, protect creation, and respect other basic moral values at home and abroad. We can also make conscious efforts to consume less.[9]

- All human beings have unique talents, gifts from God that we are called to develop and share. We should celebrate this diversity. People who use their skills and expertise for the common good, the service of others, and the protection of creation, are **good stewards** of the gifts they have been given. When we labor with honesty, serve those in need, work for justice, and contribute to charity, we use our talents to show our love—and God's love—for our brothers and sisters.[10]

- As **citizens** in the world's leading democracy, Catholics in the United States have special responsibilities to protect human life and dignity, to stand with those who are poor and vulnerable. We are also called to welcome the stranger, to combat discrimination, and to pursue peace. Catholic social teaching calls us to practice civic virtues and offers us principles to shape participation in public life. We cannot be indifferent to or cynical about the obligations of citizenship. Our political choices should not reflect simply our own interests, partisan preferences or ideological agendas but should be shaped by the principles of our faith and our commitment to justice, especially to the weak and vulnerable. The voices and votes of lay Catholics are needed to shape a society with greater respect for human life, economic and environmental justice, cultural diversity, and global solidarity. Catholic involvement in public life and legislative advocacy are important ways to exercise responsible citizenship. Participation in politics is a worthy vocation and a public trust. Believers who serve in public office have unique responsibilities and opportunities to stand up for human life and dignity, to pursue justice and peace, and to advance the common good by the policies, priorities, and program they support or oppose.[11]

Supporting the "Salt of the Earth"

Church statements, structures, and initiatives are important for Catholic formation and action. Social ministry programs and structures provide valuable opportunities for believers to learn to act on the justice demands of their faith. Church social ministry efforts should encourage and complement the vital roles of believers in family, economic, and public life. However, there is simply no substitute for Catholic men and women carrying their faith into the world. Everyday discipleship for justice and the Church's organized social ministry can reinforce one another and help shape a more just society and more peaceful world. We hope these reflections can serve as an opportunity for increased dialogue on the demands of discipleship in our time.

Parishes are essential sources of support and encouragement for Christian discipleship. At their best, parishes help believers prepare and go forth to live the Gospel in everything we do. The Sunday liturgy sends us forth to renew the earth and build up God's kingdom of justice and peace. We encourage our pastors and preachers to listen to their parishioners on the challenges of their daily lives and help bring the insight of the Gospel and the principles of Catholic teaching to these experiences. We affirm prayer and worship that help believers apply the Gospel to everyday situations. Across the country, there are examples of Catholic men and women gathering in small groups to examine the moral dimensions of their lives and work. They can enlarge their vision beyond the immediate and the individual experience when they are enabled to examine the structures and processes that shape social life. Catholic schools and religious education programs provide important lessons about living a life of justice and compassion and promoting participation in civic life. Many parishes participate in legislative networks and community organizing projects that involve parishioners in working for justice. And in thousands of other parishes, social ministry efforts provide valuable opportunities to help believers make choices about their time, money, and talents that reflect the justice demands of the Gospel. These parishes are convinced that the mystery of Jesus' life, death, and resurrection unfolds within human life.

We applaud these efforts and urge our parishes to do even more. Our culture often suggests that religion is a private matter, to be tolerated as long as it is detached from our lives as workers and citizens. Catholic men and women look to our parishes to find the support, tools, and concrete help they need to resist this tendency and instead proclaim Christ's love, justice, and peace in everything they do.

The measure of the Church's organized social ministry is not simply the teaching shared, the services offered, or the actions taken but also the support and challenge provided for men and women as they seek to live the Gospel in the world. Our community of faith needs to share its social teaching more clearly and comprehensively so that its principles can help shape the choices and actions of Catholics. Catholics also need to learn and further explore the links between faith and life, between theology and ethics, between what we believe and how we act every day. Catholics need to support one another as we take up these difficult tasks, helping each other to have the courage of our convictions, to stand up for what we believe, and to practice in our own lives what the Scriptures proclaim. As we approach the year 2000, our conference is promoting a Jubilee Pledge for Charity, Justice, and Peace as one concrete way for believers to commit to renewed prayer, reflection, service, and action in preparation for the third Christian millennium (see Jubilee Pledge).

Conclusion

The word of God calls believers to become "the salt of the earth, the light of the world."[12] The pope and the bishops are called to teach and to lead, but unless the Church's social teaching finds a home in the hearts and lives of Catholic women and men, our community and culture will fall short of what the Gospel requires. Our society urgently needs the everyday witness of Christians who take the social demands of our faith seriously. The pursuit of justice is an essential part of the Catholic call to holiness, which is our true vocation: to live "in Christ," and let Christ live and work in us in our world today.

Christian faith requires conversion; it changes who we are, what we do, and how we think. The Gospel offers "good news" and guidance not just for our spiritual lives but for all the commitments and duties that make up our lives. Living our faith in the ordinary tasks of everyday life is an essential part of what it means to be holy today.

As the third Christian millennium approaches, the call to live our faith in everyday choices and actions remains at the heart of what it means to be a disciple of Jesus. This call takes on renewed urgency as we approach the great jubilee, but it is not new. The task of disciples today was probably best and most simply expressed in the words of the prophet Micah:

> *He has told you, O mortal, what is good;*
> *and what does the LORD require of you*
> *but to do justice, and to love kindness,*
> *and to walk humbly with your God?* (Mi 6:8)

Jubilee and the Lay Call to Justice
A Call to Jubilee Justice

Pope John Paul II has declared the year 2000 to be a jubilee year. The beginning of the next millennium is especially significant for followers of Jesus. The year 2000 is a holy year, a time of favor, a reminder that we live and work in a time of special grace between the Incarnation of Jesus and his Second Coming. Amidst all the clamor that will surround the millennium believers need to ask, "What does the jubilee mean for us? How should Catholic women and men respond to this call for a jubilee?"

The jubilee was an ideal, a reminder that Yahweh, the Creator of all, was the true owner of creation and that those who live in a covenant relationship with Yahweh must also seek right and just relationships with all people. The pious Israelite knew that the land was a gift from God. The land and all it signified—work, material goods, financial security, the practices of economic and everyday life—were to be understood within the context of one's relationship with God. All gifts of creation, including personal talents and abilities, first of all belong to God. The devout Israelite was a steward of God's goods. Natural resources and human talents were to serve all with a particular concern for the poor and weak.

The "year of the Lord's favor" was a time to proclaim "liberty in the land for all" (Lev 25:10), to "bring glad tidings to the lowly" and "release to the prisoners" (Is 61:1). It was a time to restore freedom and justice among people, to reestablish relationships of equality, remedy the conditions that kept people oppressed (Is 61), and to cancel debts (Dt 15). The jubilee was intended to relieve the burdens of the weak and give people an opportunity to start anew. There was a clear social message in the jubilee. The jubilee year was an invitation for people to see their lives from a divine perspective: all that they were and all they did should be in accord with God's will for building a community of justice, mercy, love, and peace.

Like the ancient Israelites in their time, Catholic lay persons today ought to see the coming jubilee as a call to renewed practice of charity, pursuit of justice, welcome to the stranger, and new efforts to permit all to participate in the life of the community. As followers of Christ transformed by the power of the Holy Spirit, Catholics must strive to open their hearts to Christ's truth, love, and justice, and to grow in virtue. Each generation of believers must take up this task. This is an essential part of what it means to be holy today.

As the jubilee approaches, there are a variety of ways to take up this task. Among the possibilities is the special Jubilee Pledge for Charity, Justice, and Peace being promoted by our conference, which offers individuals and families an opportunity to commit themselves to ongoing prayer, reflection, service, and action in preparation for the new millennium (see Jubilee Pledge). Another opportunity is the Jubilee Justice Gathering in Los Angeles in July 1999, sponsored by a broad range of Catholic organizations to bring together Catholics from across the nation to explore the demands of charity, justice, and peace as we approach the third Christian millennium.

Jubilee Pledge for Charity, Justice, and Peace

A Catholic Commitment for the New Millennium

This Jubilee Pledge for Charity, Justice, and Peace is being offered to individuals, families, and parishes as a sign of commitment in preparation for the millennium:

> *The Jubilee of our Lord's birth calls us "to bring glad tidings to the poor. . . . to proclaim liberty to captives and recovery of sight to the blind, to let the oppressed go free"* (Lk 4:18).

As disciples of Jesus in the new Millennium, I/we pledge to

Pray regularly for greater justice and peace.

Learn more about Catholic social teaching and its call to protect human life, stand with the poor, and care for creation.

Reach across boundaries of religion, race, ethnicity, gender, and disabling conditions.

Live justly in family life, school, work, the marketplace, and the political arena.

Serve those who are poor and vulnerable, sharing more time and talent.

Give more generously to those in need at home and abroad.

Advocate public policies that protect human life, promote human dignity, preserve God's creation, and build peace.

Encourage others to work for greater charity, justice, and peace.

_____

Signature

Love for others, and in the first place love for the poor, in whom the Church sees Christ himself, is made concrete in the promotion of justice.

Pope John Paul II, *Centesimus Annus*, 1991 (no. 58).

Note: This pledge is being promoted by the United States Conference of Catholic Bishops and other organizations as a practical response to the Holy Father's designation of 1999 as "the year of charity."

NOTES

1   Other major documents address in a more comprehensive way the vocation of the laity (i.e. the *Dogmatic Constitution on the Church, Decree on the Apostolate of the Laity, On the Role of Laity, Called and Gifted, Called and Gifted for a New Millennium*). Catholic teaching also outlines our broader social mission in a series of documents (i.e. *Pastoral Constitution on the Church in the Modern World, Justice in the World, On the Hundredth Anniversary of Rerum Novarum, A Century of Social Teaching, Communities of Salt and Light, Called to Global Solidarity.*)

2   Mt 25:31-46, Mt 5:1-10.

3   Lk 4:18.

4   Second Vatican Council, *Dogmatic Constitution on the Church* (*Lumen Gentium*), no. 31.

5   Second Vatican Council, *Pastoral Constitution on the Church in the Modern World* (*Gaudium et Spes*), no. 43

6   See Pope John Paul II, *On the Family* (*Familiaris Consortio*).

7   See Pope John Paul II, *On Human Work* (*Laborem Exercens*).

8   See Catholic Bishops of the United States, *Tenth Anniversary Edition of Economic Justice for All.*

9   Ibid.

10   See Catholic Bishops of the United States, *To Be a Christian Steward.*

11   See Pope Paul VI, *Octogesima Adveniens; Catholic Bishops of the United States, Political Responsibility.*

12   Mt 5:13-14.

Themes from Catholic Social Teaching

United States Conference of Catholic Bishops, 1998, 2005

The Church's social teaching is a rich treasure of wisdom about building a just society and living lives of holiness amidst the challenges of modern society. Modern Catholic social teaching has been articulated through a tradition of papal, conciliar, and episcopal documents. The depth and richness of this tradition can be understood best through a direct reading of these documents. In these brief reflections, we highlight several of the key themes that are at the heart of our Catholic social tradition.

Life and Dignity of the Human Person

The Catholic Church proclaims that human life is sacred and that the dignity of the human person is the foundation of a moral vision for society. This belief is the foundation of all the principles of our social teaching. In our society, human life is under direct attack from abortion and euthanasia. Human life is threatened by cloning, embryonic stem cell research, and the use of the death penalty. The intentional targeting of civilians in war or terrorist attacks is always wrong. Catholic teaching calls on us to work to avoid war. Nations must protect the right to life by finding effective ways to prevent conflicts and resolve them by peaceful means. We believe that every person is precious, that people are more important than things, and that the measure of every institution is whether it threatens or enhances the life and dignity of the human person.

Call to Family, Community, and Participation

The person is not only sacred but also social. How we organize our society—in economics and politics, in law and policy—directly affects human dignity and the capacity of individuals to grow in community. Marriage and family are the central social institutions that must be sup-

United States Conference of Catholic Bishops, *Themes from Catholic Social Teaching* (Washington, DC: USCCB, 2005).

ported and strengthened, not undermined. We believe people have a right and a duty to participate in society, seeking together the common good and well-being of all, especially the poor and vulnerable.

Rights and Responsibilities

The Catholic tradition teaches that human dignity can be protected and a healthy community can be achieved only if human rights are protected and responsibilities are met. Therefore, every person has a fundamental right to life and a right to those things required for human decency. Corresponding to these rights are duties and responsibilities—to one another, to our families, and to the larger society.

Option for the Poor and Vulnerable

A basic moral test is how our most vulnerable members are faring. In a society marred by deepening divisions between rich and poor, our tradition recalls the story of the Last Judgment (Mt 25:31-46) and instructs us to put the needs of the poor and vulnerable first.

The Dignity of Work and the Rights of Workers

The economy must serve people, not the other way around. Work is more than a way to make a living; it is a form of continuing participation in God's creation. If the dignity of work is to be protected, then the basic rights of workers must be respected—the right to productive work, to decent and fair wages, to the organization and joining of unions, to private property, and to economic initiative.

Solidarity

We are one human family whatever our national, racial, ethnic, economic, and ideological differences. We are our brothers' and sisters' keepers, wherever they may be. Loving our neighbor has global dimensions in a shrinking world. At the core of the virtue of solidarity is the pursuit of justice and peace. Pope Paul VI taught that "if you want peace, work for justice."[1] The Gospel calls us to be peacemakers. Our love for all our sisters and brothers demands that we promote peace in a world surrounded by violence and conflict.

Care for God's Creation

We show our respect for the Creator by our stewardship of creation. Care for the earth is not just an Earth Day slogan, it is a requirement of our faith. We are called to protect people and the planet, living our faith in relationship with all of God's creation. This environmental challenge has fundamental moral and ethical dimensions that cannot be ignored.

This summary should only be a starting point for those interested in Catholic social teaching. Text for this card is drawn from Sharing Catholic Social Teaching: Challenges and Directions *(English: Pub. No. 5-281; Spanish: Pub. No. 5-803) and* Faithful Citizenship: A Catholic Call to Political Responsibility *(English: Pub. No. 5-561; Spanish: Pub. No. 5-894). A full understanding can only be achieved by reading the papal, conciliar, and episcopal documents that make up this rich tradition. For a copy of the complete texts and other social teaching documents, call 800-235-8722.*

Notes

1   Paul VI, *For the Celebration of the Day of Peace* (Rome: January 1, 1972).

Faithful Citizenship:
A Catholic Call
to Political Responsibility

United States Conference of Catholic Bishops, 2003

INTRODUCTION

Elections are a time for debate and decisions about the leaders, policies, and values that will guide our nation. Since the last presidential election and our last reflection on faithful citizenship, our nation has been attacked by terrorists and has gone to war twice.[1] We have moved from how to share budget surpluses to how to allocate the burdens of deficits. As we approach the elections of 2004, we face difficult challenges for our nation and world.

Our nation has been wounded. September 11 and what followed have taught us that no amount of military strength, economic power, or technological advances can truly guarantee security, prosperity, or progress. The most important challenges we face are not simply political, economic, or technological, but ethical, moral, and spiritual. We face fundamental questions of life and death, war and peace, who moves ahead and who is left behind.

Our Church is also working to heal wounds. Our community of faith and especially we, as bishops, are working to face our responsibility and take all necessary steps to overcome the hurt, damage, and loss of trust resulting from the evil of clerical sexual abuse. While working to protect children and rebuild trust, we must not abandon the Church's important role in public life and the duty to encourage Catholics to act on our faith in political life.

These times and this election will test us as American Catholics. A renewed commitment to faithful citizenship can help heal the wounds of our nation, world, and Church. What we have endured has changed

United States Conference of Catholic Bishops, *Faithful Citizenship: A Catholic Call to Political Responsibility* (Washington, DC: USCCB, 2003). See http://www.usccb.org/faithfulcitizenship/index.htm (accessed May 10, 2005).

many things, but it has not changed the fundamental mission and message of Catholics in public life. In times of terror and war, of global insecurity and economic uncertainty, of disrespect for human life and human dignity, we need to return to basic moral principles. Politics cannot be merely about ideological conflict, the search for partisan advantage, or political contributions. It should be about fundamental moral choices. How do we protect human life and dignity? How do we fairly share the blessings and burdens of the challenges we face? What kind of nation do we want to be? What kind of world do we want to shape?

Politics in this election year and beyond should be about an old idea with new power—the common good. The central question should not be "Are you better off than you were four years ago?" It should be "How can 'we'—all of us, especially the weak and vulnerable—be better off in the years ahead? How can we protect and promote human life and dignity? How can we pursue greater justice and peace?"

In the face of all these challenges, we offer once again a simple image—a table.[2] Who has a place at the table of life? Where is the place at the table for a million of our nation's children who are destroyed every year before they are born? How can we secure a place at the table for the hungry and those who lack health care in our own land and around the world? Where is the place at the table for those in our world who lack the freedom to practice their faith or stand up for what they believe? How do we ensure that families in our inner cities and rural communities, in *barrios* in Latin America and villages in Africa and Asia have a place at the table—enough to eat, decent work and wages, education for their children, adequate health care and housing, and most of all, hope for the future?

We remember especially the people who are now missing at the table of life—those lost in the terror of September 11, in the service of our nation, and in the bloody conflicts in Iraq, Afghanistan, the Middle East, and Africa.

A table is also a place where important decisions are made in our communities, nation, and world. How can the poorest people on Earth and those who are vulnerable in our land, including immigrants and those who suffer discrimination, have a real place at the tables where policies and priorities are set?

For Catholics, a special table—the altar of sacrifice, where we celebrate the Eucharist—is where we find the direction and strength to take what we believe into the public square, using our voices and votes to defend life, advance justice, pursue peace, and find a place at the table for all God's children.

TASKS AND QUESTIONS FOR BELIEVERS

Our nation has been blessed with freedom, democracy, abundant resources, and generous and religious people. However, our prosperity does not reach far enough. Our culture sometimes does not lift us up but brings us down in moral terms. Our world is wounded by terror, torn apart by conflict, and haunted by hunger.

As we approach the elections of 2004, we renew our call for a new kind of politics—focused on moral principles not on the latest polls, on the needs of the poor and vulnerable not the contributions of the rich and powerful, and on the pursuit of the common good not the demands of special interests.

Faithful citizenship calls Catholics to see civic and political responsibilities through the eyes of faith and to bring our moral convictions to public life. People of good will and sound faith can disagree about specific applications of Catholic principles. However, Catholics in public life have a particular responsibility to bring together consistently their faith, moral principles, and public responsibilities.

At this time, some Catholics may feel politically homeless, sensing that no political party and too few candidates share a consistent concern for human life and dignity. However, this is not a time for retreat or discouragement. We need more, not less engagement in political life. We urge Catholics to become more involved—by running for office; by working within political parties; by contributing money or time to campaigns; and by joining diocesan legislative networks, community organizations, and other efforts to apply Catholic principles in the public square.

The Catholic community is a diverse community of faith, not an interest group. Our Church does not offer contributions or endorsements. Instead, we raise a series of questions, seeking to help lift up the moral and human dimensions of the choices facing voters and candidates:

- After September 11, how can we build not only a safer world, but a better world—more just, more secure, more peaceful, more respectful of human life and dignity?

- How will we protect the weakest in our midst—innocent unborn children? How will our nation resist what Pope John Paul II calls a "culture of death"? How can we keep our nation from turning to violence to solve some of its most difficult problems—abortion to deal with difficult pregnancies; the death penalty to combat crime; euthanasia and assisted suicide to deal with the burdens of age, illness, and disability; and war to address international disputes?

- How will we address the tragic fact that more than 30,000 children die every day as a result of hunger, international debt, and lack of development around the world, as well as the fact that the younger you are, the more likely you are to be poor here in the richest nation on Earth?

- How can our nation help parents raise their children with respect for life, sound moral values, a sense of hope, and an ethic of stewardship and responsibility? How can our society defend the central institution of marriage and better support families in their moral roles and responsibilities, offering them real choices and financial resources to obtain quality education and decent housing?

- How will we address the growing number of families and individuals without affordable and accessible health care? How can health care better protect human life and respect human dignity?

- How will our society combat continuing prejudice, overcome hostility toward immigrants and refugees, and heal the wounds of racism, religious bigotry, and other forms of discrimination?

- How will our nation pursue the values of justice and peace in a world where injustice is common, desperate poverty widespread, and peace is too often overwhelmed by violence?

- What are the responsibilities and limitations of families, community organizations, markets, and government? How can these elements of society work together to overcome poverty, pursue the common good, care for creation, and overcome injustice?

- When should our nation use, or avoid the use of, military force—for what purpose, under what authority, and at what human cost?

- How can we join with other nations to lead the world to greater respect for human life and dignity, religious freedom and democracy, economic justice, and care for God's creation?

We hope these questions and the 2004 campaigns can lead to less cynicism and more participation, less partisanship, and more civil dialogue on fundamental issues.

A CALL TO FAITHFUL CITIZENSHIP

One of our greatest blessings in the United States is our right and responsibility to participate in civic life. Everyone can and should participate. Even those who cannot vote have the right to have their voices heard on issues that affect their communities.

The Constitution protects the right of individuals and of religious bodies to speak out without governmental interference, favoritism, or discrimination. Major public issues have moral dimensions. Religious values have significant public consequences. Our nation is enriched and our tradition of pluralism is enhanced, not threatened, when religious groups contribute their values to public debates.

As bishops, we have a responsibility as Americans and as religious teachers to speak out on the moral dimensions of public life. The Catholic community enters public life not to impose sectarian doctrine but to act on our moral convictions, to share our experience in serving the poor and vulnerable, and to participate in the dialogue over our nation's future.

A Catholic moral framework does not easily fit the ideologies of "right" or "left," nor the platforms of any party. Our values are often not "politically correct." Believers are called to be a community of conscience within the larger society and to test public life by the values of Scripture and the principles of Catholic social teaching. Our responsibility is to measure all candidates, policies, parties, and platforms by how they protect or undermine the life, dignity, and rights of the human person—whether they protect the poor and vulnerable and advance the common good.

Jesus called us to "love one another."[3] Our Lord's example and words demand care for the "least of these"[4] from each of us. Yet they also require action on a broader scale. Faithful citizenship is about more than elections. It requires ongoing participation in the continuing political and legislative process.

A recent Vatican statement on Catholic participation in political life highlights the need for involvement:

> Today's democratic societies . . . call for new and fuller forms of participation in public life by Christian and non-Christian citizens alike. Indeed, all can contribute, by voting in elections for lawmakers and government officials, and in other ways as well, to the development of political solutions and legislative choices which, in their opinion, will benefit the common good.[5]

In the Catholic tradition, responsible citizenship is a virtue; participation in the political process is a moral obligation. All believers are called to faithful citizenship, to become informed, active, and responsible participants in the political process. As we have said, "We encourage *all citizens*, particularly Catholics, to embrace their citizenship not merely as a duty and privilege, but as an opportunity meaningfully to participate [more fully] *in building the culture of life*. Every voice matters in the public forum. Every vote counts. Every act of responsible citizenship is an exercise of significant individual power."[6] Even those who are not citizens are called to participate in the debates which shape our common life.

CATHOLIC ASSETS IN THE PUBLIC SQUARE

Our community of faith brings three major assets to these challenges.

A Consistent Moral Framework

The *Word of God and the teachings of the Church* give us a particular way of viewing the world. Scripture calls us to "choose life," to serve "the least of these," to "hunger and thirst" for justice and to be "peacemakers."[7]

Catholic teaching offers consistent moral principles to assess issues, political platforms, and campaigns for their impact on human life and dignity. As Catholics, we are not free to abandon unborn children because they are seen as unwanted or inconvenient; to turn our backs on immigrants because they lack the proper documents; to create and then destroy human lives in a quest for medical advances or profit; to turn away from poor women and children because they lack economic or political power; or to ignore sick people because they have no insurance. Nor can we neglect international responsibilities in the aftermath of war because resources are scarce. Catholic teaching requires us to speak up for the voiceless and to act in accord with universal moral values.

Everyday Experience

Our community also brings to public life *broad experience in serving those in need*. Every day, the Catholic community educates the young, cares for the sick, shelters the homeless, feeds the hungry, assists needy families, welcomes refugees, and serves the elderly.[8] In defense of life, we reach out to children and to the sick, elderly, and disabled who need help. We support women in difficult pregnancies, and we assist those wounded by the trauma of abortion and domestic violence. On many issues, we speak for those who have no voice. These are not abstract issues for us; they have names and faces. We have practical expertise and daily experience to contribute to the public debate.

A Community of People

The *Catholic community* is large and diverse. We are Republicans, Democrats, and Independents. We are members of every race, come from every ethnic background, and live in urban, rural, and suburban communities in all fifty states. We are CEOs and migrant farm workers, senators and persons on public assistance, business owners and union members. But all Catholics are called to a common commitment to protect human life and stand with those who are poor and vulnerable. We are all called to provide a moral leaven for our democracy, to be the salt of the earth.[9]

THE ROLE OF THE CHURCH

The Church is called to educate Catholics about our social teaching, highlight the moral dimensions of public policies, participate in debates on matters affecting the common good, and witness to the Gospel through our services and ministries. The Catholic community's participation in public affairs does not undermine, but enriches the political process and affirms genuine pluralism. Leaders of the Church have the right and duty to share Catholic teaching and to educate Catholics on the moral dimensions of public life, so that they may form their consciences in light of their faith.

The recent Vatican statement on political life points this out:

> [The Church] does not wish to exercise political power or elim-
> inate the freedom of opinion of Catholics regarding contingent
> questions. Instead, it intends—as is its proper function—to
> instruct and illuminate the consciences of the faithful, particu-
> larly those involved in political life, so that their actions may
> always serve the integral promotion of the human person and
> the common good.[10]

We urge our fellow citizens "to see beyond party politics, to analyze campaign rhetoric critically, and to choose their political leaders according to principle, not party affiliation or mere self-interest."[11] As bishops, we seek to form the consciences of our people. We do not wish to instruct persons on how they should vote by endorsing or opposing candidates. We hope that voters will examine the position of candidates on the full range of issues, as well as on their personal integrity, philosophy, and performance. We are convinced that a consistent ethic of life should be the moral framework from which to address issues in the political arena.[12]

For Catholics, the defense of human life and dignity is not a narrow cause, but a way of life and a framework for action. A key message of the Vatican statement on public life is that Catholics in politics must reflect the moral values of our faith with clear and consistent priority for the life and dignity of the human person.[13] This is the fundamental moral measure of their service. The Vatican statement also points out:

> It must be noted also that a well-formed Christian conscience
> does not permit one to vote for a political program or an indi-
> vidual law which contradicts the fundamental contents of faith
> and morals. The Christian faith is an integral unity, and thus it is
> incoherent to isolate some particular element to the detriment of
> the whole of Catholic doctrine. A political commitment to a sin-
> gle isolated aspect of the Church's social doctrine does not
> exhaust one's responsibility towards the common good.[14]

Decisions about candidates and choices about public policies require clear commitment to moral principles, careful discernment and prudential judgments based on the values of our faith.

The coming elections provide important opportunities to bring together our principles, experience, and community in effective public witness. We hope parishes, dioceses, schools, colleges, and other Catholic institutions will encourage active participation through non-partisan voter registration and education efforts, as well as through ongoing legislative networks and advocacy programs.[15] As Catholics we need to share our values, raise our voices, and use our votes to shape a society that protects human life, promotes family life, pursues social justice, and practices solidarity. These efforts can strengthen our nation and renew our Church.

THEMES OF CATHOLIC SOCIAL TEACHING

The Catholic approach to faithful citizenship begins with moral principles, not party platforms. The directions for our public witness are found in Scripture and Catholic social teaching. Here are some key themes at the heart of our Catholic social tradition.[16]

Life and Dignity of the Human Person

Every human person is created in the image and likeness of God. Therefore, each person's life and dignity must be respected, whether that person is an innocent unborn child in a mother's womb, whether that person worked in the World Trade Center or a market in Baghdad, or even whether that person is a convicted criminal on death row. We believe that every human life is sacred from conception to natural death, that people are more important than things, and that the measure of every institution is whether it protects and respects the life and dignity of the human person. As the recent Vatican statement points out, "The Church recognizes that while democracy is the best expression of the direct participation of citizens in political choices, it succeeds only to the extent that it is based on a correct understanding of the human *person*. Catholic involvement in political life cannot compromise on this principle."[17]

Call to Family, Community, and Participation

The human person is not only sacred, but social. The God-given institutions of marriage—a lifelong commitment between a man and a woman—and family are central and serve as the foundations for social life. Marriage and family should be supported and strengthened, not undermined. Every person has a right to participate in social, economic, and political life and a corresponding duty to work for the advancement of the common good and the well-being of all, especially the poor and weak.

Rights and Responsibilities

Every person has a fundamental right to life—the right that makes all other rights possible. Each person also has a right to the conditions for living a decent life—faith and family life, food and shelter, education and employment, health care and housing. We also have a duty to secure and respect these rights not only for ourselves, but for others, and to fulfill our responsibilities to our families, to each other, and to the larger society.

Option for the Poor and Vulnerable

Scripture teaches that God has a special concern for the poor and vulnerable.[18] The prophets denounced injustice toward the poor as a lack of fidelity to the God of Israel.[19] Jesus, who identified himself with "the least of these,"[20] came to preach "good news to the poor, liberty to captives . . . and to set the downtrodden free."[21] The Church calls on all of us to embrace this preferential option for the poor and vulnerable,[22] to embody it in our lives, and to work to have it shape public policies and priorities. A fundamental measure of our society is how we care for and stand with the poor and vulnerable.

Dignity of Work and the Rights of Workers

The economy must serve people, not the other way around. Work is more than a way to make a living; it is a form of continuing participation in God's act of creation. If the dignity of work is to be protected, then the basic rights of workers, owners, and others must be respected—the right to productive work, to decent and fair wages, to organize and choose to join a union, to economic initiative, and to ownership and private property. These rights must be exercised in ways that advance the common good.

Solidarity

We are one human family. We are our brothers' and sisters' keepers, wherever they may be. Pope John Paul II insists, "We are *all* really responsible for all."[23] Loving our neighbor has global dimensions in a shrinking world. At the core of the virtue of solidarity is the pursuit of justice and peace. Pope Paul VI taught that "if you want peace, work for justice."[24] The Gospel calls us to be "peacemakers."[25] Our love for *all* our sisters and brothers demands that we be "sentinels of peace" in a world wounded by violence and conflict.[26]

Caring for God's Creation

The world that God created has been entrusted to us. Our use of it must be directed by God's plan for creation, not simply for our own benefit. Our stewardship of the Earth is a form of participation in God's act of creating and sustaining the world. In our use of creation, we must be guided by a concern for generations to come. We show our respect for the Creator by our care for creation.

These themes anchor our community's role in public life. They help us to resist excessive self-interest, blind partisanship, and ideological agendas. They also help us avoid extreme distortions of pluralism and tolerance that deny any fundamental values and dismiss the contributions and convictions of believers. As the Vatican's statement on public life explains, we cannot accept an understanding of pluralism and tolerance that suggests "every possible outlook on life [is] of equal value."[27] However, this insistence that there are fundamental moral values "has nothing to do with the legitimate freedom of Catholic citizens to choose among the various political opinions that are compatible with faith and the natural moral law, and to select, according to their own criteria, what best corresponds to the needs of the common good."[28]

MORAL PRIORITIES FOR PUBLIC LIFE

We wish to call special attention to issues that we believe are important in the national debate in this campaign and in the years to come. These brief summaries do not indicate the depth and details of the positions we have taken in the documents which are cited at the end of this statement.

Protecting Human Life

Human life is a gift from God, sacred and inviolable. Because every human person is created in the image and likeness of God, we have a duty to defend human life from conception until natural death and in every condition.

Our world does not lack for threats to human life. We watch with horror the deadly violence of terror, war, starvation, and children dying from disease. We face a new and insidious mentality that denies the dignity of some vulnerable human lives and treats killing as a personal choice and social good. As we wrote in *Living the Gospel of Life*, "**abortion and euthanasia** have become preeminent threats to human life and dignity because they directly attack life itself, the most fundamental good and the condition for all others."[29] Abortion, the deliberate killing of a human being before birth, is never really acceptable. The destruction of human embryos as objects of research is wrong. This wrong is compounded when human life is created by **cloning** or other means only to be destroyed. The purposeful taking of human life by **assisted suicide and euthanasia** is never an act of mercy. It is an unjustifiable assault on human life. For the same reasons, the **intentional targeting of civilians in war or terrorist attacks** is always wrong.

In protecting human life, "We must begin with a commitment never to intentionally kill, or collude in the killing, of any innocent human life, no matter how broken, unformed, disabled or desperate that life may seem."[30]

We urge Catholics and others to promote laws and social policies that protect human life and promote human dignity to the maximum degree possible. Laws that legitimize abortion, assisted suicide, and euthanasia are profoundly unjust and immoral. We support constitutional protection for unborn human life, as well as legislative efforts to end abortion and euthanasia. We encourage the passage of laws and programs that promote childbirth and adoption over abortion and assist pregnant women and children. We support aid to those who are sick and dying by encouraging health care coverage for all as well as effective palliative care. We call on government and medical researchers to base their decisions regarding **biotechnology** and human experimentation on respect for the inherent dignity and inviolability of human life from its very beginning, regardless of the circumstances of its origin.

Catholic teaching calls on us to work to **avoid war**. Nations must protect the right to life by finding ever more effective ways to prevent conflicts from arising, to resolve them by peaceful means, and to promote post-conflict reconstruction and reconciliation. All nations have a right and duty to defend human life and the common good against terrorism, aggression, and similar threats. In the aftermath of September 11, we called for continuing outreach to those who had been harmed, clear resolve in responding to terror, moral restraint in the means used, respect for ethical limits on the use of force, greater focus on the roots of terror, and a serious effort to share fairly the burdens of this response. While military force as a last resort can sometimes be justified to defend against aggression and similar threats to the common good, we have raised serious moral concerns and questions about **preemptive or preventive use of force**.

Even when military force is justified, it must be discriminate and proportionate. Direct, intentional attacks on civilians in war are never morally acceptable. Nor is the use of weapons of mass destruction or other weapons that cause disproportionate harm or that cannot be deployed in ways that distinguish between civilians and soldiers. Therefore, we urge our nation to strengthen barriers against the use of **nuclear weapons**, to expand controls over existing nuclear materials and other weapons of mass destruction, and to ratify the Comprehensive Test Ban Treaty as a step toward much deeper cuts and the eventual elimination of nuclear weapons. We also urge our nation to join the treaty to ban anti-personnel **landmines** and to address the human consequences of cluster bombs. We further urge our nation to take immediate and serious steps to reduce its own disproportionate role in the scandalous **global trade in arms**, which contributes to violent conflicts around the world.

Society has a right and duty to defend itself against violent crime and a duty to reach out to victims of crime. Yet our nation's increasing reliance on the **death penalty** cannot be justified. We do not teach that killing is wrong by killing those who kill others. Pope John Paul II has said the penalty of death is "both cruel and unnecessary."[31] The antidote to violence is not more violence. In light of the Holy Father's insistence that this is part of our pro-life commitment, we encourage solutions to violent crime that reflect the dignity of the human person, urging our nation to abandon the use of capital punishment. We also urge passage of legislation that would address problems in the judicial system, and restrict and restrain the use of the death penalty through use of DNA evidence, a guarantee of effective counsel, and efforts to address issues of racial justice.

Promoting Family Life

God established the family as the basic cell of human society. Therefore, we must strive to make the needs and concerns of families a central national priority. **Marriage** must be protected as a lifelong commitment between a man and a woman and our laws should reflect this principle. Marriage, as God intended, provides the basic foundation for family life and the common good. It must be supported in the face of the many pressures working to undermine it. Policies related to the definition of marriage, taxes, the workplace, divorce, and welfare must be designed to help families stay together and to reward responsibility and sacrifice for children. Because financial and economic factors have such an impact on the well-being and stability of families, it is important that **just wages** be paid to those who work to support their families and that generous efforts be made to aid poor families.

Children must be protected and nurtured. We affirm our commitment to the protection of children in all settings and at all times, and we support policies that ensure that the well-being of all children is safeguarded. This is reflected within our Church in the *Charter for the Protection of Children and Young People* and other policies adopted by our bishops' conference and dioceses to ensure the safety of children.

The **education** of children is a fundamental parental responsibility. Educational systems can support or undermine parental efforts to educate and nurture children. No one model or means of education is appropriate to the needs of all persons. Parents—the first and most important educators—have a fundamental **right to choose the education** best suited to the needs of their children, including private and religious schools. Families of modest means especially should not be denied this choice because of their economic status. Government should help provide the resources required for parents to exercise this basic right without discrimination. To support parents' efforts to share basic values, we believe a national consensus can be reached so that students in all educational settings have opportunities for moral and character formation to complement their intellectual and physical development.

Communications play a growing role in society and family life. The values of our culture are shaped and shared in the print media as well as on radio, television, and the Internet. We must balance respect for freedom of speech with concern for the common good, promoting responsible regulations that protect children and families. In recent years, reduced government regulation has lowered standards, opened the door to increasingly offensive material, and squeezed out non-commercial, religious programming.

We support regulation that limits the concentration of control over these media; disallows sales of media outlets that attract irresponsible owners primarily seeking a profit; and opens these outlets to a greater variety of program sources, including religious programming. We support a TV rating system and technology that assist parents in supervising what their children view.

The Internet has created both great benefits and some problems. This technology should be available to all students regardless of income. Because it poses serious dangers by giving easy access to pornographic and violent material, we support vigorous enforcement of existing obscenity and child pornography laws, as well as efforts by the industry to develop technology that assists parents, schools, and libraries in blocking out unwanted materials.

Pursuing Social Justice

Our faith reflects God's special concern for the poor and vulnerable and calls us to make their needs our first priority in public life.

Church teaching on **economic justice** insists that economic decisions and institutions be assessed on whether they protect or undermine the dignity of the human person. We support policies that create **jobs for all who can work** with decent working conditions and adequate pay that reflects a **living wage**. We also support efforts to overcome barriers to equal pay and employment for women and those facing unjust **discrimination**. We reaffirm the Church's traditional support of the **right of workers to choose to organize**, join a union, bargain collectively, and exercise these rights without reprisal. We also affirm the Church's teaching on the importance of **economic freedom, initiative, and the right to private property**, through which we have the tools and resources to pursue the common good.

Efforts to provide for the basic financial needs of poor families and children must enhance their lives and protect their dignity. The measure of **welfare reform** should be reducing **poverty** and dependency, not cutting resources and programs. We seek approaches that both promote greater responsibility and offer concrete steps to help families leave poverty behind. Welfare reform has focused on providing work and training, mostly in low-wage jobs. Other forms of support are necessary, including tax credits, health care, child care, and safe, affordable housing. Because we believe that families need help with the costs of raising children, we support increasing **child tax credits and making them fully refundable.** These credits allow families of modest means with children to keep more of what they earn and help lift low-income families out of poverty.

We welcome efforts to recognize and support the work of **faith-based groups** not as a substitute for, but as a partner with, government efforts. Faith-based and community organizations are often more present, more responsive, and more effective in the poorest communities and countries. We oppose efforts to undermine faith-based institutions and their identity, integrity, and freedom to serve those in need. We also vigorously resist efforts to abandon civil rights protections and the long-standing protections for religious groups to preserve their identity as they serve the poor and advance the common good.

We are also concerned about the income security of low- and average-wage workers and their families when they retire, become disabled, or die. In many cases, women are particularly disadvantaged. Any proposal to change **Social Security** must provide a decent and reliable income for these workers and their dependents.

Affordable and accessible health care is an essential safeguard of human life, a fundamental human right, and an urgent national priority. We need to reform the nation's health care system, and this reform must be rooted in values that respect human dignity, protect human life, and meet the needs of the poor and uninsured. With tens of millions of Americans lacking basic health insurance, we support measures to ensure that decent health care is available to all as a moral imperative. We also support measures to strengthen Medicare and Medicaid as well as measures that extend health care coverage to children, pregnant women, workers, immigrants, and other vulnerable populations. We support policies that provide effective, compassionate care that reflects our moral values for those suffering from HIV/AIDS and those coping with addictions.

The lack of safe, affordable **housing** is a national crisis. We support a recommitment to the national pledge of "safe and affordable housing" for all and effective policies that will increase the supply of quality housing and preserve, maintain, and improve existing housing. We promote public/private partnerships, especially those that involve religious communities. We continue to oppose unjust discrimination or unjust exclusion in housing and support measures to help ensure that financial institutions meet the credit needs of local communities.

The first priority for **agriculture** policy should be **food security for all**. Food is necessary for life itself. Our support for Food Stamps, the Special Nutrition Program for Women, Infants, and Children (WIC), and other programs that directly benefit poor and low-income people is based on our belief that no one should face **hunger** in a land of plenty. Those who grow our food should be able to make a decent living and maintain their way of life. **Farmers** who depend on the land for their livelihood deserve a decent return for their labor. Rural communities deserve help so that they can continue to be sources of strength and support for a way of life that enriches our nation. Our priority concern for the poor calls us to advocate especially for the needs of **farm workers**, whose pay is generally inadequate, whose housing and working conditions are often deplorable, and who are particularly vulnerable to exploitation. We urge that public policies support **sustainable agriculture** and careful stewardship of the Earth and its natural resources.

The Gospel mandate to love our neighbor and welcome the stranger leads the Church to care for and stand with **immigrants**, both documented and undocumented. While affirming the right and responsibility of sovereign nations to control their borders and to ensure the security of their citizens, especially in the wake of September 11, we seek basic protections for immigrants, including due process rights, access to basic public benefits, and fair naturalization and legalization opportunities. We oppose efforts to stem migration that do not effectively address its root causes and permit the continuation of the political, social, and economic inequities that contribute to it. We believe our nation must remain a place of refuge for those fleeing persecution and suffering exploitation—refugees, asylum seekers, and victims of human trafficking.

All persons, by virtue of their dignity as human persons, have an inalienable right to receive a quality **education**. We must ensure that our nation's young people—especially the poor, those with disabilities, and the most vulnerable—are properly prepared to be good citizens, to lead productive lives, and to be socially and morally responsible in the complicated and technologically challenging world of the twenty-first century. This requires that all educational institutions have an orderly, just, respectful, and non-violent environment where adequate professional and material resources are available. We support the necessary initiatives that provide adequate funding to educate all persons no matter what school they attend—public, private, or religious—or their personal condition.

We also support providing salaries and benefits to all teachers and administrators that reflect the principles of economic justice, as well as providing the resources necessary for teachers to be academically and personally prepared for the critical tasks they face. As a matter of justice, we believe that when services aimed at improving the educational environment—especially for those most at risk—are available to students and teachers in public schools, these services should be available to students and teachers in **private and religious** schools as well.

Our schools and our society in general must address the growing "**culture of violence.**" We need to promote a greater sense of moral responsibility, to advocate a reduction in violence in the media, to support gun safety measures and reasonable restrictions on access to assault weapons and hand guns, and to oppose the use of the **death penalty**. We also believe a Catholic ethic of responsibility, rehabilitation, and restoration can become the foundation for the necessary reform of our broken **criminal justice system**.

Our society must also continue to combat **discrimination** based on sex, race, ethnicity, disabling condition, or age. Discrimination constitutes a grave injustice and an affront to human dignity. It must be aggressively resisted. Where the effects of past discrimination persist, society has the obligation to take positive steps to overcome the legacy of injustice. We support judiciously administered **affirmative action** programs as tools to overcome discrimination and its continuing effects.

In the words of Pope John Paul II, care for the Earth and for the environment is a "moral issue."[32] We support policies that protect the land, water, and the air we share. Reasonable and effective initiatives are required for energy conservation and the development of alternate, renewable, and clean-energy resources. We encourage citizens and public officials to seriously address global climate change, focusing on prudence, the common good, and the option for the poor, particularly its impact on developing nations. The United States should lead the developed nations in contributing to the sustainable development of poorer nations and greater justice in sharing the burden of environmental neglect and recovery.

Practicing Global Solidarity

September 11 has given us a new sense of vulnerability. However, we must be careful not to define our security primarily in military terms. Our nation must join with others in addressing policies and problems that provide fertile ground in which terrorism can thrive. No injustice legitimizes the horror we have experienced. But a more just world will be a more peaceful world.

In a world where one-fifth of the population survives on less than one dollar per day, where some twenty countries are involved in major armed conflict, and where poverty, corruption, and repressive regimes bring untold suffering to millions of people, we simply cannot remain indifferent. As a wealthy and powerful nation, the United States has the capacity and the responsibility to address this scandal of **poverty and underdevelopment**. As a principal force in globalization, we have a responsibility to **humanize globalization**, and to spread its benefits to all, especially the world's poorest, while addressing its negative consequences. As the world's sole superpower, the United States also has an unprecedented opportunity to work in partnership with others to build a system of cooperative security that will lead to a more united and more just world.

- The United States should take a leading role in helping to **alleviate global poverty** through a comprehensive development agenda, including substantially increased development aid for the poorest countries, more equitable trade policies, and continuing efforts to relieve the crushing burdens of debt and disease.
- More concerted efforts to ensure the promotion of **religious liberty** and other basic human rights should be an integral part of U.S. foreign policy.

- It is a moral imperative that the United States work to reverse the spread of **nuclear, chemical, and biological weapons**, and to reduce its own reliance on weapons of mass destruction by pursuing progressive nuclear disarmament. It also should reduce its own predominant role in the conventional arms trade.

- The United States should provide more consistent political and financial support for appropriate **United Nations** programs, other **international bodies**, and international law, so that these institutions may become more effective, responsible, and responsive agents for addressing global problems.

- Asylum must be afforded to all refugees who hold a well-founded fear of persecution in their homelands. Our country should support protection for **persons fleeing persecution** through safe haven in other countries, including the United States, especially for unaccompanied children, single women, women heads of families, and religious minorities.

- The United States should adopt a more generous **immigration and refugee policy** based on providing temporary or permanent safe haven for those in need; protecting immigrant workers from exploitation; promoting family reunification; safeguarding the right of all peoples to return to their homelands; ensuring that public benefits and a fair and efficient process for obtaining citizenship are available to immigrants; extending to immigrants the full protection of U.S. law; offering a generous legalization program to undocumented immigrants, and addressing the root causes of migration.

- Our country should be a leader—in collaboration with the international community—in addressing **regional conflicts** in the Middle East, the Balkans, the Congo, Sudan, Colombia, and West Africa. Leadership on the **Israeli-Palestinian conflict** is an especially urgent priority. The United States should actively pursue comprehensive negotiations leading to a just and peaceful resolution of this conflict that respects the legitimate claims and aspirations of both Israelis and Palestinians, ensuring security for Israel, a viable state for Palestinians, and peace in the region. The United States, working with the international community, must also make the sustained commitment necessary to help bring stability, democracy, freedom, and prosperity to **Iraq and Afghanistan**.

Building peace, combating poverty and despair, and protecting freedom and human rights are not only moral imperatives; they are wise national priorities. Given its enormous power and influence in world affairs, the United States has a special responsibility to ensure that it is a force for justice and peace beyond its borders. "Liberty and justice for all" is not only a profound national pledge; it is a worthy goal for any our nation in its role as world leader.

CONCLUSION

We hope these reflections will contribute to a renewed political vitality in our land. We urge all Catholics to register, vote, and become more involved in public life, to protect human life and dignity, and to advance the common good.

The 2004 elections and the policy choices we will face in the future pose significant challenges for our Church. As an institution, we are called to be **political but not partisan**. The Church cannot be a chaplain for any one party or cheerleader for any candidate. Our cause is the protection of the weak and vulnerable and defense of human life and dignity, not a particular party or candidate.

The Church is called to be **principled but not ideological**. We cannot compromise our basic values or teaching, but we should be open to different ways to advance them.

We are called to be **clear but also civil**. A Church that advocates justice and charity must practice these virtues in public life. We should be clear about our principles and priorities, without impugning motives or name-calling.

The Church is called to be **engaged but not used**. We welcome dialogue with political leaders and candidates, seeking to engage and persuade public officials. But we must be sure that events and "photo-ops" are not substitutes for work on policies that reflect our values.

The call to faithful citizenship raises a fundamental question for all of us. What does it mean to be a Catholic living in the United States in the year 2004 and beyond? As *Catholics*, the election and the policy choices that follow it call us to recommit ourselves to carry the values of the Gospel and church teaching into the public square. As *citizens and residents of the United States*, we have the duty to participate now and in the future in the debates and choices over the values, vision, and leaders that will guide our nation.

This dual calling of faith and citizenship is at the heart of what it means to be a Catholic in the United States. Faithful citizenship calls us to seek "a place at the table" of life for all God's children in the elections of 2004 and beyond.

MAJOR CATHOLIC STATEMENTS ON PUBLIC LIFE AND MORAL ISSUES

The following documents from the United States Conference of Catholic Bishops explore in greater detail the public policy issues discussed in *Faithful Citizenship*. To obtain copies, call 800-235-8722 or go to *www.usccbpublishing.org*.

Protecting Human Life

A Matter of the Heart: A Statement on the Thirtieth Anniversary of Roe v. Wade, 2002
Living the Gospel of Life, 1998
Faithful for Life: A Moral Reflection, 1995
Resolution on Abortion, 1989
Pastoral Plan for Pro-Life Activities: A Reaffirmation, 1985
Documentation on the Right to Life and Abortion, 1974, 1976, 1981
Statement on Iraq, 2002
A Pastoral Message: Living with Faith and Hope After September 11, 2001
Sowing the Weapons of War, 1995
The Harvest of Justice Is Sown in Peace, 1993
A Report on the Challenge of Peace and Policy Developments 1983-1888, 1989
The Challenge of Peace: God's Promise and Our Response, 1983
Welcome and Justice for Persons with Disabilities, 1999
Nutrition and Hydration: Moral and Pastoral Reflections, 1992
NCCB Administrative Committee Statement on Euthanasia, 1991
Pastoral Statement of U.S. Catholic Bishops on Persons with Disabilities, 1989, 1984
A Good Friday Appeal to End the Death Penalty, 1999
Confronting a Culture of Violence, 1995
U.S. Bishops' Statement on Capital Punishment, 1980
Community and Crime, 1978

Promoting Family Life

A Family Guide to Using the Media, 1999
Renewing the Mind of the Media, 1998
Statements and testimony by the USCCB Department of
     Communications before Congress and the Federal
     Communications Commission
Sharing Catholic Social Teaching: Challenges and Directions, 1998
Principles for Educational Reform in the United States, 1995
In Support of Catholic Elementary and Secondary Schools, 1990
Value and Virtue: Moral Education in the Public School, 1988
Sharing the Light of Faith; National Catechetical Directory, 1979
To Teach As Jesus Did, 1972
When I Call for Help, 2002
A Family Perspective in Church and Society, 1998
Always Our Children, 1997
Statement on Same-Sex Marriage, 1996
Walk in the Light, 1995
Follow the Way of Love, 1993
Putting Children and Families First, 1992

Pursuing Social Justice

Strangers No Longer: Together on the Journey of Hope, 2003
*A Place at the Table: A Catholic Recommitment to Overcome Poverty
     and to Respect the Dignity of All God's Children,* 2002
Global Climate Change, 2001
*Responsibility, Rehabilitation, Restoration: A Catholic Perspective on Crime
     and Criminal Justice,* 2000
A Commitment to All Generations: Social Security and the Common Good,
     1999
In all Things Charity, 1999
Ethical and Religious Directives for Catholic Health Care Services, 1995
One Family Under God, 1995
Confronting a Culture of Violence, 1995
Moral Principles and Policy Priorities for Welfare Reform, 1995
The Harvest of Justice Is Sown in Peace, 1993
A Framework for Comprehensive Health Care Reform, 1993
Renewing the Earth, 1992

Putting Children and Families First, 1992
New Slavery, New Freedom: A Pastoral Message on Substance Abuse, 1990
Brothers and Sisters to Us, 1989
Food Policy in a Hungry World, 1989
*Called to Compassion and Responsibility: A Response to the HIV/AIDS Crisis,
1989*
Homelessness and Housing, 1988
Economic Justice for All, 1986

Practicing Global Solidarity

A Call to Solidarity with Africa, 2001
A Jubilee Call for Debt Forgiveness, 1999
Called to Global Solidarity, 1998
Sowing the Weapons of War, 1995
One Family Under God, 1995
The Harvest of Justice Is Sown in Peace, 1993
War in the Balkans: Moral Challenges, Policy Choices, 1993
Statements on South Africa, 1993, 1994
Refugees: A Challenge to Solidarity, 1992
The New Moment in Eastern and Central Europe, March 1990
The Harvest of Justice Is Sown in Peace, 1993
Toward Peace in the Middle East, 1989
Relieving Third World Debt, 1989
USCC Statement on Central America, 1987

NOTES

1   Since 1975, the United States Conference of Catholic Bishops has developed a reflection on
     "faithful citizenship" in advance of each presidential election. This statement continues that tra-
     dition. It summarizes Catholic teaching on public life and on key moral issues. These reflections
     build on past political responsibility statements and integrate themes from a recent statement
     on Catholics in public life from the Congregation for the Doctrine of the Faith, as well as themes
     from several recent bishops' statements, including *Living the Gospel of Life* and *A Place at the Table*.
     To provide additional information on Catholic teaching on these matters, major Catholic state-
     ments on public life and moral issues are listed at the conclusion of these reflections.

2   Cf. United States Conference of Catholic Bishops, *A Place at the Table: A Catholic Recommitment
     to Overcome Poverty and to Respect the Dignity of All God's Children* (Washington, D.C.: United
     States Conference of Catholic Bishops, 2002).

3   Jn 13:34-35.

4   Mt 25:40-45.

5   Congregation for the Doctrine of the Faith, *Doctrinal Note on Some Questions Regarding the Participation of Catholics in Political Life Questions Regarding the Participation of Catholics in Political Life* (November 24, 2002), no. 1.

6   United States Conference of Catholic Bishops, *Living the Gospel of Life: A Challenge to American Catholics* (Washington, D.C.: United States Conference of Catholic Bishops, 1998), no. 34.

7   Dt 30:19-20, Mt 25:40-45, Mt 5:3-12.

8   The Catholic community has a presence in virtually every part of the nation, including almost 20,000 parishes, 8,600 schools, 237 colleges and universities, 1,062 hospitals and health care facilities, and 3, 044 social service agencies. The Catholic community is the largest non-governmental provider of education, health care, and human services in the United States.

9   Mt 13:33, Mt 5:13-16.

10   Congregation for the Doctrine of the Faith, *Doctrinal Note on Some Questions Regarding the Participation of Catholics in Political Life Questions Regarding the Participation of Catholics in Political Life*, no. 6.

11   United States Conference of Catholic Bishops, Living the Gospel of Life, no. 34. 12 Cf. Congregation for the Doctrine of the Faith, *Doctrinal Note on Some Questions Regarding the Participation of Catholics in Political Life Questions Regarding the Participation of Catholics in Political Life*, no. 4.

13   Ibid.

14   Ibid.

15   Resources designed to help parishes and dioceses share the message of faithful citizenship and develop non-partisan voter registration, education, and advocacy programs are available from the United States Conference of Catholic Bishops. For more information, call 800-235-8722 or go to *www.usccb.org/faithfulcitizenship/index.htm.*

16   Catholic social teaching is a rich tradition that is rooted in the Scriptures and the lived experience of the people of God. It has been developed in the writings of church leaders through the ages, and has most recently been articulated through a tradition of modern papal, conciliar, and episcopal documents. For a more thorough discussion of the themes identified here and their roots, see the *Catechism of the Catholic Church* (Washington, D.C.: United States Conference of Catholic Bishops, 1994), *Sharing Catholic Social Teaching: Challenges and Directions* (Washington, D.C.: United States Conference of Catholic Bishops, 1998), the USCCB website *www.usccb.org/publishing/index.htm* and the Vatican web site *www.vatican.va.*

17   Congregation for the Doctrine of the Faith, *Doctrinal Note on Some Questions Regarding the Participation of Catholics in Political Life Questions Regarding the Participation of Catholics in Political Life*, no. 3.

18   Ex 22:20-26.

19   Is 1:21-23; Jer 5:28.

20   Mt 25:40-45.

21   Lk 4:18-19.

22   John Paul II, Apostolic Letter *Novo Millennio Ineunte* (January 6, 2001), no. 49. 23 John Paul II, *On Social Concern (Sollicitudo Rei Socialis)* (Washington, D.C.: United States Conference of Catholic Bishops, 1987), no. 38.

24   John Paul II, World Day of Peace Message, (January 1, 1972).

25   Mt 5:9.

26   John Paul II, Angelus (February 23, 2003), no. 1.

27   Congregation for the Doctrine of the Faith, *Doctrinal Note on Some Questions Regarding the Participation of Catholics in Political Life Questions Regarding the Participation of Catholics in Political Life*, no. 2.

28   Ibid, no. 3.

29   United States Conference of Catholic Bishops, *Living the Gospel of Life*, no. 5.

30   Ibid, no. 21.

31   John Paul II, *Homily in St. Louis* (January 27, 1999).

32   John Paul II, *The Ecological Crisis: A Common Responsibility* (January 1, 1990), no. 15.

Catholics in Political Life

United States Conference of Catholic Bishops, 2004

We speak as bishops, as teachers of the Catholic faith and of the moral law. We have the duty to teach about human life and dignity, marriage and family, war and peace, the needs of the poor and the demands of justice. Today we continue our efforts to teach on a uniquely important matter that has recently been a source of concern for Catholics and others.

It is the teaching of the Catholic Church from the very beginning, founded on her understanding of her Lord's own witness to the sacredness of human life, that the killing of an unborn child is always intrinsically evil and can never be justified. If those who perform an abortion and those who cooperate willingly in the action are fully aware of the objective evil of what they do, they are guilty of grave sin and thereby separate themselves from God's grace. This is the constant and received teaching of the Church. It is, as well, the conviction of many other people of good will.

To make such intrinsically evil actions legal is itself wrong. This is the point most recently highlighted in official Catholic teaching. The legal system as such can be said to cooperate in evil when it fails to protect the lives of those who have no protection except the law. In the United States of America, abortion on demand has been made a constitutional right by a decision of the Supreme Court. Failing to protect the lives of innocent and defenseless members of the human race is to sin against justice. Those who formulate law therefore have an obligation in conscience to work toward correcting morally defective laws, lest they be guilty of cooperating in evil and in sinning against the common good.

As our conference has insisted in *Faithful Citizenship*, Catholics who bring their moral convictions into public life do not threaten democracy or pluralism but enrich them and the nation. The separation of church and state does not require division between belief and public action, between moral principles and political choices, but protects the right of

United States Conference of Catholic Bishops, *Catholics in Political Life* (June, 2004). See http://www.usccb.org/bishops/catholicsinpoliticallife.shtml (accessed May 10, 2005).

believers and religious groups to practice their faith and act on their values in public life.

Our obligation as bishops at this time is to teach clearly. It is with pastoral solicitude for everyone involved in the political process that we will also counsel Catholic public officials that their acting consistently to support abortion on demand risks making them cooperators in evil in a public manner. We will persist in this duty to counsel, in the hope that the scandal of their cooperating in evil can be resolved by the proper formation of their consciences.

Having received an extensive interim report from the Task Force on Catholic Bishops and Catholic Politicians, and looking forward to the full report, we highlight several points from the interim report that suggest some directions for our efforts:

- We need to continue to **teach** clearly and help other Catholic leaders to teach clearly on our unequivocal commitment to the legal protection of human life from the moment of conception until natural death. Our teaching on human life and dignity should be reflected in our parishes and our educational, health care and human service ministries.

- We need to do more to **persuade** all people that human life is precious and human dignity must be defended. This requires more effective dialogue and engagement with all public officials, especially Catholic public officials. We welcome conversation initiated by political leaders themselves.

- Catholics need to **act** in support of these principles and policies in public life. It is the particular vocation of the laity to transform the world. We have to encourage this vocation and do more to bring all believers to this mission. As bishops, we do not endorse or oppose candidates. Rather, we seek to form the consciences of our people so that they can examine the positions of candidates and make choices based on Catholic moral and social teaching.

- The Catholic community and Catholic institutions should **not honor** those who act in defiance of our fundamental moral principles. They should not be given awards, honors or platforms which would suggest support for their actions.

- We commit ourselves to **maintain communication** with public officials who make decisions every day that touch issues of human life and dignity.

The Eucharist is the source and summit of Catholic life. Therefore, like every Catholic generation before us, we must be guided by the words of St. Paul, "Whoever, therefore, eats the bread or drinks the cup of the Lord in an unworthy manner will be guilty of profaning the Body and Blood of the Lord" (1 Cor 11:27). This means that all must examine their consciences as to their worthiness to receive the Body and Blood of our Lord. This examination includes fidelity to the moral teaching of the Church in personal and public life.

The question has been raised as to whether the denial of Holy Communion to some Catholics in political life is necessary because of their public support for abortion on demand. Given the wide range of circumstances involved in arriving at a prudential judgment on a matter of this seriousness, we recognize that such decisions rest with the individual bishop in accord with the established canonical and pastoral principles. Bishops can legitimately make different judgments on the most prudent course of pastoral action. Nevertheless, we all share an unequivocal commitment to protect human life and dignity and to preach the Gospel in difficult times.

The polarizing tendencies of election-year politics can lead to circumstances in which Catholic teaching and sacramental practice can be misused for political ends. Respect for the Holy Eucharist, in particular, demands that it be received worthily and that it be seen as the source for our common mission in the world.

Appendix

A wide range of documents regarding Catholics and political life can be found at the following websites:

www.vatican.va

www.usccb.org/faithfulcitizenship

www.usccb.org/prolife

www.usccb.org/comm

www.usccb.org/education

www.usccb.org/mrs

www.usccb.org/prolife

www.usccb.org/sdwp

www.usccbpublishing.org

Index

A

Abortion, 22-24, 37, 72-74, 160-67, 183, 190, 193
    imperfect legislation, voting for, 28-29, 103
    law and, 24-29, 73, 103, 142, 154-56, 169n6, 198, 213-15
    medical terminology, 22
    Resolution on Abortion, 149, 208
    Roe v. Wade, 155-56, 196n6, 208
    Second Vatican Council on, 11, 166-67
    See also Right to life.
Abstinence, 63
Action,
    Christian laity called to, 3-4, 7, 39-40, 80, 93, 103, 106, 137
    Christian organizations and, 5, 30
    and Christian witness, 135, 154
    Church and, 89, 129, 144
    citizens and, 125-26
    and the common good, 93, 137, 143, 145, 194
    ecclesial, social doctrine and, 132-45
    for justice, 174
    options for, 5, 125-26, 172
    political, 102, 120-21, 191
    social, 93, 137, 138
    volunteer work, 126
    See also Participation.
Ad Limina, 151, 167-68, 169n12
Adoption, 165, 198
Affirmative action, 204
Affluence. *See* Wealth.
Afghanistan, 188, 206
Africa, 188, 206
Aging, 31, 153, 167, 193
    See also Elderly.
Agnosticism, 19, 120, 141
Agriculture, 203
AIDS, 202-3, 210
Alcohol, 77
America,
    American Catholics, 151-69
    "American Century," 151-69
    foreign policy, 205-6
    See also specific topics.
Amputation, 78

Anger, 15, 69, 70, 76, 79-80
Animals, 87-88
Apostles, 46, 61
Aquinas, St. Thomas. See Thomas Aquinas, St.
Armed conflict, 21-22, 80-83, 153, 199, 205
    See also Conflict; War.
Armed forces, 81, 82, 199
    See also War.
Arms,
    production, 82
    trade, 21-22, 82, 206
    weapons of mass destruction, 15, 199, 206
    See also War.
Arts, x, 138-39
Ascesis, 63
Assisted suicide. See under Suicide: assisted.
Associations (organizations), 4, 5, 15, 124-25, 174, 189
    appropriate tasks assigned to, 112
    Catholic, 107, 179
    and Catholic social mission, 172
    and Christian witness, 174
    and the common good, 14, 44, 104, 113, 159, 190
    faith-based groups, 202
    religious, State and, 127, 129
    responsibility of, 5, 91
    right to form, 42, 128-29
    secret, 140
    socialization, 36
    subsidiarity and, 111, 112, 113
    the "third sector," 125-26
    See also specific topics.
Atheism, 10, 89
Augustine, St., 29n97, 55n51, 84n98
Authority, Church, 40, 54, 61-62, 144
    teaching authority of the Church (see Magisterium)
Authority, definition of, 56
    See also Authority, public (below).
Authority, public, 26-28, 30, 41-46, 55-57, 114-19
    abuse by, 43
    the Church and, 11, 68
    citizens and, 44, 66-68

cures, scientific research and, 12
respectful treatment during, 74
the sick, Church and, 11
the sick, treatment of, 85
terminal, 74-75, 154
See also Death and dying; Health;
Health care; *specific topics.*
Simple lifestyle, 14, 85, 175
Sin,
causing children to, 76
confession of, 63
hatred and, 79-80
and involuntary ignorance, 54-55
mortal sin, 79, 82
original sin, 69, 95
structure of, cultural, 23, 36
tempting others to, 76
See also Forgiveness; Scandal.
Slander, 38
Slavery, 11, 37, 87, 203
Social doctrine of the Church, 17-18, 88-90, 143, 195-97
Socialism, 89-90
Socialization, 36, 44
Social justice, 15, 201-5
and economic activity, 90-92
and working conditions, 201
See also Human rights; Justice.
Social nature, human, 35-36, 195-96
Social order,
Church and, 18, 61, 109n6
development of, 15
disturbances in, 36, 89
foundations of, 37
Social Security, 202
Social Teaching, 18, 89, 106-7, 141, 144, 175, 177, 181, 183, 191, 193, 214
See also Catholic social teaching;
Social doctrine of the Church.
Society, 183-84
participation in, 55-59
service in, 135-39
See also Community.
Soldiers, 81, 82, 199
See also War.
Solidarity, 5, 85, 126, 184
among nations, 92-93
bearing witness to, 14
and the common good, 15
definition of, 15
and freedom, 3
global, 205-7
and peace, 25-26

political, 15
See also Cooperation.
Sollicitudo Rei Socialis, 15
Son of God. *See* Jesus Christ.
Souls,
of others, respecting, 75-76
salvation of (*see* Salvation)
Sovereignty. *See* Authority, public.
Spirit of God. *See* Holy Spirit.
Spiritual formation, 17
Spirituality, 138-39
Spiritual life: integration with secular life.
See Unity, integral.
Spiritual worship, 60-61
State. *See* Church-State relationship; Political community; *specific topics.*
Stealing, 84-87
Stem cell research. *See* Embryo.
Sterilization, 78
Stewardship, 175, 185, 197, 204-5
and private property, 84-85
and simple living, 85, 175
Strangers, welcoming, 175, 179, 203
Strikes, 92
Subsidiarity, 111-13
and civil society, 125-26
See also Social doctrine of the
Church.
Substance abuse, 77, 104
Sudan, 206
Suffering, 8n7, 11
See also Misery, human; Social justice; *specific topics*, e.g.: Poverty.
Suicide, 11, 37, 75
assisted, 27-28, 183, 198 (*see also* Euthanasia)
Sunday; Sunday rest, 37, 63, 171, 176
Supernatural values, 141

T

Talents. *See* Christian vocation; Gifts of
the Spirit.
Taxes, 62, 200
tax evasion, 86
Teachers, 11, 159
bishops as, ix, 61, 177, 213, 214
responsibility of, 78
Teaching authority of the Church. *See*
Magisterium.
Teaching, Church. *See* Church teaching.
See also Catholic social teaching;
Social doctrine of the Church.

working conditions, 11, 37, 92, 201, 203
See also Wages.
Works (faith and), 64, 94-96, 163
Works of mercy. *See under* Mercy: works of.
Worship, 39, 105, 176
freedom of, 128
moral life as, 60-61
Wrath. *See* Anger.

Y

Yahweh, 178
See also God.
Young People, 10, 45, 75, 190, 204
See also Children; *specific topics.*